PR

UNMARKETABLE

ALSO BY ANNE ELIZABETH MOORE

Hey, Kidz! Buy This Book:
A Radical Primer on Corporate and Governmental Propaganda and
Artistic Activism for Short People

The Best American Comics 2006
(series editor)

The Best American Comics 2007
(series editor)

UNMARKETABLE

Brandalism, Copyfighting, Mocketing, and the Erosion of Integrity

Anne Elizabeth Moore

THE NEW PRESS

NEW YORK
LONDON

Published in the United States by The New Press, New York, 2007
Distributed by W. W. Norton & Company, Inc., New York

LIBRARY OF CONGRESS CATALOGING-IN-PUBLICATION DATA

Moore, Anne Elizabeth.
    Unmarketable : brandalism, copyfighting, mocketing, and the erosion of integrity /
Anne Elizabeth Moore.
      p.   cm.
    Includes bibliographical references and index.
    ISBN 978-1-59558-168-6 (pbk)
    1. Market segmentation.   2. Green marketing.   3. Brand name products.   I. Title.
    HF5415.127.M663   2007
    658.8'02—dc22   2007023498

The New Press was established in 1990 as a not-for-profit alternative to the large,
commercial publishing houses currently dominating the book publishing industry. The
New Press operates in the public interest rather than for private gain, and is committed
to publishing, in innovative ways, works of educational, cultural, and community value
that are often deemed insufficiently profitable.

www.thenewpress.com

Composition by dix!

Printed in the Canada

10   9   8   7   6   5   4   3   2   1

CONTENTS

ACKNOWLEDGMENTS

The auspicious occasion of you reading this book was made possible by the support of several individuals who said the things I wrote down to put in it. Particularly generous with their time were Elisa Harkins, Rob Walker, Kristin Lingrin, and Ian MacKaye, who, in consort with Nancy J. Arms Simon, Roman Mars, Thurber, Cake, and a particularly moving cover of "Straight Outta Compton" by ex–Veruca Salt Nina Gordon, acted as a moral compass for this project. Particularly generous with their libraries were Stephen Duncombe and Logan Bay, without whom way too much of this would be wild speculation. Rob Carmichael's cover design and modeling efforts established the tone for this volume, and last-minute legal assistance was provided by David Bruce Wolf, by which I do not mean to imply that he sprung me from the clink.

Next up, we cannot overlook the contributions of the subscribers, readers, contributors, and staff of *Punk Planet* magazine, who closely monitored the matters addressed herein for almost a decade and a half, and responded to early drafts of this work enthusiastically. Thank you for your careful attention: my couch is always open when you're in town.

Finally, the moment you've all been waiting for: the 2007 Anne Elizabeth Moore Award for Excellence in Awesomeness goes to Sarah Fan. It marks a new direction for this award, as for several years running it's gone to a single contender, one Anne Elizabeth Moore in Chicago, Illinois. This year, however, the judges were particularly impressed by Ms. Fan's meticulous editing skills, endless patience, near ridiculous ability to grasp the meaning and import of this book far better than the author herself, and all-around awesomeness.

Please enjoy the rest of your night responsibly.

UNMARKETABLE

1

FREE CANDY

Several years ago, a friend and I held a series of pedagogical sessions called "free candy" workshops throughout the country as a way of addressing integrity within the punk and do-it-yourself (DIY) underground. Actually they were more like interactive stand-up comedy routines—riffs on the Man, selling out, payola, and makin' the deal—held at self-publishing conferences, anarchist bookstores, and zine libraries.[1] Yet because getting together to discuss abstract theories like "the preservation of integrity" sounds a little dry to those who would rather be tuning guitars, doodling in sketchbooks, or interviewing band members for pirate radio shows, and because no self-respecting punk kids believe they will give up the authenticity, sincerity, honor, and personal vision they refer to as integrity, we promised free candy. And people came. We knew our audience: zinesters are hungry folk. Hell, we *were* our audience.

We were kind of dirty, dressed funny, and swore without provocation. We associated with people who both ate out of garbage bins and fixed up bikes as political acts. We relentlessly documented our disgust with mainstream culture, our never-ending frustrations with governments both Republican and Democratic, and our desire to live lives free of corporate influence. This amounts to very little of what most people would consider success, and thus our clothes, food, mode of transportation, and lifestyle were often handmade or greatly modified versions of what polite society had already rejected.

For over a decade I sold funny little booklets for a dollar through zine distros, independent bookstores, and at self-publishing conferences, scrounging out work in writing as a legitimate career evolved. I am now a publisher at Independents' Day Media, where my business partner Daniel Sinker and I edit and publish the no-major-media thirteen-year-old cultural politics magazine *Punk Planet* and Punk Planet Books (in partnership with Akashic Books in Brooklyn, founded by Johnny Temple when his punk band Girls Against Boys signed to Geffen Records in 1997). My wardrobe was acquired through friends and thrift stores and retooled to fit my needs. And my food, although not grown in my garden (at least not all of it), is usually prepared by my own hands. Unlike many of my peers, I do watch TV, although because I am surrounded by talented people, the vast majority of the music I listen to, books I read, art I hang, and zines I keep in the bathroom are created—conceived, executed, published, and distributed—by just a few individuals with vibrant, crushing passions they feel driven to share with the world.

Mark Hosler describes the art-making practice of his band Negativland as a "natural response to growing up in a mediated world," and this was how I came to zine making. My decision to write and publish my own work for an audience of whomever I ran into after I photocopied it was a reaction to the information I was fed daily about how to live my life. Without advertisers, sponsors, or funders I was beholden neither to publishing dates nor content that would (or more likely would not) ultimately please them. Without an editorial staff I re-created language to suit my message, and without a design team I explored my own vision of what a periodical might look like. I published whatever I agreed with or found interesting, and urged the creators of work I found objectionable, malformed, or boring to publish themselves. It wasn't, to be sure, a financially rewarding decision. It was merely the only one I was interested in making.

But this is no memoir. My experience is merely one among many comprising the current punk and DIY underground. The series of decisions that go into living a life of intentionality, where one chooses goods and services based on some knowledge of the history of their production, are deeply political yet rarely chosen for lofty ideological reasons. They are often made initially out of necessity and originate in an awareness of poverty, social class, and the race and gender biases of mainstream culture. When a certain kind of individual stumbles across barriers to stability like these, which in our consumerist culture hold real economic consequences, a certain kind of logic emerges. DIY: Do It Yourself. "If you boil punk down to remove all the hair dye, power chords, typewriters, colored vinyl, leather jackets, glue sticks, show flyers, and combat boots," Dan Sinker wrote in the introduction to *Punk Planet*'s collected interviews *We Owe You Nothing*, the culture "has always been about asking 'why' and then doing something about it." [2]

Musicians start labels when it becomes clear no one else will release their music; writers self-publish because the publishing world doesn't feel their perspective is marketable; visual artists go unfunded and unrepresented and yet still feel compelled to make work. There are myriad reasons *why* the labels, the publishing companies, the galleries—and, in turn, the music fans, the bookclubbers, the art collectors—may outright reject or simply fail to embrace a particular artist's point of view. Far too often, however, these can all can be reduced to a single essential problem that no cultural movement has yet been able to eradicate: the artist's point of view is considered unmarketable by the label manager, publisher, or gallery owner—whether, for example, due to her skin color, his low-class manner of dress, her feminist themes, his language of choice, her lack of access to proper social networking channels, his failure to come up with an entrance fee, or perhaps the artist's transgender identity. These are curatorial and editorial decisions made primarily out of fear that the keepers of culture will be unable to make back what they invest in supporting the work. While this has led to the creation of a vital, hand-forged independent underground, this is not a culture visible—or accessible—to most. For years sacrificing merit to the market has affected what the vast majority can see, experience, or purchase in the world; now, as we will see in the following chapters, the dwindling viability of independent media is beginning to influence what we believe to be possible.

This book is primarily concerned with integrity, a notion that lately has inspired confusion: it topped the list of most looked-up words in Merriam-Webster's online dictionary in 2005. Equally confusing may be the other words that form the subtitle of this book (although they may not yet appear in most dictionaries): brandalism, vandalism committed as an advertising campaign; graffadi, or graffiti that is advertising; copyfighting, or activist projects that take on copyright and intellectual property issues; and mocketing, or product placement that is integrated into parody-based entertainment media content.

There has been a similar confusion over the word "organic," particularly regarding foodstuffs. The definition of organic most of us are accustomed to describes living beings; refers to something that develops gradually and without force; and implies the use of agricultural practices reliant on naturally occurring pesticides, fertilizers, and other growing aids but without the use of synthetic chemicals. We think of "organic" as a synonym for natural, untrammeled, sustainable.

Yet the definition of organic used on food packaging is a technical and tautological one, describing a lack of synthetic fertilizers, toxic pesticides, or herbicides, and an adherence to a set of standards put in place by the U.S. Department of Agriculture to regulate the commercial use of the word "organic." While the definition has been pared down from its original, the word has also become popular in packaging, advertising, and the media; it's a promotional tool. The word "organic" has therefore grown (inorganically, I would argue) to comprise such methods as those used by Earthbound Foods in farming arugula, as described by the *New Yorker*'s Steven Shapin in a review of Michael Pollan's book *The Omnivore's Dilemma*: "Earthbound's compost is trucked in; the salad-green farms are models of West Coast monoculture, laser-leveled fields facilitating awesomely efficient mechanical harvesting; and the whole supply chain from California to Manhattan is only four percent less gluttonous a consumer of fossil fuel than that of a conventionally grown head of iceberg lettuce."[3] Thus, he argues, "the growing of the arugula is indeed organic, but almost everything else is late-capitalist business as usual. . . . 'Organic' isn't necessarily 'local,' and neither 'organic' or 'local' is necessarily 'sustainable.'"[4]

So the schism between what we believe organic means (naturally occurring, created without using damaging substances or force, and eminently reproducible) and what it means in the commercial sphere (grown by aid only of other products also labeled "organic") is vast. Marketers have done more than take full advantage of this schism. They have created it.

For those of you who may not pay attention to such things (in my world, you are much less likely to pay attention to what farmers in California may be doing than what's coming out of your radio), remarkably similar sleights of hand have occurred with the terms "independent," "alternative," and "punk."

Similar to markets such as Whole Foods, which has profited by widely marketing organic produce, back in the 1990s major record labels attempted to capitalize on independent, alternative, and punk music. This was a switch from earlier decades, notes Naomi Klein; the original punks of the 1970s "were only half-heartedly sought after as markets. In part this was because seventies punk was at its peak at the same times as the infinitely more mass marketable disco and heavy metal, and the gold-mine of high-end preppy style."[5] When it came a few decades later, the drive to capitalize on the punk and DIY underground seemed to happen fast, as if all the A&R reps woke up one morning, heard Nirvana for the first time, and suddenly realized that throughout the country small groups of kids were getting together and creating their own music. These kids had been doing so for decades, of course, inspired not only by the energy and ubiquity of the Sex Pistols and the Clash but also by bands like the Minutemen and the Ramones, each made up of a few scruffy losers who happened to know each other and have access to guitars.

Almost overnight, these had been decreed marketable.

The music of bands like Fugazi, Bratmobile, Screeching Weasel—and Girls Against Boys, Le Tigre, and Green Day, when they started out—was independent, meaning it was made without corporate support, remained free of conceptual or artistic meddling, and explored previously untested sounds. It was alternative: there was a musical mainstream you could hear on the radio and these sounds did not fit into it. Such music also forged an alternative path for success, one that depended not on record sales or radio plays but on consistent touring schedules, a national fan base, a devoted local following, and the admiration of peers. Most important, this music was punk; like those earlier angry white mostly male musicians, it was self-righteous, inappropriate, and dirty. Punk therefore seemed safely immune to widespread popularity and thus served as a protected space from which to voice sociopolitical criticism. At the time, the official, on-the-books definition of "punk" included phrases like "unwashed," "obscene," and "violent." (My dictionary's definition still uses those words.[6])

But by fall of 1991, "there was a sudden and intense interest in underground and independent music . . . largely due to the phenomenal success of the Nirvana *Nevermind* album," musician and founder of Dischord Records Ian MacKaye recalled. The major corporate record labels were right to take note of the vast audience interested in what they weren't providing. By the time they noticed it there *was* an entire network of people—fans, mostly, but also artists, businesspeople, and general supporters of subculture—who had devoted themselves to creating an existence outside of major media. We wrote our own literature, from zines to comics, and sold them for cheap. We made our own T-shirts and traded them for home-recorded tapes; we held concerts in our basements advertised with flyers we'd carefully designed using tape, scissors, and white-out, then copied at Kinko's using any number of well-known free-copy scams, and circulated among friends and friends of friends. This was a culture you couldn't see on TV (the most ubiquitous mass media at the time), and when you eventually did hear it on the radio it was watered down and wrong.

Now the establishment wanted to cash in on this unestablished culture. MacKaye recalled, "Fugazi, the band that I started with Brendan [Canty] and Guy [Picciotto] (from Rites of Spring) and Joe Lally in 1988 was one of the largest in the underground, and soon attracted the interests of many major labels. The band's decision to remain on Dischord led to offers from the majors to buy the entire label, but selling it was never even a consideration. We understood the value of self-determination." [7]

The majors were slightly more successful with bands on newer independent labels, however, and punked up their recording dockets in no time by luring struggling artists away with big-money promises. Warner Brother's Reprise Records scored biggest with Green Day—like Nirvana, the band had developed a substantial following before the major-label jump—but other bands were duped into bad contracts, loss of creative control, and unbearable tour schedules that frequently cost more than their albums ever brought in. [8] Yet selling out held tangible appeal to band members, who were eager to quit day jobs, wanted the big advance checks, and deserved the increase in audience the promotional teams at major labels could offer. Given the sudden recognition of their products as widely marketable, smaller labels couldn't give much enticement to stay. They couldn't, in some cases, even meet increased demands for merchandise.

Major record labels, however, weren't the only ones waiting to cash in on the underground. News and other entertainment media were closely following the riot grrrl movement, a brash combination of second-wave feminism and punk-rock music. Named for the 1991 zine *Riot Grrrl*, written by political organizer and musician Tobi Vail, Kathleen Hanna of Bikini Kill (and later Le Tigre), Allison Wolfe of Bratmobile, and a few others, riot grrrl came out of young punk women's simple desires to express their personal voices. "In a way," Wolfe recalled, "it was like announcing, 'Hey us girls are here, we're doing something, we're making our voices heard in this scene.'" [9] Riot grrrl shows and zines were confrontational and loud but aimed to create safe spaces for female (and eventually less traditionally gendered) fans.

It was a straightforwardly sexual movement and therefore ripe for misrepresentation. By 1992, the press was already getting everything wrong. "A lot of riot grrrls don't shave and deliberately give each other bad haircuts," declared *Seventeen* magazine.[10] "Also popular is a deliberately nerdy or dowdy appearance," the *New York Times* stated, further explaining that antisocial fashion decisions were to be read as "a challenge to the cultural expectation that women should strive to be pretty."[11] Such stories ran in direct opposition to what riot grrrls were calling for: to not have their appearance up for evaluation by the *New York Times* or *Seventeen* at all.

So riot grrrl participants developed a sophisticated response: a media blackout. It didn't entirely take, of course, but for the most part the mainstream media was forced to describe what they could comprehend of the burgeoning scene from the outer edge of a sweaty mosh pit. A movement that embraced sexuality was too enticing to ignore, however, and even though participants refused to talk to the press, reporters continued to misconstrue the messages. "During a performance [Kathleen Hanna of Bikini Kill] might take off her top screaming, 'Suck my left one,'" the *Chicago Reader* reported before postulating incorrectly what this might mean. "Such acts probably confuse and terrify the teenage boys in the audience who've been waiting for this moment."[12] In fact, riot grrrl deliberately deprioritized concern for boys' feelings, occasionally going so far as to emasculate male fans: sometimes men were charged extra for not wearing dresses or bras to shows.[13] Still, the *Washington Post* rushed to preserve heteronormativity: "Make no mistake," it reassured readers. "Most riot grrrls still find boys useful for the usual teenaged things."[14]

The barest trace of revolutionary ideas still filtered through such reporting—available in stronger doses through the zines and shows whose audiences began to grow. Usually, though, to major media this was a style, not a social, revolution. "The media usually served to water down our message and turn it into fashion statements," Wolfe acknowledged.[15] To some, the movement proved the viability of the market, and although few grrrls were offered the same major-label opportunities their male counterparts were, the market found a way to appropriate the grrrl-style revolution into its sales pitch. A slogan from the cover of *Bikini Kill* #2 read "Girl Power," which quickly became the rallying cry of the patently unradical Virgin Records creation the Spice Girls.

It was only the most egregious co-optation from the mid-1990s frenzy for underground culture. Zines also received major media attention, with zinesters appearing on the pages of glossy magazines like *Details* and *Sassy* and on talk shows—Dishwasher Pete, for example, who pledged to document his experiences washing dishes in every state in the union, was invited to appear on *Late Night with David Letterman* but sent a friend in his stead. (I was invited to the *Jim J and Tammy Faye Show*; sadly the program was canceled before I could reply.) Graffiti and street art were all the decorative rage, and the messy DIY/punk fashion aesthetic was packaged and sold at Urban Outfitters.

Despite the underground's newfound acceptance as an aesthetic, genuine and well-founded fears of major media misrepresentation remained, fueling the debates about selling out and co-optation that plagued the period (and, to some degree still rage). Something was perceived to have been lost from the definitions of the words "independent," "alternative," and "punk" as "without corporate support," "created and experienced outside of the mainstream," and "made out of passion and not for profit." Each were eroded, and now only denoted a slightly different flavor of mass-produced entertainment. The loss of the original senses of these terms, which had once held serious political implications vital to our ability to describe life outside of corporate support, seemed only a short step away from the loss of our ability to imagine what they describe.

The surge of interest in the punk and DIY underground didn't last long, though, and within a few years it was over. "There are no A&R people at major labels looking for punk bands anymore," stated Ruth Schwartz in 1997. Schwartz ran Mordam Records, the independent distributor smack-dab in the middle of the major-label boom. "It's over. There have been layoffs because of it." [16]

By then, of course, a major policy change in media ownership had taken place. The Telecommunications Act of 1996 eliminated caps on the number of outlets single-media conglomerates could control. Formerly independent radio stations and newspapers were bought up or sold out. Resources for small media withered; teeny, almost one-on-one media—home-recorded music, street art, zines—became less visible. And debates formerly about selling out and co-optation—about integrity—were recast as necessary sacrifices in pursuit of an audience, if they were raised at all.

Punk music, at its most basic, was created in reaction to what could be purchased elsewhere, and it reclaimed the joy inherent in making something by hand. The same was true for zines, graffiti, underground comics, and stencils. In a way, these provide exactly what we think we are buying when we buy organic produce: a locally produced, delectable commodity created not to be sold to you but to speak to you. This can be seen even more directly in the cultural products and activities of activist communities. Traditional punk culture and its more accessible (and feminine) post–riot grrrl iteration, DIY culture, remain inherently political acts, responses to and critiques of rampant consumerism, social class differences, and access to media resources. It's a culture established by people unwilling to live by the standards set for youth in society. It can't claim a terribly large membership, nor can it define itself any more succinctly than as "vaguely anarchic." Kids involved simply felt removed, subterranean, buried, and forgotten about. Underground.

Although this culture may not be readily apparent to everyone, it remains a rich potential space from which to voice dissent. "Up close, the DIY punk scene can seem an effective strategy for resisting branded culture," Alissa Quart writes in her 2003 investigation of youth marketing, *Branded*. These youth "have developed a distinctly anticorporate edge that extends past their distaste for commercial music spaces. They stage 'actions' that combine these two elements, as on the occasion in summer 2001 when fifty kids took over a Kinko's copy shop at the Roosevelt Field Mall in Garden City, New York, and put on an illegal concert." [17]

Because sociopolitical ideals are so deeply woven into punk culture—and simply because the DIY methodology demanded it—integrity of message and of medium has always been a punk mainstay. In her memoir, *Weird Like Us*, former *New York Times* rock critic Ann Powers asked her friend Jone Stebbins, the bassist in Imperial Teen and a former member of the 1980s all-girl punk band the Wrecks, to define the values of punk rock. She responded: "Integrity. . . . [T]aking an active part in your life, rather than just being a consumer. Being ready to blaze a different path or try something new." [18]

Yet the marketability of punk in the mid-1990s and changes in media ownership policy had buffed over concerns about integrity, which by then had mostly been consigned to well-worn debates over co-optation and selling out anyway. "Talk of who has sold out or bought in has become impossibly anachronistic," [19] Klein wrote in 2000.

Of course, the watering down of these terms has been advanced by their use in advertising and corporate entertainment media, which, as with the word organic, have a vested interest in relaxing the original definitions. Soon, the repositioning of these terms led to increasingly weird cultural products. Friends in recovery ran alcohol ads in their zines; brilliant underground comics artists took jobs with major animation studios that had worked actively to squelch the work of their peers just a few years earlier; radical anti-establishment newsletters were sold in Borders and Tower Records; nonsmoking former straight-edgers signed contracts with conglomerates that also owned tobacco firms. Yet addressing core issues of integrity directly has always been exceedingly difficult without restating worn-out tropes: bitching about whether or not your favorite band sold out by signing to a major label, reminiscing about the first time you noticed that chain stores had co-opted your fashion sense, or what exactly a barcode on the cover of a zine denoted.

This was because the terms we used to discuss integrity—co-optation and selling out—relied on differing sets of assumptions about underground practices, human behavior, intellectual property (IP), and corporate strategy. The standard punk line on co-optation, for example, assumes:

1. That a strict membership makes up a community at risk of co-optation.
2. That the practices of this community are the intellectual property of this strict membership.
3. That a corporate entity is the sole agent in all acts of co-optation, which it sees as a necessary prelude to future sales.
4. That co-optation is never inflicted upon a willing community; it is always unwelcome.

Similarly, punk notions of giving up one's autonomy and integrity in exchange for money or other benefits—selling out—rely on the following assumptions:

1. That selling out is a purely black-and-white proposition; you either sign on the dotted line or walk away from the deal, and either option is whole and complete and affects every future thing that you do.
2. That selling out is always fully acknowledged by all parties in advance: it is not done accidentally or without full consent.
3. That a corporate entity is the sole agent in all acts of selling out, which it sees as a necessary prelude to future sales.
4. That selling out always affects the greater community negatively, and is done exclusively for personal gain.
5. That the personal gain to be had by selling out is enormous and financial.

Unfortunately, however popularly held these assumptions may be, not one of them is true. Yet they still seem to dictate how members of the underground assess the integrity of their own work. Which, increasingly, and whether they acknowledge it or not, is now being used to sell and improve corporate products.

To skirt the self-protective instincts that arise when addressing the authenticity, sincerity, honor, and personal vision of work made within the punk community, my friend Tizzy Asher and I decided to give away free candy in 2003. Of course there was a catch. To get the big candy bar—the monster Kit Kat or the super-sized M&Ms bag—you had to agree to certain stipulations. Those stipulations involved artistic and ethical compromises. Otherwise you just got the lame "fun"-size bar.

At the time, Tizzy and I ran an ultimately short-lived online magazine called *To Whom It May Concern* that was primarily a joke, an excuse to insert links into words that contained the letters C-A-T—"catalog" or "scatological"—that when clicked on would display pictures of our household pets. To begin the workshops, we described in as straightforward a manner as possible our personal publishing agenda, known as the To Whom It May Concerns:

1. To forward the vitality and awareness of our pet cats via any means possible
2. To encourage the support of cats throughout the world in general
3. To encourage awareness of *To Whom It May Concern*, in support of all previously listed factors
4. To support the work of Anne and Tizzy in particular, encouraging secondary awareness of *To Whom It May Concern* and all previously listed factors

Big candy bars were given to those individuals who agreed to authentically adopt one or more of these concerns as their own, through their videos, zines, radio shows, independent films, or radical distribution networks. A verbal promise was not enough to win participants the king-sized Snickers, however. Workshop attendees had to fill out our handwritten, photocopied contracts. They were messy—not what you'd expect from a legally binding contract—but that's what they were. The transaction was deliberately transparent: all of us in that room were friends, and we honestly didn't want to force anyone to do anything they weren't

comfortable with. So the documents left large blank spaces for attendees to list whichever concerns, from those listed previously,
they agreed to forward as their own. Participants were then, in
marketing terminology, "invited"—and by that I mean cajoled,
teased, bribed, and otherwise tricked—into agreeing to add the To
Whom It May Concerns to their independent media projects as if
such concerns were their own.

For a piece of candy.

After each workshop we walked away with signed and dated
contracts that assured us influence over several DIY media outlets.
One woman who had come to the underground publishing conference in an attempt to connect with her son, who, she complained, had recently developed an addiction to publishing his own
poetry, promised us a minimum of five cat poems in his next volume. Several zinesters agreed to mention our names and our Web
site within six months. (It is important to note that we weren't
looking for advertising; we already knew independent media
producers mistrust the stuff, as we did.) A video game maker suggested an innovative plan to create greater cat awareness with a
game in which players ran over cats, Grand Theft Auto III–style.
We liked his spunk but not his message; we were eventually convinced to let him join our team when we grasped the potential
media opportunities that would surely arise from the backlash
against his game. A man who did not currently possess a media
outlet agreed to start one in our honor based on our concerns.
And a popular underground Northwest publisher signed away all
ownership to his small but influential media empire.

Our one failure—the single individual who refused, outright,
to put anything to paper—happened to be a lawyer. Because as fun
as the atmosphere was, and as much as we laughed while discussing
these ridiculous demands and stupid contracts, they remain, even

now, legally binding documents. And since the candy promised in exchange has been delivered, we could hold the signers to the bargain at any time. (In theory, at least. Technically I lost the contracts in my last move.)

Ultimately, the free-candy workshops were conducted, and experienced, as a joke. They involved a lot of candy for an educational session, and there was little ultimate point to them: the *To Whom It May Concern* Web site was abandoned before the workshops ended, so the marketing potential yielded little value. Plus, we were just goofy self-publishers (sometimes, just one goofy self-publisher) with nothing to offer in exchange for participants' souls but candy.

Nonetheless, the free-candy workshops were a success, if we measure success solely by the gains made by our *To Whom It May Concern* enterprise: in exchange for a few seventy-five-cent candy bars, we seeded a vast, dedicated promotional team that our company's target demographic—activists, anarchists, and independent media producers—could really trust. They had not agreed to any stipulations that they could not uphold with authenticity and sincerity and that did not jibe with their sense of honor or personal vision. These independent cultural producers had simply agreed to adjust their own belief systems to comfortably accommodate what we asked.

We had turned a tired debate over integrity into an experiment that answered a central question for participants about integrity: how little will it take to give yours up?

Souls come sort of cheap in the underground. I had been giving mine out in the form of hand-colored, photocopied, limited-edition pieces of literature for around ten years at that point. I had most certainly never made enough money to cover my costs, not to mention my time, and when my income from my day job grew, so too did my production values, although never the price of my zines.

In fact, the spring before the free-candy workshop series, I had finally gotten what seemed a dream job when two friends and I were asked by a local arts festival to organize a zine-making workshop. I could fly in any of my awesome zinester friends from all over the country and have them talk about whatever parts of zine making they knew best. Supplies—fancy art-making ones like glitter, colored papers, and collage materials, as well as the standard paper cutter, 8½-inch-by-11-inch white paper, and stapler—were all made available free of charge to all workshop attendees. And the coup de grâce: two free-standing, full-color, large-format photocopiers with on-call tech support completely at our disposal for the duration of the festival. For someone who has snuck photocopies from law firms, temp jobs, and office supply stores for a decade, the free photocopies alone were a great reason to take the job. That I was being paid, in no uncertain terms, to make zines *during work hours* and *as a part of my job* was simply too much. Turning the offer down never occurred to me, until it was too late to back out.

Because everything has a price, and in this case, mine was Starbucks sponsorship.

So when I was asked later that summer to talk about issues of integrity at an independent self-publishing conference, I'm sure it was expected that I would give a straight-up play-by-play of how I had sold out to Starbucks. But selling out didn't accurately describe how my work for Starbucks had unfolded; moreover, it presented no concrete lessons I could use to alert others to the insidious nature of dealing with big business. More disheartening was the fact that telling people never to sign anything that has the

Starbucks—or Toyota or Nike or Sony or Tylenol—name on it only works sometimes. In my case, Starbucks was not originally involved in the project I had committed to. In other cases, corporate participation is deliberately obfuscated. Anyway, corporations have endless amounts of money and can almost always find a way to buy you out; if you refuse, they can find someone else who is willing to be bought. These are the facts of late-stage capitalism.

A discussion, however, that focuses on the evil that certain corporations do, and how we get tricked into playing along, misses the point. Because what we fail to acknowledge in debates about selling out and co-optation is that we all do have a price. For some the price of integrity is about the same as a candy bar.

The trick seems to be offering it up in the right context.

This worked in our favor as Tizzy and I set up our free-candy workshops. We advertised them in advance as selling-out workshops that would highlight issues of integrity and personal voice in independent cultural production; in the moments before they began we would abandon the ruse of propriety and race through the halls yelling, "Free candy!" and passing out flyers with our room number on them. It is true that we stacked the deck: if you came to a workshop because you wanted candy, you would probably be willing to do almost anything for it. One almost-attendee came to the door and peeked in. "Free candy?" he asked, disappointed. "I thought this was the selling-out workshop," he said, and left. Which leads me to conclude: the only way you could really win the game we were playing was by somehow failing to play.

Yet because it was fun and social; because we exist in a small and friendly community of independent cultural producers; because we had come up with a way to give out free candy to people we liked; and because what we were asking was not all that harmful, or crazy, or hard to get behind, no one (except one lawyer) refused our demands. Our project-within-a-project, the marketing of *To Whom It May Concern*, was done in a totally straightforward manner. Our concerns were listed on the board! Right there to accept, deny, or ignore as participants saw fit! They got to choose whatever campaign they agreed with! It was a marketing campaign, sure, but it was a totally transparent one, designed to work in tandem with our community's authentic concerns about selling out and co-optation.

When opposition arose we dealt with it the same way, I imagine, as the managers of Tylenol's Ouch! campaign might have, as the planners of the Lucasfilm underground ad blitz would, or as the leaders at the BzzAgent marketing firm do: acknowledge the naysayers, note the transparency of the project, ask politely that further disruptions be kept to a minimum, and underscore that participation in all aspects of the project is voluntary.

What our campaign generated was phenomenal buzz: people asked us to repeat the workshops throughout the country that summer—and, ignoring travel fees, the cost (perhaps $20 per session in candy and $3 in photocopies) was minimal (and paid with Starbucks money). If we can pretend for a moment that Tizzy and I had a valid project to market, we'd have what any boardroom in America would call a smashing success, especially when we compare these costs to a traditional ad campaign to reach out to this elusive demographic. Admittedly, ads in zines (if publishers take them) are cheap to begin with, although we could have purchased perhaps only one or two for the cost of each session we held. We would have had a more difficult time getting our message out through pirate radio broadcasts, blogs, or independent video games because these venues don't usually offer advertising. But we sought wider and more entrenched support from our target demographic, knowing that ads don't have much credibility with them.

We aren't the only ones. In recent years corporate marketers have gained access to independent media projects and have successfully targeted punk and even dedicated activist communities. This was done seamlessly enough that radical leftists, anticorporate artists, and independent cultural producers—as well as marketers and advertisers—can all state with equal force that *Adbusters* magazine, *Star Wars Episode III: Revenge of the Sith*, Reverend Billy, American Girl dolls, Negativland, Pepsi, Tony Trujillo, Sony, Ian MacKaye, Tylenol, pirate radio, and (speaking for myself now, in acknowledgment of the unseen corporate donor behind the free-candy purchases) Starbucks have all contributed to their work dismantling the corporate machine.

That first free-candy workshop was held with the hope that forcing independent media producers to consider their own integrity would prepare them for the unimaginable enchantments—notoriety, validation, money, and health insurance—that, it turns out, lay just around the corner, soon to be offered up by those same corporations listed above, and more. Unfortunately, we didn't hold enough workshops.

Or, perhaps we did. And Sophie Wong, the street-level force behind Tylenol's Ouch! Campaign, just happened to attend one.

2

SCENE FOR SALE

Love conjures up many sensual images in our national consciousness: moonlit beach strolls, bouquets of flowers, a passionate embrace. Marketers would like to expand this repertoire to include, among other things: a decoupaged compact car; a dirty, sullen skateboarder wearing a certain kind of athletic shoe; an excessively hip headache remedy; a city wall mural displaying a perfume for men. They're doing so by circumventing the process of rational thought that dictates our spending habits and trying to connect directly with our very real and very human need for love. Unfortunately, they're trampling integrity—artistic, intellectual, personal—in the process.

The desire to tap into the lucrative potential of carefree devotion is not new to ad men, but it was given a name in 2004: lovemarks. Invented by Saatchi & Saatchi CEO Kevin Roberts, lovemarks in his explanation is always capitalized, as if to demarcate it as its own brand, to separate it from actual love, and to provide it a weight more significant than either that mere emotion or mere branding. Roberts, a balding Aussie, got his start at Procter & Gamble, who he calls "the people who invented brand management."[1] This is important, for in Roberts's view lovemarks is the next movement in marketing, the future of consumerism, and a happy solution to many ills of the world.

Lovemarks is a strategy reliant on cultivating passion, as opposed to the reason-based desire to improve one's image promised by branding. The way Roberts explains it, it's a culmination of several years' worth of advancements in marketing. We've been moving toward lovemarks since products were first sold.

"In the beginning," Roberts writes in his book on the subject, "products were just, well, . . . products. One product was pretty much indistinguishable from another." This was fine when consumer goods and trade were still new and customers depended on local wares, but it soon became restrictive to producers hoping to expand their markets. "Over the centuries, trade increasingly stretched past local boundaries and the importance of trademarks increased. . . . Trademarks moved up a notch from simple name-tags to marks of trust and quality."[2]

Trade restrictions based on national or continental boundaries soon fell away, however, and international trade became more common. Simple trademarks, then, weren't enough—as we are now reminded daily. "Brands were developed to create differences for products that were in danger of becoming . . . hard to tell apart," explains Roberts.[3] This innovative strategy became the way to distinguish a product throughout the world as well as inspire a greater need than was justified by just, well . . . products. As branding took hold it gained an importance beyond the stature of a sales gadget. According to the strategy's most eloquent detractor, Naomi Klein, "the product always takes a backseat to the real product, the brand, and the selling of the brand acquired an extra component that can only be described as spiritual."[4]

Each of these advancements in shopping awareness technologies brought about entirely new legislation, legal restrictions put in place to provide these inventions protection within an increasingly predatory capitalist culture. It was important that these protective measures be written into law, too, stronger prohibitions than mere propriety might dictate. Propriety—for example, those guidelines that govern the borrowing of spiritual or religious traditions between sects or across national boundaries or, more relevant to our purposes, the intrinsically felt notions of decorum in the underground that govern what is borrowed from whom and when credit is given—has its own system of punishment when violated, but that system is not directly financial. The ever-growing corporate culture dictated that all goals and punishments be profit-minded; thus, the invention of trademarks was followed immediately by the invention of trademark law and a system of monetary fines was devised to punish violators. Similarly, the invention of branding[5]—the deliberate association of a product not just with a mere name but with an almost spiritual image, an idea—was followed by more stringent controls over what would and would not be subject to claims of intellectual property rights ownership, as well as an increased number of accusations of copyright violation, justified and not, and stricter punishments for those found in violation (a subject I will address in more detail in Chapter 4).

Each marketing advancement colonized new territory, additional space in individual human lives now available for corporate ownership. Klein refers to the colonization of space inside the individual under branding as not being merely physical but also mental.[6] Now, with lovemarks, it is emotional as well.

It seems obvious that Roberts would claim lovemarks a wholly natural development in business history, and his enthusiasm for his own invention would be easy to discount. Many have, dismissing lovemarks as simply more marketing, an effort on Roberts's part to forward "his own brand of branding."[7] But doing so misses the concurrent legions of youthful members of the contemporary underground—a wide category into which I would place not only punks but hipsters, skaters, B-boys, and any number of assorted subcategories all devoted to a life outside (or set against) corporate culture—who are working mighty hard to create art out of cars, illegally paint logos on city streets, and make handcrafted zines, comics, and flyers that promote brands, companies, and mass-produced goods.

The marketing of products, the legal restrictions created to protect the marketing of products, and the resounding cultural climate created by the protection of the marketing of products have all combined into a situation in which some of contemporary American society's most dirty, hostile, and poor members will work hard on behalf of companies seemingly intent on destroying their integrity. Most aren't doing it in exchange for big paychecks, either. In fact, most are selling out for almost no money at all.

It's true, though: branding isn't hacking it anymore. Spam fills our e-mail boxes, ads abound in our supermarkets, and we're constantly hearing pitches that may or may not relate directly to our lives. While most complain that the sheer volume of messages is the problem, marketers feel otherwise. Not enough of it works, they say instead. The frenzy of purchasing based solely on image association has finally proven hollow, and brands are now "out of juice," as Roberts contends. "They can't stand out in the marketplace, and they are struggling to connect with people."[8]

It's a big problem for those stuck making products—now two steps behind the rest of the business world, most of whom have moved on to creating image—but an even bigger problem for marketers, who have manufactured the culture of branding *and* set themselves up as examples of it. Weiden+Kennedy, Faith Popcorn's BrainReserve, and even Saatchi & Saatchi are all distinct marketing companies with distinct personalities that are totally devoid of actual products, instead offering an expensive set of potentials prepared to work on behalf of any paying customer. Still, many marketing companies forward products and therefore qualify as advertisers, a practice Roberts suggests they cease entirely. Lovemarks tap into pure passion, where products, and ads for them, are crass and unwelcome. Marketers wishing to stay competitive will connect with consumers emotionally, tapping directly into their snap decision-making skills and bypassing the need for product information entirely.

None of this is news to marketers, who have been trying for years to distance themselves from advertising. So have consumers. A group called Anti-Marketing even posted a little poem about it on their Web site:

> People are becoming smarter.
> They don't like to be deceived, or have their intelligence
>   insulted . . .
> People either ignore ads, or become annoyed by them . . .
> It's easy to get lost in the crowd.
> Everyone is selling something.

It's startlingly true and concisely written—people *do* hate ads and *don't* like to be lied to or talked down to by salespeople. It's also honest on a meta level that advertising can never approach: *Everyone is selling something.* Not least the writer of this candid little 2003 poem. Because, although the descriptions of its services could have appeared in the anticonsumerist magazine *Adbusters*, Anti-Marketing is a marketing firm. The poem concludes with the firm's pitch:"If traditional marketing is lying, then antimarketing is telling the truth." [9] While Anti-Marketing's clients are primarily minor Web-based entities (a few online bingo sites, a referral source for Internet bookies, and a fashion-ratings page) the firm *has* somehow distilled a contemporary truth to its essence with this anticommercial poem—and its use as a commercial object.

Roberts, therefore, may have coined the term lovemarks—which we'll use to denote our current postbranding ethos that relies on the word-of-mouth and small-media techniques we discuss in this book—but countless firms both large and small have been exploring the use of the deep emotional appeal for years. In some ways this strategy would appear to be a manifestation of the desire to link more brands with the trappings of authenticity. Yet lovemarks also strive to genuinely *be* more authentic, which is where things become odd. Should it seem deranged, for example, to promote the authenticity of a Web site where you can post pictures of your co-workers' bad clothes, it will seem even more ridiculous to tout the hard-won integrity of the marketing campaigns of blockbuster motion pictures (Chapter 6), sweatshop-produced athletic wear (Chapter 7), or video-game systems (Chapter 8).

But this is the strategy at the heart of lovemarks, which seeks to locate iconic brands that are infused with mystery, sensuality, and intimacy—and exploit the hell out of them for money. Those, as Roberts told Douglas Rakoff on *Frontline* in 2004, "are going to be the brands where the premium profits lie." [10]

One of these is Coke, the ubiquity of which makes clear the crisis of marketers who stay in the advertising game. We know it is unnecessary to advertise Coke. The brand is already everywhere; the name is even a synonym for soda. Often we aren't in much of a position to "Choose Coke," as the outdated slogan goes: sometimes it is the only supplier to restaurants, high schools, convenience stores, and hospitals, making Coke (or a Coke product) the only option in certain spaces by contract. [11] Television commercials for the product don't need to make claims about taste or describe what soda is to unfamiliar consumers. They only have to show the Coke logo at the end of any number of enjoyable and expensively produced Rockwellian scenes of feel-goodness. This serves to remind us: hey, Coke still exists. Maybe you'd like one right now? Surely one can't be far away.

This sort of thorough and holistic branding, not of products so much as our feelings about them, only works for a few dominant brands in big-money product areas. These Roberts deems lovemarks. And while second-place Pepsi makes a good showing, brand-wise—in fact occasionally surpassing Coke in sales—its youth-focused advertising campaign and alternative-to-the-mainstream image (initiated in 1968's "Join the Pepsi Generation" campaign) still rings true with consumers today, bolstered even by such arty projects as Negativland's album *Dispepsi* (which we'll discuss more in Chapter 5). The branding of Pepsi is so reliant on its oppositional status, the cola must work mighty hard to become a lovemark.

Because a lovemark is distinct from a brand. Where branding relies on metaphor (where things seen in close proximity to each other over and over become confused) and reification (where things are confused with their descriptions), lovemarks are meant to inspire "loyalty beyond reason." (In fact, this is the tagline of the word lovemarks, and Roberts's constant description of their use). Brands create identities we can borrow and adopt and meld with our own, but lovemarks take hold of our reptilian brains, striving to be so very special that we do not consider them in any way at all; we merely purchase. Reason, Roberts explains, problematically leads to conclusions. Emotion, however, creates action. Love urges decision making not based on consumers' sense of logic—*if I purchase this product I will be more like its brand image*—but on no information whatsoever. *I need this. Period.* With lovemarks there is no need for communication, no need for facts. Just need, of a particular brand-name, trademarked product.

And so lovemarks not only describe those certain big-name products for whom consumers have special feelings, it also describes the entire current ethos intent on cutting through the clutter of branding with intense emotional connections. Take, for example, the torrent of soda advertising messages even beyond Coke or Pepsi that we've taken in over the course of our lives, which both marketers and consumer watch groups will argue has exhausted our capacity to distinguish individual messages. And this is just one product field of many (some with even bigger ad budgets). Frankly, the sense of "truthiness"—as opposed to a full accounting of facts, which clearly is not in evidence in any of these strategies—to be had by reading such messages as Anti-Marketing's "Everyone is selling something" is a relief, a lapse in the demand for our attention constantly called for by such messages as "Drink Coke" or "Join the Pepsi Generation." Yet when "Everyone is selling something" gets followed immediately by any range of selling propositions, from "take our ad firm, for example," to "and here's another product you can buy," it becomes clear what the strategy of lovemarks really is. It's a forged connection to authenticity, a borrowed veil of integrity, a disingenuous stab at honesty. Because, in the end, "lovemarks" describes not an emotional connection but a financial transaction.

This is not to say that emotion doesn't play a significant role in postbranding strategies. Love is important to people, as Kevin Roberts notes in *Lovemarks*: "Without it, they die." Yet tired old notions of romance, long-lasting marriages, familial love, the bond of friendship: these are all perfectly acceptable, if slightly outmoded, forms of love. There are others, he reminds us, like the love of "a cold Becks beer." [12] Such consumerist passions—and close studies of how cults and other close-knit communities operate—got him thinking. "Love was the only way to ante up the emotional temperature and create the new kinds of relationships brands needed," he realized. [13] If the din of branding isn't distinguishable any longer, there needed to be a new way to sell more effectively to more people. Getting them to like marketers was key. "Connect with people's emotions," Roberts urges, "and—despite all their concerns about privacy—they will tell you almost anything." [14]

It's true: people can sense emotional commitment. Claire Ramsey, director of trends for the teen-focused market research group Youth Intelligence, uses this same falsely symbiotic relationship model. The teens she works with, she told Alissa Quart for her book *Branded*, can "feel the difference if they think we are stealing ideas from them and when we are forming relationships with them. We want them to like us and we want the relationships to last." Her motives are understandable. Without those relationships, she would have no youth to gather intelligence from, and her job and entire business would be in peril. Ramsey's method for forming these lasting relationships with youth? "We act like friends," she says unapologetically. [15]

But Quart isn't falling for it. Calling such professional trend spotters "faux teens," she notes that they act and dress decades younger than their actual ages. "The marketers put the adolescents at ease by cocking their heads drolly and layering speech with 'like' and 'whatever' and 'cool,'" Quart writes. [16] It's all a put-on, with distinct goals of financial reward just over the pretty, but fake, horizon.

Quart may not be impressed, but the girls who hang out with faux teens are. The marketers "acknowledge they have an easier time reaching teens because of the teens' increasingly bleak and atrophied family relationships."[17] Some girls Quart talks to feel more isolated and are more solitary than those of years past, due in part to divorce and the lack of after-school programs, and they clearly appreciate the attention of an older but still cool adult.

It all reeks of charlatanism, something Roberts warns against stringently. "The trick is not to exploit this thirst for personal connections," Roberts says. (You know, that thing without which we could *die*.) "But to slake it with integrity."[18]

The meaning of *slake* is central, both to Roberts's plan and to the stories we will tell in this book. Distinct from something so arcane as "provide," to "slake" means "to appease a desire for." To fill marketing with *authentic* passion would be, we know instinctively, a difficult task. But to give the *appearance* of providing a deep emotional connection and uncompromised integrity, that's a little bit easier.

A vast network of people devoted to integrity, respectful of creativity, and united by a disinclination to buy what the mainstream might wish to sell, the DIY punk underground—whatever categorical descriptions are used to describe its members—has always been a tough market to break into. This is especially true if you're a major media star, corporate shill, or multimillionaire. To the underground, you're the enemy, antithetical to its purpose. If you can break in, though, it's worth your marketing team's effort, because when the underground's abuzz over your movie, your soda, your footwear, your drug of choice, it sells like hotcakes.[19]

Take Pabst Blue Ribbon, for example, which, after a series of calculated endorsements by select members of fringe culture (bike messengers, specifically), enjoyed "a highly unlikely comeback," marketing critic Rob Walker notes. "In 2002, sales of the beer, which had been sinking steadily since the 1970s, actually rose 5.3 percent. From the start of 2003 through April 20, [2003] super-market beer sales are up another 9.4 percent. It is endorsed in *The Hipster Handbook*, a paperback dissection of cool, and is popping up in trendy bars from the Mission District to the Lower East Side." [20] How did the notoriously cheap swill become the toast of the town, everyone wanted to know? By fostering a natural incli-nation on the part of certain beer fans toward PBR's accidental lack of image following several years of failing to devote a signifi-cant budget to ad campaigns. Yet once their market was identified, this changed dramatically: cash payments, free beer parties, and swag were all employed to solidify the beer's emotional relation-ship with the rowdy and influential bike messenger crowd.

Exploiting a connection to punk and DIY communities, which many bike messengers would claim to be a part of, is a re-cent phenomenon. Yet it's only one of the latest in a long line of identifiably countercultural demographics to be pillaged for sales potential. Thomas Frank and others have demonstrated that coun-tercultures are little more than scenic stops along the highway of all-encompassing, all-American consumerism. Frank's *The Con-quest of Cool* documents the selling of 1960s underground culture through the marketing industry's surprisingly natural adaptation of rock-and-roll music, Nehru jackets, and psychedelic artwork. Frank refutes the idea that this wave of ad images represented the co-optation of a genuinely political subculture, and argues that the counterculture and its well-advertised mirror image were a single large national shift in approaches to culture evident both in the boardroom and on the streets. This is a theme taken up by *Na-tion of Rebels*'s co-authors Joseph Heath and Andrew Potter as well.

To some degree, this is true. As noted in Chapter 1, the mythology of co-optation implies that the cultures at risk of being co-opted are private and protected entities. They are not; cultures are by definition created by people and, as people change, so does the culture. So at least as far as *legal* protection goes—and the financial muster to back it up—one of the few "cultures" afforded protection is the corporate. Punk and DIY communities even strive to be deliberately accessible and eminently reproducible, transmissable through the mail or inspired by a song heard on the college radio station.[21] They were viral before viral was a marketing strategy.

Yet what distinguishes this current fascination with the underground and its particular values and tactics is not that it might be new but that it appears, at least from a marketing standpoint, worthless. Punk and DIY communities are notoriously poor, remember. However popular it may be with the Martha Stewart types, DIY culture did not emanate from the idle rich. This is in contrast to the underground of the 1960s, the dominant youth culture: a vast, moneyed demographic that invented the term antiestablishment and had the numbers to qualify as an oppositional force, becoming a kind of establishment itself. The counterculture was made up of desirable spokespeople on the hunt for shiny markers for their newly constructed identities, willing to test innovative modes of consumption with the bucks to back their efforts. Punk, however, evolved in opposition to that counterculture as well as to the culture at large. Punk was thought to be the thing that simply couldn't sell out, because it was by definition ugly and nasty and based on an opposition to money and fame and success. It was constituted against the concept of a market, particularly against the concept of a mass market. That someone could define and sell to its members at all was preposterous, because membership was based on the principle that what was made by hand for yourself and your friends was better than what could be purchased.

Punk was founded on integrity above all else, on a dedication to personal artistic expression free of financial influence, intended primarily to share talents, and secondarily to foster a separate but sustainable economy based, for the most part, on social networks. Money earned from the sale of goods went into making more copies (or paying off the debt accrued making the originals), and while large sums of money bring about immediate accusations of selling out, these accusations stood for a deeper legitimate concern that artists would sacrifice vision in order to make a buck. That's why the tapes and CDs were cheap, the zines often free, the flyers crumpled, and the T-shirts torn and ratty. They were explicitly designed to remain unmarketable.

Yet if Frank and others are right and even radical fringe cultures are simply holding pens for the next edgy marketing plan, it is to be expected that marketing would eventually encompass unmarketability. What makes the use of punk and DIY culture as advertising tools so unique, however, is that it not only coincides with the shift in marketing toward the youth demographic and furthers a trend toward media consolidation to a nearly ridiculous extent but also dovetails neatly with marketing's new desire for passion and integrity. The gray area created when punk and DIY meet marketing offers several compelling and extreme examples of contemporary consumerism. Unfortunately, this combination of forces is wreaking some serious havoc on how we can imagine our individual influence over the world.

If the question is, how did a distinctly anticorporate subculture even start to absorb the whims of the market, the answer may be something called fufu berry soda. Hot on the heels of the mid-1990s major-label frenzy, which made it clear that punks could be sold to on a mass scale, a soda appeared on the scene that started to bring marketing and the underground a bit closer together. It was a weird soda; you couldn't really order it in restaurants or get it out of vending machines in places where you normally found vending machines, and it didn't, therefore, compete with Coke or Pepsi. It came in flavors like green apple, blue bubblegum, and—*Christ*—turkey and gravy (although this was seasonal). Perhaps most important, it had a minimalist, low-key, totally straightforward logo that almost wasn't a logo at all, just a generic name: Jones Soda. Rather than forward a single iconic image on which to build its brand, the Jones Soda labels featured limited-edition photographic images pulled from customers' submitted artwork. In contrast to standard operating procedure (read: branding), the audience was able to dictate the Jones Soda image. With whatever their hearts desired.

This was no OK Cola, a foul-tasting concoction and cynical marketing move by Coca-Cola, who in 1994 had apparently read the hype about "slackers" and brought in the coolest rising stars of underground comics to market their product to disaffected youth. Turkey-and-gravy soda was not delicious, true, but in comparison to OK's carefully test-marketed flavor (an odd mix of down-market cola and watery orange drink), it had *guts*. This was a beverage of the people—if by people we mean the urban youth demographic—discovered in local hangouts like tattoo parlors and skate shops, unaffiliated with any discomfiting parent company, and adorned, unassumingly, with photos sent in by fans like you. It was a welcome change from the mandated identities of brands like Coke and Pepsi.

Founder and CEO Peter van Stolk makes sure you know how unique his beverage and company are, too. As his bio on the Jones Soda Web site explains, "He entered the highly competitive beverage industry, learned the rules, and then promptly rejected them."

In interviews he talks about his ski-bum past and not giving "a rat's ass" about your opinions of him or of his little drink company.[22] "His skateboard-dude persona might be a bit unorthodox for the boardroom," *Beverage World* reported, neglecting to note that van Stolk had had plenty of time to tone down that persona during the decade spent as a beverage distributor, during which the Jones Soda lovemark was conceived.[23]

Anyway, the members of the board were not the ones making Jones Soda popular—skateboard dudes were. When it first hit, Jones Soda was targeted to the thirteen- to twenty-four-year-old set, as evidenced by the odd locations chosen for their vending machines: skate parks, bike shops, record stores. Jones Soda RVs (still in operation) even brought free drinks to snowboarding competitions, concerts, and other hip locales to connect directly with its target demographic. And they went further than that: "Jones Soda was one of the first companies to enter into sponsorship deals in alternative sports," one writer noted.[24]

This was a brilliant and previously untested strategy: van Stolk had thoroughly entrenched a product within a youth subculture and grown the brand as if it were a natural part of that scene. But of course it wasn't natural at all—it had been artificially grafted onto that milieu. And van Stolk's iconoclasm may not run as deep as his Web site bio claims. He told *Fast Company*, "The very first case of Jones Soda went to the founder of Nike, Phil Knight. He got the first case of Jones Soda. I don't know if he ever saw it. But he sent a letter—I don't know if he signed it or if his secretary signed it. I don't care; it's framed in the boardroom. I just really like what he was doing. One of the things about Jones Soda, I always viewed Jones as an accessory."[25]

An accessory, though, on par with pet rocks, black-rubber bracelets, and maybe even stylish athletic shoes: the soda is now carried in Target, Starbucks, Panera, and 7-Eleven stores. And although it's currently only a $30 million-ish company in a $66 billion industry, in the third quarter of 2006 alone it pulled in revenues in the $10 million range, a growth spurt that only seems to be beginning its rise.[26] One financial analyst on *Seeking Alpha*, an online stock market opinion and analysis blog, noted that the company's reliance on young adults (and those now moving into their thirties) has led to a slow but "still respectable double-digit annual revenue growth. From an investment perspective, what's important is the potential path of future earnings growth." A smaller company competing against mainstays like Coke and Pepsi isn't expected to pull in more than a tiny margin of their profits, but smaller companies spend less, too. "Efficiencies of scale could also drive Jones' net profit margins much higher as revenue grows in the years ahead," the financial analyst continues. "In the consumer products area, brand acceptance determines survival and growth, especially for a small company like Jones. . . . Though difficult to measure, the unique way that Jones chooses to do business does, in my opinion, help to grow the brand."[27]

All without a penny spent on advertising, because the demographic Jones relies on doesn't pay attention to the stuff. A *Business Week* article on Jones Soda and van Stolk explains, "His target consumers are increasingly hard to find through conventional mass media as they spend more time on the computer. So Jones Soda's marketing has been more promotions-driven, with the company establishing street credibility with this generation of young consumers, who are cynical of conventional advertising and media savvy beyond their years."[28] Van Stolk concurs: "Our competition spends over a billion dollars a year. We can't play by their rules. When you're marketing without money, you have to stay true to the fact that you need to make an emotional connection."[29] This is the company's founding concept. Jones Soda was not chasing after approval from alternative cultures; it defined itself from the beginning as an integral part of alternative cultures in order to attract their members. "They discover us in environments where they hang out," van Stolk told *USA Today*. "It makes us legitimate."[30]

If Jones Soda successfully relied on the underground as a legitimizing force, it had wider cultural implications as well. For example, van Stolk is called an inspiration by Proctor & Gamble, which, in 2001, created the highly successful (and much reviled) Tremor program for marketing young adult products to young adults by young adults. A word-of-mouth campaign based on van Stolk's infiltration methods, Tremor today claims close to two hundred fifty thousand dedicated youth who, after being encouraged to visit the Web site by friends, signed up to receive free products (P&G's and others'—Tremor is available for hire) in exchange for chatting them up to other pals.[31] They have now started a program for moms called VocalPoint and inspired the Girl's Intelligence Agency (GIA), a slumber party–based word-of-mouth provider. Also in 2001, a similar peer-to-peer marketing style was adopted by the Boston firm BzzAgent, which places a relatively austere sixty thousand volunteer marketers on the streets for a wide variety of products to perform one-on-one promotions for the books, frozen dinners, and cosmetics BzzAgent represents. Word-of-mouth marketing is estimated to be used by 85 percent of the country's most cutting-edge advertising firms.[32]

Commercial watchdog group Consumer Alert questions the legality of buzz marketing, calling its methods deceptive and in possible violation of Federal Trade Commission standards. Jonah Bloom, executive editor of *Advertising Age*, is equally skeptical: "This is a practice that may be illegal," he told *USA Today*.[33] Word-of-mouth campaigns may be criminal, but so are wheat-pasting and graffiti in many cities, and, as we will soon see, marketers don't seem to care about breaking those laws, either. For now, however, legal issues don't seem to keep people from signing up.

Nor, for that matter, do ethical concerns. According to the participants I talked to, Tremor and GIA seem to operate on the simple principle that kids love free stuff. They love trying it out, they love being experts on it, and they love talking about it. They might not love every free thing they get, and they don't have to pretend they do—following one Consumer Alert awareness campaign, buzz marketing volunteers were explicitly urged to be completely honest in their product promotions—but they do love getting those things. They're not the only ones; adults love free stuff, too, which is why BzzAgent and VocalPoint exist.[34] These marketing volunteers seem to feel that a connection to a company is, at least, better than nothing. "I've already been giving word of mouth campaigns for free all by myself," says Shannon, a BzzAgent in Ontario on a blog she keeps called *Tales from the Fairy Godmother*. "I can't wait to tell everybody and anybody when I use an exceptional product (I talked for days about my Mr. Clean Magic Eraser. . . . everybody with kids should have one BTW), get a great price (Cool Quenchers drink mix at No Frills On for 77 cents and I had 30 cent off coupons) or receive incredible service somewhere."[35]

Yet between the love of free stuff and the urge to belong to something, word-of-mouth marketing volunteers disassociate from the practice of marketing. "They tend to see themselves as not being involved in marketing at all," Rob Walker wrote in his groundbreaking 2004 *New York Times Magazine* article "The Hidden (in Plain Sight) Persuaders."[36]

It's clear how participants could be confused about what they're really doing: they make no money, working instead for points that can be traded in for "free gifts" they rarely pick up; have no professional affiliation with the company; and feel no obligation to claim ownership of the products hyped in campaigns. Moreover, volunteers are never given fiscal tallies on the success of campaigns, as would be expected in a job; they're simply given personal feedback.

It is, however, *very* personal feedback, which starts to explain the appeal of joining something like BzzAgent. BzzReports, the description of a successful word-of-mouth endeavor, are filed with the site after each campaign's completion, and BzzAgents read them carefully, offering specific feedback or joking about the contents of the report so it is clear that they are being read. "Nice job in Bzzing your chef friends," one such feedback e-mail sent in response to a crème liqueur campaign reads. "We are very excited and can't wait to hear about your chef friends' drink recipe. . . . Have fun experimenting, who knows, you may create a most delicious drink and Happy Bzzing!" [37]

It begins to seem as though all people need to be persuaded to incorporate marketing into their personal lives is a little targeted attention. Agents feel valuable because they have an emotional connection to something larger than themselves; they *are* valuable, however, because that emotional connection is extremely profitable, although tenuous—an "act," faux teen and demographic researcher Claire Ramsey called it. And that's just weird.

"There's something truly creepy about the notion of marketers manipulating what ordinary people say to one another," one reporter noted.[38] "Word-of-mouth marketing agencies catch people's attention because they freak people out," Rob Walker confirmed over the phone. Once his buzz marketing story came out, he told me, "a lot of people were really horrified. On the other hand, a lot of people immediately told me they signed up to be a part of the BzzAgent team." This was verified by both the founder of BzzAgent and several individuals who wrote to him in appreciation of his story. How many joined? I asked; Walker's not sure. A couple of thousand, he recalled being told, all of whom signed up almost immediately after his story ran.[39]

And it just gets weirder. Word-of-mouth agencies build their teams through their own clandestine word-of-mouth campaigns, which, in Tremor's case, can be safe from the prying eyes of parents and teachers because they're communicated directly and exclusively from kid to kid—no adults allowed. Over at BzzAgent, kids and adults alike visit the Web site and sign up, then recruit their closest friends to join. And when the parade of free stuff begins, so too do the marketing campaigns for hundreds of products aimed at their exact demographic, made clear by both the initial online application and subsequent (highly personal) reports: shampoo, candy, music, deodorant, movies, chicken sausage, cosmetic cream, a book about changing your life. Cynics may call it Product Placement X-treme, a direct infiltration of daily life, but marketing strategists—and psychologists—just know it works.

A 2005 report in the academic periodical *Sport Journal* found that, at least among teens, recommendations from peers (aka "socialization agents" the report calls them) carry the most weight in a young adult's decision to purchase certain goods. Public products—those purchased or consumed outside the home, such as the clothing, food, or books that make up most of a word-of-mouth agency's clients—are, it seems, susceptible to public pressures. "Peers exert a relatively strong influence on purchasing public products," states the report, which focused on peer influence in athletic shoe purchasing. In fact, among the more than five hundred teens studied, friends' opinions heavily outweighed the competing influences of family and television. "The most important socialization agent when teens purchase athletic shoes appears to be the peers. . . . [They] provide the greater influence for teens' consumer behavior than other agents," the report finds. And it goes on to note: "From a business perspective, athletic shoe marketers who target teenagers might consider consumers' social structural and individual position status to design more valuable marketing strategies. . . . [But] marketers should keep in mind that not all teens are susceptible to TV advertisings and they are skeptical. Therefore, marketers need to exercise caution to communicate sincerely." [40]

The notion of some large international megacorporation with all the ad money in the world sending a team of suits to a sit-down with a blue-haired girl who does a zine about her crappy coffee shop job, comical thought it may be, isn't wholly unthinkable anymore. Marketers seem to have realized that underground media tactics "communicate sincerity" better, faster, and cheaper than an exquisitely staged TV commercial or downtown billboard.

Through well-planned word-of-mouth campaigns and, as we will start to see in the next chapter, ill-conceived activist endeavors alike, more and more nonmarketers are doing the work of marketing. Kids in high school are shilling for youth clothing companies and blockbuster films; branding efforts can be seen both on Madison Avenue and in antisweatshop actions in front of athletic-wear stores; office workers across the country are touting the wonders of motor oil and chicken sausage to co-workers; and some of the most devoted fringe elements of our society, unwashed antiauthoritarian punk rockers, are selling headache remedies, foreign cars, and well-known bourgeois coffee.

In its efforts to "cut through the clutter," marketing is becoming decentralized and diffuse. One might start to wonder if perhaps marketers weren't working themselves right out of their jobs.

The keen strategists behind such campaigns are all prime examples of what Thomas Frank described in *The Conquest of Cool* as "people in more advanced reaches of the corporate world [who] deplored conformity, distrusted routine, and encouraged resistance to established power."[41] Take the zinester, writer, punk-music fan, and Lucasfilm, Ltd., employee, for example, who saw no irony in using small media in a promotional campaign for the big-budget media event *Star Wars: Episode III—Revenge of the Sith*. How about the anonymous skateboarders at Nike who needed an image that spoke to their genuine enthusiasm for and knowledge of skate-punk culture and simply appropriated an image they all already loved? Then there's the ad firm OMD Worldwide that was hired by Sony PlayStation to reach out to the underground with art that appears right in the urban landscape—by artists who mastered their form by running from cops, working at night, and reveling in the noncorporate work environment of the city streets. The marketers we'll meet in this book simply love punk and DIY culture and crave the integrity it conveys. That they're usurping that integrity and misapplying it to their own big-money projects rarely seems to enter their minds. They believe they're just being edgy.

While it may be easy to write this off as the way of the world—or more specifically, the way of our late-capitalist society—we would do well to remember what influence marketing does have over national consciousness. The use of a subculture's trappings to sell products devalue that subculture's essential message, as it did with the 1970s peace movement. Today's underground-inspired and -bred fleet of marketers, with their desire to circumvent logic, tap directly into our emotions, and claim this as integrity, may be more destructive.

While corporate entities that feel no discomfort appropriating underground media methods forged in direct response to their lack of access to the corporate world may strike some as distasteful, few have been able to pinpoint the exact problem. None of the campaigns I discuss in this book used underground media exclusively as primary campaigns, making it even more surprising that they would be used at all. All of them—every corporate-sponsored zine, every professionally printed and wheat-pasted flyer, every paid piece of graffiti—begs the same question: with endless money, reach, and talent at your disposal, why waste time and energy emulating the sloppy DIY aesthetic?

It's a good question, and the obvious answer can be found in a GoGorilla Media guidebook from 2001. The booklet outlines a series of what were at the time cutting-edge marketing techniques but are now common venues for corporate logos: street teams, posters, coasters, textbook covers, and street-painted stencils. GoGorilla was founded, the opening missive reads, "to bombard and overwhelm consumers with advertising messages as they go about their daily lives. In our view, there is nothing more regrettable than an empty space with no advertising printed on it. . . . The GoGorilla team has painstakingly researched, planned, and developed every one of our products with one goal in mind: maximum intrusion." [42] If this is the goal of cutting-edge marketing, of course underground methods are to be utilized. So are any others that come along.

Fun is important to GoGorilla, too. "The best advertising is fun advertising. Advertising that takes chances and never takes itself too seriously," [43] the guidebook states. But fun can get out of hand, as in their most famous campaign, which involved applying ads to

U.S. currency—technically defacing money, which is illegal. They acknowledge that their techniques may cross "the limits of good taste, respectability, and even legality," yet GoGorilla goes on to prophesy, "Advertising will never be the same."[44]

And it hasn't been. The company is behind the nearly ubiquitous GoCard, a free postcard rack mounted in bars, restaurants, and cafés and filled with postcard-sized ads for Altoids, Biore Strips, Nike, Levis, Bacardi, and probably every feature film that's come out since 2001. And its more "edgy" tactics—street teams, stencils, etc.—have been used by big-name clients like Snapple, ABC's *The Bachelor*, and XM Satellite Radio, to name just a few.

Scott Johnson, columnist for the trade magazine *Advertising Age* and the executive creative director of Tribal DDB Worldwide from 2003 to 2006, offers a bit more insight into the corporate desire to emulate underground techniques. "As the media landscape becomes increasingly fragmented, mass media inevitably lose credibility with young people and others with pretense to hipness (whatever that happens to mean at a given moment)," he told me via e-mail. "If 50 million people watch something, how cool can it be? The notion of exclusivity, after all, is a key part of being cool. Small media messages can feel more personal, more targeted, more relevant. In addition, there is a belief that people are bored with the media they've become familiar with. That being the case, if you can put an ad in a place that will surprise someone, you increase your likelihood of breaking through the clutter and getting noticed."[45] (At Tribal DDB, Johnson was responsible for accounts including Sierra Mist, the U.S. Air Force, and Wal-Mart, so when he offers advice on getting noticed, it seems fairly well-tested.) The argument for using underground media techniques, distinguished by their shoddy craftspersonship, street-level placement, and accessible materials, would then seem primarily to be one of novelty.

But Johnson continues his explanation, offering a case study from his own repertoire of former clients. " 'Smaller' media tend to be better at building relationships with consumers. The Internet is a great example. More than 9 million people have signed up to be part of the Pepsi X-tras program because they want to have some sort of relationship with the brand." [46] Despite the giant brands behind these small media tactics, individual consumers crave singularity, a sense of connection, a similar experience to being handed a mix tape at a show and being asked to check it out because they might like it. It's personal, touching, and sweet. It's unfortunate that it's all part of a well-organized, big-money effort described in violent terms like "bombardment" and "maximum intrusion" within the industry.

That marketing would try to infiltrate a community as hostile to its methods as punk and DIY communities shocks no one. Once we abandon the tired arguments over co-optation and selling out, we see clearly that marketing strategies are constantly evolving in new directions, any directions, all directions. It is a business dependent upon both expansion and innovation to survive. Although we have begun to see what machinations lie behind the interest in marketing punk, what remains startling is the sheer number of zinesters, graffiti artists, and punk-rock musicians joining such campaigns, sometimes without even bothering to question the continued integrity and essential independence of their work.

What is at stake here is not simply the ethos of punk. That's been used to sell Good Charlotte, Hot Topic T-shirts, and any number of books about zines published by major houses to the mainstream for years now, not to mention its more natural use by bands, self-publishers, crafters, and street artists as an inherent part of trying to survive by doing what they are good at.

What is at stake here is far greater than even the questions of authenticity and authorial voice behind both underground marketing techniques and Anti-Marketing's oddly intentioned but still anti-advertising ad slogan. These issues spur this book: they are fun to argue about with friends when you chance upon an Astroturf (as opposed to grassroots) political protest, a piece of graffadi, a TV program that uses mocketing techniques, some street brandalism, or other realities of living in our big, fat, remix culture. Yet hidden somewhere within these jarring dichotomous cultural products, the notion of integrity—the idea that individuals can act autonomously and honestly according to a privately held system of values—abuts the corporate-sponsored assertion that, in fact, they can't. As marketing strives to burrow deeper into our social networks and bypass our reason entirely, our ability to locate and uphold personal integrity—factors that must precede a demand for democracy—is being challenged.

3

PREACHING TO THE CONVERTED

A white man preaching—loud, self-important, and seemingly filled with scorn for the decision-making abilities of the commonfolk—didn't stand out much in 2005, when white men were preaching from every TV, radio, and street corner in town. This one, though, stands in front of an international coffee shop chain, counseling a boycott of its wares while repeatedly, carefully, constantly invoking the name of this chain to those he suggests avoid it. He's surrounded by a chorus: harmonious, beatific, and perfectly cued to his speech. He's wearing black robes and a white collar. If you initially fail to notice him amid the onslaught of billboards, the din of car radio–blasted commercials, and the throngs of hawkers for off-off-Broadway shows or famous maker sales, his voice is sonorous. Hypnotic. Arresting. His message equally so. Your constant interior monologue cannot help but respond, "Wait . . . *don't* drink Starbucks?"

Reverend Billy Talen and the Church of Stop Shopping are the leaders of the spiritual movement against rampant consumerism, a fast-growing church with many devoted followers. "Oh children," one sermon begins,

> Let us pray to the God who is not a product. We ask that our message go straight into the sky, past the logo-barnacled walls, up past Cindy Crawford's lip mole. And

we ask to be protected and blessed by those whose stories are buried beneath this overlay of logos. . . . We ask for the blessing of the family that ran the Astor Riviera Diner—evicted from this corner by the speculator lawyers of Starbucks. . . . Amen.[1]

Their methods are theatrical and attention grabbing, an example of a popular form of anticorporate activism known as culture jamming. A loose network of tactics used to revolt against the onslaught of corporate creep into public space, culture-jamming methods range from the alteration of existing ads in situ (called "adbusting") to the organization of public-space reclamation parties like Critical Mass or Reclaim the Streets; from the airing of TV "subvertisements" (ads that intend to promote ideas over products) to the performance of "cultural interventions" like shopdropping as well as the street theater of groups like the Church of Stop Shopping.[2] Culture jamming meets brands where they lie in an effort to widen consumer choice to include not just more products but the idea of no products at all.

"I will be an interruption today," Talen narrates in his 2003 book, *What Should I Do if Reverend Billy Is in My Store?* as he prepares for a protest. "Our affinity group, our 'church,' will try to slide between a group of people and the cash register of Starbucks, the fastest-growing brand name in the world. We'll try to pry them apart."[3]

Despite the persuasive nature of his tactics, Reverend Billy has been accused of a central hypocrisy: his basic form of protest against shopping is to create large, impossible-to-miss anti-advertising campaigns that invariably draw a great deal of attention to the stores he targets. Reverend Billy tells people what not to buy and precisely where not to buy it. He spreads his word with actions located at the stores he boycotts and via the videos he stars in, books he writes, and CDs he records—which are available for purchase at several national chain stores owned by companies he urges passersby not to support.

This may seem disconcerting when viewed by the casual liberal unaccustomed to the ironies of manic, late-stage capitalism. The Church of Stop Shopping purports to call for a high-alert, all-products boycott. It also creates products for sale. At the very least Reverend Billy is complicit in the act of shopping; at times he must actively support it. The paradox is so blatant it was pointed out by the Chicago *RedEye*, a paper no stranger to irony itself. The free tabloid version of the *Chicago Tribune*, targeted to young professionals who don't usually read newspapers, melds news and advertising so seamlessly it regularly runs front-page headlines such as "Why You Should Buy the New X-Box." In a short feature on a Reverend Billy protest in Chicago, the paper nonetheless criticized the activist, correctly positioning him in the consumerist framework within which he operates, against which he rails, and from which he profits: "Talen acknowledges the conflicts, saying he fears his own hypocrisy. And he admits he must sometimes dance with the enemy in an effort to spread his word."[4]

This cookie-cutter critique of Reverend Billy does miss the context he provides for unchecked consumerism: the rampant gentrification that encompasses the loss of organically popularized, independently owned spaces (the Astor Riviera Diner, as he is quoted mentioning earlier) in favor of the purely profitable (Starbucks). Yet the parody of sanctimoniousness that Reverend Billy engages in is a dangerous game: when a free tabloid can find fault in your faux religious, anticonsumerist message, it may be time to rethink it. But the activist has an easy answer, one that happens to be true. "Everyone's a sinner," Billy glibly proclaims.[5] Although the paper is itself the product of crass market calculations, it's nonetheless impressive that Reverend Billy's project prompted the Chicago *RedEye* to address the existence of anticonsumerist urges at all.

All activist strategies that attempt to take on branding, however, contain substantive contradictions. "Anticorporate activism enjoys the priceless benefits of borrowed hipness and celebrity—borrowed, ironically enough, from the brands themselves," explains Naomi Klein.[6] The Church of Stop Shopping is no exception. The faux religiosity Reverend Billy engages in encourages dogmatic adherence to and blind faith in principles he himself has established—much like a real preacher's demands, except for the divine part, and very much like the advertising to which culture jamming is fundamentally opposed. (His appropriation of gospel music has also prompted accusations of racism.) Frustratingly, the mode of instruction employed by the Church and its charismatic leader discourages critical engagement in the actual issues that underlie brand fervor. The Church of Stop Shopping provides an easy fix, a palliative that becomes increasingly problematic the more products they offer as safe, anticonsumerist shopping alternatives. Soon, the entire notion of stopping shopping is seen as impossible to achieve, a joke. Then the project becomes participatory entertainment about political things instead of an engaged activist endeavor, an anecdote to share with the customer behind you at Starbucks: merely "amusing," as I recall a high school friend dubbing a cigarette billboard ad reworked with crossed-out eyes and gaunt cheeks to evoke the cancerous effects of smoking.

We'll look more closely at activist strategies that specifically rely on parody in Chapter 5, but for now it should be clear that the insurmountable problem of culture jamming is that marketing has already surpassed it. This is not Reverend Billy's fault but stems in part from a fundamental and widespread misunderstanding of the boycott—the withholding of support for a product, company, or government in the face of objectionable practices—as a political strategy. The story of the very first boycott, named for its recipient, Charles C. Boycott, will provide a more complete picture of how contemporary activism has failed to predict and combat current marketing practices and may help us develop an effective language of dissent.

An Englishman working in Ireland as an agent for an absentee landlord, Boycott unfairly evicted several tenants of an apartment house in 1780. Charles Parnell, a politician and a member of the Irish Land League, a group focused on land-reform issues, urged Boycott's servants and community to abandon him in punishment. For several months Boycott's entire family was denied service in stores and did not get mail in recognition of his act of injustice. A message was received anyway: by the end of that calendar year Boycott had left his job and taken his family back home to England. The first boycott was a success, and the word became the name for the practice of refusing to cooperate with those who commit unfair actions.

As a demand that individuals bear responsibility for deeds committed in the name of business, the boycott holds great potential for contemporary anticorporate activists, struggling with a legal system that defines a corporation as an individual. Personal responsibility, however, is often overlooked. As Parnell originally saw it, the full strategy was one of organized isolation, and complete community support was necessary for it to succeed. Support for the boycott was not based exclusively on abstract ethics or principles, either; Charles Boycott was a local man who had wronged his neighbors.

Now, however, a boycott is generally understood as a campaign to withhold *financial* support for an unethical product or a company using egregious business practices (we are, clearly, a consumer-oriented society). Thus, contemporary boycott targets are most often corporations or the products of corporations. And although citizens have continued to wage small boycotts against the United States and other governments—whether by refusing to pay taxes, moving to Canada, and renouncing citizenship; or demanding divestment from companies that deal with unfair governments (a leverage boycott)—it is direct corporate influence with which we are primarily concerned here. In a corporate boycott, withholding financial support by refusing to buy certain products is important, certainly. That is the fiscal message the media, also focused on the consumerist aspects of our society, can embrace and disseminate. It is important to remember, however, that although the loss of profit on certain products may be a contributing factor in a company's decision to reevaluate its habits, a boycott will likely enlist more backers and work more quickly if nonfinancial support is withheld, too.

In fact, today nonfinancial aspects of a boycott may be more effective precisely because they cannot be explained away by phrases like "whims of the market" or erased by a loan. (It is clearly not a "cash-flow problem" if you don't receive your mail and your neighbors ignore you.) Profit loss, in our logomaniacal culture, is not the sole motivating factor in a corporation's decision to change its procedures. It is brand devaluation.

Negative publicity is the primary aim of any well-organized boycott, although you won't find that phrase in the how-to guides disseminated by Co-op America and other organizations founded to assist, sustain, and spread awareness of national actions. Instead, you'll find affirmatively worded phrases like "make your demands specific and behavior-oriented" and "get endorsements from non-profit organizations."[7] Of course, you need a target first, plus an eye-catching image or heartbreaking story that describes the horrors your target company commits. But then you need to get that image or story out. The largest undertaking for any successful boycott, therefore, is PR. Press releases, leaflets, petition cards, educational films, advertisements, online networking with boycott support organizations, public service announcements (PSAs), celebrity endorsements, T-shirts, event sponsorships, press conferences, demonstrations, and letters to the editor are all standard—and all built on a single compelling picture of the damage one brand can inflict.

"The negative publicity associated with a boycott (or threat of a boycott) can affect a company's image in addition to its sales," one guideline for boycott organizers suggests. For this reason, companies that create consumer goods—specifically, goods that are consumed in public—are thought to be more effective targets. "Products that are not publicly purchased or consumed are more difficult to boycott effectively," the guide warns.[8] It is a company's popular image that more often than not determines its choice as a boycott target. Brand jujitsu, it's been called: the use of a company's own power against itself. In many cases a strong brand will be the primary target of a boycott, even if that brand is not the most egregious violator of fair practices. Thus, because Nike is a universally recognized brand, it will be a boycott target, while Adidas, Reebok, New Balance, and Aktiv Shoes may not even if all utilize the same sweatshops. The hope is that targeting the most visible brand will cause competitors to comply with boycotters' demands of their own accord.

Effective though this interpretation of boycotting may be, it's

easy to see that emphasizing brand strength more than the violation of fair practices in choosing the targets of activism is kind of
a strange concession to the power of branding. More frustrating
is that contemporary boycotts fail to incorporate what was so
charming about the strategy as it was conceived: that an entire
community personally held Charles C. Boycott accountable for an
unjust act. His boycott was meted out through a network of individuals personally unwilling to interact with him, refusing even to
acknowledge him. And in a world where, as we will see in Chapter 5, even negative publicity is good publicity, we may wish to re-
consider the full scope of Parnell's original boycott strategy by
responding more fully to acts of wrongdoing by fellow members
of our society.

Still, it is easy to comprehend why this part of boycotting has
fallen away. Corporations were invented to unite groups toward
common profit-making goals, thus negating the individual human
assignment of responsibility. Moreover, the purpose of the heavily
branded culture within which we operate is to create a network of
product support so diffuse few realize they participate in it. But it
is this diffuse support that makes, for example, Reverend Billy and
the Church of Stop Shopping's actions so troubling. Consider, for
example, his decision to allow a national music megastore to offer
his product as one of several profit-making ventures for the company. It just doesn't quite register with his call for an end to consumerism, nor does his regular repetition of brand names. These
glitches in Reverend Billy's message means that he has failed to
note (or is choosing to ignore) the nonfinancial support lent to
corporations when promoting their name, even when speaking
negatively of it.

Reverend Billy Talen and the Church of Stop Shopping are

not, however, simply advertising. The message this church preaches *is* different from what is found in magazine ads, on billboards, in TV commercials, and on radio spots—but it's not *that* different. For me, "*don't* drink Starbucks" is a little too similar to "drink Starbucks," and the antisweatshop movement's culture jam "just stop it" sounds too much like its target Nike's "just do it." By the same token "Stop shopping (unless you're buying anticonsumerist product)" is merely a new, improved flavor of "Buy this." "Research shows that it is dangerous to use negatives," David Ogilvy warned. The revered founder of Ogilvy & Mather and author of the seminal ad handbook *Confessions of an Advertising Man*, Ogilvy was sharp and knew his craft. He explained, "Many readers will miss the negative" in ad copy.[9] Activists may wish to heed his warning.

Critics argued that the fun family of strategies known as culture jamming had fast become a different brand of consumerism.[10] Sure, culture jamming hopes to wrest citizens from the haze of consumption in order to decrease fuel emissions, for example, and increase quality of life. But it does so with magazines, T-shirts, books, and ticketed lectures, seeming to participate in the same consumerist agenda as the companies it speaks out against.[11]

Although this recent breed of activism has been popularized by Kalle Lasn, publisher of the magazine *Adbusters* and author of the book *Culture Jam*, the band Negativland originally coined the phrase "culture jam" more than two decades ago when they titled an album with the phrase in 1984.[12] Culture jamming as invented by Negativland added an aural aspect to traditional collage work, which the band attributed to the increased social reliance on television, radio, and film for entertainment and information. In theory, culture jamming is vandalism of mass media, the activist arm of our remix culture. In the 1995 Craig Baldwin film *Sonic Outlaws*, the prophetic documentary heralding the arrival of the new mash media, founding Negativland member Mark Hosler describes the process as a "totally natural response to growing up in a mediated world."[13] By relying on a melding of the images, advertisements, and self-representations we regularly stumble across to create a situationist détournement, a reworking of the familiar in order to force a schism into our constant consumption, the spectacle of consumerism. Culture jamming uncovers the hidden meanings in familiar advertising messages, creating in the viewer a flash of recognition, a bolt of truth.

But that lightning-quick moment never seems to last. Naomi Klein describes the ethos of culture jamming as "go-for-the-corporate-jugular"[14] in *No Logo*, although she does not go on to acknowledge that the jugulars of corporations are not advertisements, brand names, commercials, or representations—the targets of culture jamming. She therefore stops short of noting the inherent irony we have already discovered with Reverend Billy and the Church of Stop Shopping. The jugulars of corporations are profits, and profits—at least in the world of popular consumer goods—come from name recognition. Unfortunately for the dreams of many activists, trading in name recognition is what culture jamming does best.[15]

Critics call it preaching to the converted: to understand the message you must already believe it. And if you don't already believe, say, that Starbucks is a destructive force in both neighborhoods and rainforests (as plenty of people seem not to), the man in the preacher's outfit—however hypnotic he may be—isn't necessarily engaged in explaining it to you. He must remain intent on his campaign of negative publicity. And newcomers that could be diverted from their haze of consumption continue to enjoy the spectacle but may miss its message.

We've already witnessed the bizarre clash between emotion and reason that can result when marketing adopts an antimarketing stance. Some culture jams merely reverse this technique, blatantly promoting a different kind of consumption, but consumption nonetheless. *Adbusters* magazine's early plan for a Buy Nothing Day T-shirt initiative, thankfully dropped before sales began, was one ludicrous example.[16] "It's true that Adbusters has become some sort of a brand," Lasn admitted to me in a 2003 interview.[17] The confusion of messages goes both ways, too, allowing some marketing firms to name themselves unabashedly after culture-jamming activities. GoGorilla Media is clearly a play on the word "guerrilla," the street-level tactics from which all culture-jamming methods derive. And Critical Massive, the company that offers real graffiti artists the opportunity to deface city walls with brand-name, corporate-sponsored graffadi, is named after the popular alternative transportation event and nonorganization Critical Mass.

And this is only natural. Many antimarketing activist techniques were derived from advertising principles—Lasn, for example, used to work in advertising—just as many of the marketers we will meet in this book have organically adopted antimarketing strategies into their marketing plans out of a genuine discomfort with traditional marketing. Those who work in advertising are most capable of subverting it, the conventional wisdom goes. While true, the question of who is being subverted, and to what end, is rarely voiced, much less answered.

What we're left with after all this melding and mixing of techniques and messages is the distinctly uncomfortable sense that much of what we call culture jamming achieves the same effect as traditional marketing. Both rely on the bedrock principle that branding works. Yet marketing has moved on from branding toward a more direct emotional connection to our reptilian brains, which makes it immune to the cognitive dissonance culture jamming creates. In the meantime, the brands being promoted by some activists retain the full integrity of their original message.

4

PLAYING FAIR

Like a lot of eight-year-old girls, Fiona loved American Girl dolls. *Loved them.* She even wrote a letter to the company to express her feelings:

> I really like A. G. dolls. . . . I would buy a 1000 A. G. dolls if I could. . . . I would really like it if you could adopt me, because I buy a lot of your products. I would like to live at the store because of the yummy food at the restaurant and it's giving you more money if I eat at the restaurant too. I really love your books and if I live at the store then I could read all of your books. I buy them all the time!

Fiona's parents even wrote their own hilariously playful letter of support:

> Dear Execs at American Girl Store,
> I am writing to recommend my daughter, Fiona, as a fine girl, who happens to be American. She would make a wonderful addition to your corporation. She represents all of the qualities Americans like to see in their children. She's hard working, smart, strong, and fun. As your daughter, she would put those qualities to good use, helping to sell your product. In return you'd only have to feed and clothe her

and ultimately, send her to business school to take over as President of your doll empire.

Please consider this plan, for though we would miss her, we feel the corporate environment combined with extensive doll play and glittery doll-girl matching outfits would be ideal for our daughter.

Thank you,

Fiona's parents

P.S. This question has been on our minds, for awhile: Are your dolls made by American Adults?

I met Fiona when I was on tour with my first book, a radical media and anticorporate primer for middle schoolers. Fiona and her parents came to a workshop during my Radical Education Roadshow, a series of small-campaign activist projects and discussions held in place of a traditional reading tour. The mixed group of participants—from older adults to very young children—had agreed to send letters to corporate entities as a first step toward engaging in critical dialogue with the faceless businesses that dominate our world. My suggestion was that should a response fail to come we could perhaps decide that our emotional attachment to these corporations was misplaced and undeserved.

Yet Fiona's love was heartfelt and unwavering, and her parents' desire to give their daughter over to the American Girl experience isn't all that unusual. American Girl Place—"Girl Xanadu," writer Terri Kapsalis called it, and "Taj McDoll" [1]—a shiny, clean, neoclassical doll emporium owned by parent company Mattel, is thought by many to be the idyllic environment in which to raise girls, or at the very least to raise their self-esteem. Although the cost of the dolls is high, their popularity and ubiquity indicate that those who can afford to will likely make the investment: in the company's own marketing speak, the American Girl brand is recognized by 95 percent of all preteen females in the United States.[2]

The American Girl Place shopping experience is comprehensive. Not only can you buy the dolls, accessories, clothing, furniture, and books, you can also purchase services such as health and hair care for your toy (anything from braids to head replacement) or dine with her at a restaurant. Afterward, the two of you can take in a show in the downstairs theater, a movie in the lobby, or simply browse the rooms of glass-encased tableaux enacting the dolls' historical fictions—the individual elements of which are available for purchase at any of the several cash registers silently guarding each floor.

Did I mention the expense? A modestly outfitted doll, book, sampling of period-style furniture, decent array of clothing reproductions, and one each of a pet, hobby, and recreational pastime can easily cost $1,000. Doll and book sets start at $87, and your purchase will get you such wonderful stories as that of Kit, who wears a sweater set and lives in 1934, or Josefina from 1824, whose accessories include a fringed shawl ("called a *rebozo*," the catalog instructs). Bespectacled Molly is also available. She gets a lot of attention these days because she's from 1944, so her dad's at war, too, just like some of the girls Mattel hopes will take home their dolls. The books alone are less expensive, but face it: they're gateway purchases to the engaging, miniature world inhabited by the dolls. "You can't just buy the doll," one mother lamented to the *Wall Street Journal*.[3] And those accessories *are* charming: escaped slave girl Addie's undies can be purchased for only $16; a set of doll-sized hair ribbons goes for $12. Additionally, shoppers can take home logo-bedecked T-shirts, hoodies, and jeans for girls both human and plastic.

Like the home furnishings, the act of shopping is scaled down for the pre–checking account set: underneath the museumlike displays are takeaway cards bearing full-color pictures, a brief description, and the price of the object depicted. Shoppers place these cards in small maroon folders printed with the phrase "Pocket full of wishes," courtesy of American Girl Place. These pockets full of wishes can be brought to the nearest cash register and exchanged for the accessory, doll, or amazingly authentic piece of furniture shown on the cards. Or, as the folders themselves brightly suggest, they can be taken home as souvenirs, and a lucky grandparent or doting uncle can flip the card over and order the pictured good via the 800 number printed on the back.

It's a totalizing and ultimately exhausting experience, like traveling in a foreign country where, instead of everything being in a different language, everything is just smaller. And much more expensive.

But is it really an idyllic girl playground? American Girl Place imparts a lot of messages about the importance of money and no opportunities or suggestions about how to earn it in a world still predisposed toward patriarchy. Fiona had given me a pretty good idea of the dedication actual American girls have for the American Girl experience. But her parents had posed an interesting question: are these toys even created in America? How much does Mattel support the America for which the brand is named, and from which it profits?

The answer is, not very much. Although for a while the company was extremely tight-lipped about where its goods were manufactured, some Mattel toys were traced back to sweatshops in China and Korea several years ago. At first they copped the standard defense: that work contracted to one factory with decent labor standards can be subcontracted to another with poor labor standards and lower costs, and then that manufacturer might then subcontract the work to another factory with even cheaper costs and even lower standards.

It was in one of these factories with notoriously low labor standards that a nineteen-year-old in China named Li Chunmei worked producing toys similar to Mattel's. Having quit school in the third grade to help support her parents and four siblings, Li Chunmei moved seven hundred miles away from home and eventually became a "runner" at one plant in the Pearl River Delta, earning a wage of 12¢ an hour. Carrying the eyes, ears, and other parts of dolls and stuffed animals from one part of the factory to another would be hard enough under U.S. labor standards—two fifteen-minute breaks, an eight-hour workday, a half-hour lunch, and a little more than $5 per hour—but Li Chunmei worked sixteen hours a day during the holiday rush of 2001, earning about $65 a month while under constant pressure to move faster, carry more, hurry up. One day, after two months of work with no days off, Li Chunmei was exhausted and coughing up blood. She died before she made it to the hospital, her death attributed to a condition factory workers call *guolaosi*: death from overwork.[4]

One report from the group Corporate Social Responsibility in Asia estimated that by June 2006 the number of deaths attributed to *guolaosi* in China had reached six hundred thousand per year. While Chinese labor law clearly defines an allowable amount of overtime (three hours per day, not to exceed thirty-six hours per month[5]), "at present," the report states, "some companies abuse that."[6] Workers concur. Extensive overtime "may be illegal, but it's normal," one factory employee told the *Washington Post*.[7]

Embarrassed by similar conditions at its overseas factories, Mattel revised its standards and created a 112-point code of conduct called "Global Manufacturing Principles" (GMP). The company also hired a monitoring agency to ensure its manufacturers would adhere to both the GMP and the labor laws of the nations in which its goods are produced. These acts alone gave it a reputation as "one of the most socially responsible American enterprises."[8]

Yet Mattel remains well aware that the companies it works with regularly violate national labor standards. Mattel's own (and much stricter) GMP standards delimit a maximum ten-hour workday unless workers have volunteered for special overtime, in which case the workday might stretch to twelve hours, and no more than thirteen consecutive days of work. Two Mattel plant employees in Shenzhen, however, told a reporter that they regularly worked eleven-hour days six days per week; another worker in Indonesia told of thirty straight days of work on Barbie assembly lines with no time off.[9]

Despite its own claim that "if you want to work with Mattel, compliance with GMP is not an option,"[10] the 2005 GMP audit report found the following violations at a single plant in Dongguan, in the Guangdong province of China:

- Management refused to turn over work schedules for peak production periods; workers reported that management "routinely scheduled working hours which far exceeded China's national labor law" as well as Mattel's GMP. "It would seem," the report states, "that [this plant] has managed to violate even the revised and highly generous GMP standard with regard to maximum allowable overtime hours." Additionally, several workers acknowledged confusion about overtime pay; almost half of those interviewed did not understand how their wages were calculated. Others understood the wage structure but stated that they had not been properly compensated for overtime hours worked.

- Management claimed it hired through walk-ins or referrals, while the workers claimed that they were recruited and had to pay a fee to the recruiter, a practice staunchly prohibited under the GMP. Additionally, management charged workers for uniforms and ID badges, another GMP violation.

- Management required pregnancy tests in advance of hiring that, if positive, would result in workers not being hired, a violation of both Chinese labor law and Mattel's GMP. (The report further noted that this plant had been consistently cited for this violation several years running.)

- Workers were misled about Mattel's GMP standards (and therefore, their own rights), particularly regarding maternity leave. One in five employees acknowledged not understanding the company's maternity leave policy; the report calls several of the plant's stated policies "unnecessarily complicated." [11]

And that's just what goes on the books. "Before Mattel comes through twice a year for inspection," the *Los Angeles Times* reported, "managers promise to pay [workers] time-and-a-half if they repeat the company line: that they work just eight hours a day, six days a week, as allowed by Chinese law. In truth, they slog for far longer than that." A contemporary of Li Chunmei's from the same Pearl River Delta province told the National Labor Committee:

> I've been working since I was 15 years old. . . . I've been working in the spraying department for three years. I've always suspected the paints are poisonous. I've been sick ever since I started working in spraying. And they lie about the

wages. We never know how they're calculated. There's no pay stub and no way to check. We're given a sheet of paper with a lot of numbers on it to look at for a few seconds and then we have to sign it. We get what they give us.[12]

The stories of Li Chunmei and the other Chinese factory workers who risk their health and even their lives to make products for Mattel and other American companies are certainly compelling and bear a similarity to some American Girl narratives. In one American Girl story Samantha[13] gives the following speech in class:

Americans are very proud of being modern. We are proud of the machines in our factories because they make so many wonderful things for us. But Americans are proud of being truthful, too. If we were truthful we would say that factory machines make things fast and cheap, but they are dangerous, too. They can hurt the children who work in the factories. . . . They can make children sick. And children who work in factories don't have time to play or go to school. They are too tired. . . . If our factories can hurt children, then we have not made good progress in America.[14]

This speech is the cornerstone of a key friendship in American Girl mythology out of which grew two series of books, two sets of dolls and accessories, and the company's first-ever made-for-TV movie. Thus, it's probably brought in a healthy profit. Although set in Samantha's Mattelized version of 1904, the speech is one of the company's genuine attempts to teach a real(ish) history of the industrial revolution. Samantha is, after all, describing the actual experiences of her friend Nellie, a fictionalized (and slightly spruced-up) version of a real turn-of-the-century preteen factory worker. I like to imagine Samantha, still a few years younger than Li Chunmei, delivering this speech in full voice to the same group of young activists at the workshop where Fiona read her American Girl Place letter a century later.

American Girl Place appears to be a perfect site for rethinking how youth participate in culture and the economy. So, inspired by Fiona's love of the brand, Samantha's fearless voice of dissent, and Li Chunmei's story, I planned a project to prompt questions about the American Girl experience.

Although one wouldn't think it from the hubbub that resulted, Operation: Pocket Full of Wishes was really nothing more than a series of eight cards and a radical method of distributing them known in anarchist communities as shopdropping. As opposed to shop*lifting*, shop*dropping* involves bringing things inside the store and leaving them there. To disseminate the idea that not everything a girl needed to complete her happiness was available for purchase at American Girl Place to the audience that seemed to need the message most—girls seeking happiness by shopping at American Girl Place—I created some shopping aids. The cards mimicked those found in the store but featured the *actual* wishes of *actual* girls that I *actually* spoke to.[15] They addressed matters that somehow got ignored in the books, accessories, magazines, furniture, hair products, bath salts, films, plays, and tea parties celebrated by, and available for purchase at, the store. Decorated with images pulled from the American Girl catalog but recontextualized, my cards displayed the following eight wishes: Equal Pay for Equal Work; Domestic Partnership Benefits; Self-Confidence; Healthy Body Images; Safe and Effective Birth Control; Ample Career Opportunities; Safe,

Legal Abortion Access; and Free Tampons. These were described by the phrase "(not pictured)" and priced at $0. On the back the American Girl 800 number was listed with the suggestion that potential shoppers "Try ordering" these things over the phone. These cards were placed, one by one, into the Pocket Full of Wishes folders, which were then returned to the slots at an American Girl Place to be picked up by fans of the dolls.[16]

It was the distribution method that led to my getting caught at this hardly dangerous activity. It is not widely publicized that the American Girl Place on Michigan Avenue in downtown Chicago keeps close to four hundred video cameras trained on its mostly innocent shoppers at all times, nor is it well known that plain-clothes detectives roam the store frequently, keeping a watchful eye on whatever the uniformed store employees might miss—and they can't miss much, given that up to ten employees may be positioned throughout each floor at any time.[17]

The company's simultaneous celebration of presexual innocence and devoted surveillance thereof should not have surprised me. Mattel is, after all, a toy company so dedicated to its youthful audience that its employee benefits package includes financial adoption assistance for up to two children. (Such benefits do not, of course, apply to its offshore manufacturers' employees.[18])

Yet the weird juxtaposition of heavy surveillance against the company's message of girl self-sufficiency, and the hypocrisy of nurturing the maternal drive but only in U.S. employees (and, less overtly, in the girls who desire their products) that is written between the lines of the American Girl catalog, series of books, and employment manual haven't always been present. The American Girl brand first belonged to the Pleasant Company, a Wisconsin-based business started by Pleasant Rowland in 1986 with the heartfelt Midwestern desire to "enrich the lives of American girls by fostering pride in the traditions of growing up female in America and celebrating the lifestyle of girls today." [19] American Girl dolls, in comparison to the ubiquitous Barbie, were milk-fed, presexual, and entirely wholesome. While Barbie went on dates with Ken or shopped for entertainment, American Girls held healthful picnics, collected Route 66 memorabilia, or played with puppies. The books presented a palatable view of real historical time periods and encouraged reading—an unheard-of endeavor at a time when Saturday morning cartoons had become fully branded experiences, unwatchable half-hour advertisements for breakfast cereals, action figures, and major motion pictures. Yet toy giant Mattel, which had helped usher in that aggressive new strain of children's entertainment, hawkishly pursued the Pleasant Company until Rowland sold it in 1998 for $700 million.

I was, of course, aware that American Girl Place and its employees, thinking they already provide self-esteem, health education, and social justice, would not appreciate my efforts to educate their customers. In fact, among the several current and former employees I spoke to both before and after this incident—working in areas as diverse as security, editorial, sales, food service, or, in one case, as a doll hairstylist—felt that my cards were upsetting because they were unnecessary. ("Can't argue with that," one unusually kind store detective told me as he flipped through them. "We already do that," a dour female security guard scolded me.) Yet the very company that used Samantha as a mouthpiece to speak out against the mistreatment of factory workers was mistreating factory workers. Wasn't it possible, I kept asking employees, that the company was doing more local damage, too? Perhaps to the very constituency for which it is named? And how much do you make compared to a male detective? How ample are your career opportunities when you work in sales for ten-hour days over eight years and are consistently passed over for promotions, as one friend was? Are the actors in the theater paid equitably and able to work in safe conditions or forced to strike outside the store, as they did in Chicago and New York? Can you be fired for taking home an uneaten sandwich after a shift at the restaurant, as one girl was in New York? And how's your self-confidence, by the way?

Well. But the intended audience for these cards wasn't American Girl Place employees; the audience was the public. Rather, the specific, self-selecting public that shops at American Girl Place. For while the store is not exactly *public* space, it's not exactly private, either. Anyone may enter during open hours; speech in stores is not generally monitored or controlled by the shopkeepers (yelling and squealing, in fact, are thoroughly tolerated if not outright encouraged by the carefully targeted stimuli); and illogical behavior like feeding plastic homunculi gourmet plates of spaghetti is downright expected. Often, such corporate-owned, quasi-public space of the kind offered by Mattel is the only kind of public space available. (The closest you can get in the neighborhood, in fact, is a park about the size of a fast-food dining area kitty-corner from American Girl Place. It's got a sign labeling the space "public," but the same sign notes without irony that the space is owned and operated by the adjacent McDonald's.) So a small effort toward expressing my freedom of speech in a semipublic venue did not seem to me to be unreasonable—certainly not in a store that had built its empire on stories of outspoken girls. You can at least see why I would have been confused.

And confused I was when I was grabbed by a store detective and hustled into a back room, quickly and quietly. Something about my action, apparently, had been deemed unacceptable. Although I had committed no crimes or acts of civil disobedience, I had been spreading noncommercial messages in a dedicated capitalist environment. And such speech, it was made clear to me—criminal or not, critical or not—was wholly unwelcome. I was detained for two hours by a tag team of store detectives, forced to undergo a criminal background check and exuberant frisking, and escorted to the street by eight to ten angry and fully armed Chicago police officers, who permanently banned me from the store.[20] "Keep your 'freedom of speech' outside of American Girl Place," one of the cops told me (no sense of irony whatsoever) as he escorted me outside.

Cease-and-desist letters (C&Ds) are scary, as I understand it. I've never gotten one, but I've heard stories. Kembrew McLeod got one from EMI Records. He's the author of the book *Freedom of Expression*® (and owns the trademark on that phrase).[21] McLeod received his C&D on Grey Tuesday, February 24, 2004—the day 170 copyright activists, McLeod included, had made DJ Danger Mouse's corporate-kiboshed *Grey Album*, a mash-up[22] of the Beatles's *White Album* and Jay-Z's *Black Album*, available for download on their Web sites to highlight the vitality of the fair use defense against claims of copyright violation.

Fair use, as defined by Nolo, respected publisher of handy legal guidebooks of all kinds, "authorizes the use of copyrighted materials for certain purposes without the copyright owner's permission. Generally, uses intended to further scholarship, education, or an informed public are considered fair use."[23]

The C&D McLeod received demanded the removal of the album from his site and threatened swift and painful legal battles if the demand was not met. C&Ds, however, are not legal documents, and senders never need acknowledge that the supposedly offensive actions just might be permissible under fair use. A recent report by the Brennan Center for Justice, called *Will Fair Use Sur-*

vive?, found that in one sample of Web sites that had received C&Ds close to 50 percent of the letters were sent despite weak claims of copyright ownership or strong arguments for fair use. The purpose of a C&D isn't to provide information; there is no imperative to be truthful. "The purpose is to scare people," McLeod said bluntly.[24] And even though its legal claims may not hold up, C&Ds often work.

"My first reaction was what a lot of people have, which was, 'Oh shit,'" McLeod told me. Then he was hit with a thrill: "My second reaction was, 'Oh cool!'" But after a few moments of reflection on the time and energy a lawsuit would take—not to mention its effect on his new mortgage—the thrill passed. He's a nice guy with an enthusiastic bent that's odd in an academic and a relief in an activist. "There's nothing really exciting or sexy about [being threatened with a lawsuit], except that EMI has taken the time to send a letter from their legal department," he explained.

McLeod's thrill over the C&D (which, because he was participating in a group action with a network of legal advisers, he ignored, to no noticeable effect) is understandable. For a while artistic martyrhood seemed to be on the rise; artists who received lawsuit threats in pursuit of creative expression enjoyed a brief celebrity. Unfortunately, the rapid accumulation of well-publicized cases against copyright transgressors, including Jeff Koons,[25] the Girl Scouts,[26] and Napster downloaders,[27] eventually seemed to stifle cultural production communities. As a result, many artists have in recent years avoided all things brand-specific and corporate-owned, which underutilizes vital defenses like the fair-use statute, allowing them to waste away to nearly forgotten.

The Copyright Act of 1976 grants, under certain conditions, the publishing rights over a work of art to the creator, but it has always had limits. The original limits included both the fair use doctrine as well as a year, calculated from the author's death, after which works would enter the public domain. In theory, copyright is meant to protect the author of an original work. In practice, it has been revised and aggressively utilized to protect corporate licenses from comment and reuse by contemporary artists. In most cases, although not all, commercial uses aren't eligible for a fair use defense; although most interpreters agree that both commentary and news reporting are, which goes far beyond the current interpretation that only parody is eligible for a fair use defense.

The fair use statute was originally an attempt to acknowledge that releasing something into the world necessarily gives it a life of its own, one that can never be fully controlled, no matter how many lawyers you can afford to retain. And, in practice, the courts continue to support the existence of fair use. As McLeod writes in *Freedom of Expression*®, "in drafting and interpreting copyright laws, the Supreme Court, lower courts, and Congress . . . have consistently acknowledged that if we make some things totally off limits for comment, we undermine the founding principles of democracy."[28] The meaning of the fair use statute is that limiting absolute, permanent, monolithic authorial control is and has always been necessary to creativity as well as the open cultural dialogue that should be one of the hallmarks of a democracy. It's a vital lesson in an age of increasing corporate influence over physical and intellectual space. The trick in reclaiming images from tightening corporate constraints seems to lie in publicizing exactly what those limits are. One great potential for currently working artists lies in exploiting the fair use statute.

Brooklyn-based curator of the Illegal Art Exhibition and *Stay Free!* founder Carrie McLaren agrees. "There is value to leveraging publicity against corporations who threaten artists over copyright claims," she told me.[29] It's served her fairly well: her Illegal Art

Exhibition, which collects and highlights some recent contested visual art images, most of which turn out not, in fact, to be illegal, has garnered quite a bit of well-deserved attention with articles in art publications, in activist newsletters, and on news and culture sites.[30]

Leveraging publicity is a tactic rooted in the history of political art. The radical group of cartoonists called the Air Pirates used it in 1970 when they created a comic-book satire of a famous mouse couple and then dropped off copies at the board meeting of the corporation that owns these licensed characters to incite a battle. (The group also listed its phone number and address in the Yellow Pages under "Air Pirates Secret Hideout" and then waited, for four months, until detectives tracked them down through less efficient methods.)[31] They got their legal battle, a long and often hilarious one. Unfortunately, but not surprisingly, the Air Pirates lost and Disney won.

Considering both the implausibility of confusing a dope-dealing sex maniac mouse with the squeaky-voiced one from *The Mickey Mouse Club* as well as my own recent full-bore intimidation at the hands of the Chicago police force and American Girl Place employees (not to mention the fact that Mattel has a reputation for being "comically aggressive" in protecting its intellectual properties[32]), I wasn't about to wait around to see how a lawsuit against me might play out. So when an offer to publish my Operation: Pocket Full of Wishes cards came along, I declined. Intimidation tactics had worked and were all that was needed to restrict my criticism of Mattel.[33]

Intimidation has served the corporate world well: Many potential copyright transgressors—or critics—have been scared off with threats of litigation. It's not limited to the legal threats McLeod got or the physical variety I received either. It also has a direct impact on the distribution of cultural products even in forums supposedly dedicated to providing space for free speech.

Under the Digital Millennium Copyright Act (DMCA) of 1998, purported copyright owners can directly contact Internet service providers (ISPs) or search engines and demand they remove questionable material without going through a legal process. Ultimately, this means that distributors and hosts can be held liable for copyright infringements if they fail to immediately comply with any take-down letters they receive. The law is based on a ridiculous premise—that providers of access to information should be held accountable for its content, akin to holding highway construction crews liable for traffic accidents—but it plays into the fears of distributors everywhere: that the access to free speech they provide will be used illegally. Although the DMCA does allow for *registered* ISP users of the material in question to contest allegations, the rules for this counternotice are difficult to follow and don't apply to nonregistrants, such as listserv members or Web site posters. Thus, in some cases, contentious material may be removed not only without due process, but without the knowledge of the creator, who would only notice upon a later visit to the site. This stifling of creative and critical speech has therefore begun to limit the very availability of cultural products, occasionally without the creator's knowledge.

This is censorship. Marjorie Heins (the founder of the Freedom of Expression Policy Project, a fellow with the Brennan Center for Justice Democracy Program, and a former director of the American Civil Liberties Union's Arts Censorship Project) and Tricia Beckles (also of the Freedom of Expression Policy project) found in *Will Fair Use Survive?* that a strong correlation existed between the take-down letters sent under the DMCA and the critical content of the material posted. The preservation of speech critical of corporate or governmental abuse of power, of course, is one of the main reasons behind the nation's freedom of speech protection. "When companies try to use intellectual-property laws to censor speech they don't like," McLeod notes, "they are abusing the reason why these laws exist in the first place."[34] Yet Heins and Beckles charge that the DMCA has placed "censorship power . . . in the hands of IP owners."[35]

Economically speaking, overzealous intimidation via C&Ds is a good investment. Corporations want to avoid expensive legal entanglements. They'd certainly hate to lose an important case, especially if fair use becomes more widely understood. The one thing that might bring the whole construct crashing down is the revelation that the threats contained in C&Ds and take-down notices are hollow. One way that might happen is if copyright owners start losing cases against cultural producers.

"I started out photographing kitchen appliances," Utah-based photographer Tom Forsythe told me, "'cause I was trying to show how earlier technology was used in a way that was truly beneficial to people, but that we had fallen away from that and become a culture that was consuming for its own sake. But when I picked the slides up from the shop, what they didn't show was the [cultural] devolution into a more crass consumerism."[36]

Obviously, he needed to find an immediately recognizable symbol for crass consumerism. Two sprung immediately to mind. "Consumerism is different than consumption," he explained. "Consumerism is almost like a bad religion." So he naturally began working with Nike and Barbie. "It didn't take much time to figure out that Barbie had much riper photographic possibilities than Nike shoes," he said. She did, after all, own everything. In miniature. And in a wide variety of colors. As the "quintessential American consumer" she formed the basis for a series of seventy-eight images the artist started making in 1997, each of which featured a household appliance of some kind and a Barbie doll. Or sometimes two Barbie dolls. Naked. Together. Sometimes three.

But her sex-symbol status was never his photographic subject. It was her lewd, naked consumerism. His images were meant to underscore her symbolism, her status as a purchasable good that promoted the purchase of other goods. Her ease in the role was plain to Forsythe. "Her plastic smile never changed even as she got closer to the whirring blades of the blender," he joked. "I was also commenting on the slick techniques of advertising, and how easy that was," the artist added. He was playing off the entire package, the Barbie ethos, that consumers were expected to buy from Mattel.

Forsythe didn't care about the company's opinion of his work. He knew that copyright law protected the work of artists but didn't immediately think that it would apply to a mass-produced object like a doll. He knew the toy was trademarked, but he wasn't competing with the Barbie trade by using her image, only commenting on it, and he considered himself safe. In short, he said, when the project started, "I had no concerns about Mattel."

Later, though, he noticed something "on the butt of the Barbie doll: a copyright notice." [37] But it still didn't faze him. He had a working knowledge of the copyright act, and therefore understood that "according to all fair use principles, what I was doing was fair use. It's protected."

Anyway, he said, Mattel knew early on he was using the doll. "One of the first pieces I sold was given to [someone in] worldwide manufacturing at Mattel as a Christmas present."

Eventually, though, Forsythe had to worry about Mattel after all: he received a thirty-page document in 1999 informing him

that he was being sued for copyright and trademark infringement.
The company already had sued Seal Press for using the brand
name in their book on the doll phenom, *Adios, Barbie*, and the
record label MCA over Aqua's pop song "Barbie Girl." Forsythe
spent six months cobbling together a pro bono legal team who
would understand that Mattel was strong-arming cultural creatives
in an unfair way, and who would help him defend his work as
fair use.

Originally, the courts agreed only in principle. Mattel lost the
case in 2004 when the United States District Court, Central District
of California agreed with Forsythe that his art was a parody
and specifically protected under the fair use statue. Mattel, unhappy,
appealed the ruling. That's when they lost big.

The final summary judgment called the suit "groundless" and
admonished the company for pursuing it at all. "Plaintiff had access
to sophisticated counsel who could have determined that such
a suit was objectively unreasonable and frivolous," U.S. District
Court judge Ronald Lew wrote in his ruling, which went on to
speculate why the company might have ignored such counsel. "It
appears plaintiff forced defendant into costly litigation to discourage
him from using Barbie's image in his artwork."

It was a victory for cultural producers. "I couldn't have asked
for a better result," Forsythe told the *New York Times* after the ruling
came in. "This should set a new standard for the ability to critique
brands that are pervasive in our culture." [38]

Yet it was also a personal victory for Forsythe. "This is just the
sort of situation," Lew's ruling continued, "in which this court
should award attorneys fees to deter this type of litigation which
contravenes the intent of the Copyright Act." And they did, awarding
the defendant legal fees of more than $1.8 million.

"The fee decision," Forsythe explained to me, "has more far-reaching consequences because the attorneys can point to this case and say, 'I'm gonna get paid.' It's making it easier to find attorneys who want to do the right thing and now feel maybe they can actually get their money back."

The case also stands as a marker for those who may feel compelled to commit acts of *self*-censorship out of fear that they could be slapped with a lawsuit, lose, and owe tons of money. That's a fight few cultural creatives can afford to take on. "I hope I've reduced some sense of self-censorship," Forsythe said. "Because really, how can you critique a consumer culture without using the consumer items you critique?"

"Maybe now when an angry CEO picks up the phone to counsel and says, 'sue this guy,'" one intellectual property lawyer told the *New York Times*, "instead of saluting and sending the bill, the lawyer may say 'I have to warn you, this could boomerang.'"[39]

When I commented that Forsythe seemed surprisingly enthusiastic about his five-year court battle even two years later, especially in comparison to other artists I know who have undergone big, exhausting copyfights, he agreed that he was an anomaly. His explanation: "I won!"

And after all this, I asked, how do you come down now on intellectual property issues? "I actually believe in copyright," Forsythe told me, but he also believes fair use should remain open to wider interpretation. "There's no reason copyright should be used to enrich corporate coffers to the detriment of artists."

5

THE MASTER'S BLUEPRINTS

It's hard to imagine anything less politically radical than a brand-new line of foreign vehicles appearing on the market during a seemingly never-ending war over oil that raised gas prices to ridiculous highs. The team behind the Toyota Yaris nonetheless linked their latest model with do-it-yourselfness during its late summer 2006 promotional campaign, YarisWorks DIY: Drive It Yourself. Borrowing a page from the Starbucks playbook—as well as several of my compatriots in Chicago-based independent publishing and the national DIY crafting community—the Yaris version of doing it yourself meant having cool kids from the underground show you how to do what they do, albeit in the context of corporate-sponsored workshops: make cool hats, comics, and lampshades for very little cost. (This is supposed to parallel the low cost of the vehicle.) And while the Yaris is surprisingly inexpensive compared to other cars (starting at a little over $11,000 manufacturer's suggested retail price for the 2007 models), several Yaris workshop instructors may or may not have been willing to point out that buying one still costs a lot more than making a bike from parts found in the garbage. More parallels to the do-it-yourself community are presented: like the handmade wares you could purchase directly from their creators at the Renegade Craft Fair or DIY Trunk Show, this car is customizable, crafty, and hip. The Yaris Web site enthuses, "At YarisWorks DIY (Drive It Yourself) events there will be test drives (duh), hot music from indie artists cranking from the PA, and the opportunity for you (yes, you!) to decoupage a Yaris . . . quirky but fun!"[1] The links to crafters don't even end there. Actual links to DIY merch, made and sold by tried-and-true members of the DIY community, are all available, just a few clicks away from the Toyota main page.

For the people at Toyota, who may well have taken a risk by releasing a car clearly targeted to the nonwealthy (although we will return to the question of the audience for this campaign in Chapter 11), literally co-opting the term for and concept of doing it yourself was not enough. They also preempted how we might talk about the Yaris if truly left to do it ourselves: in the spring, prior to launching the line, the company paid Fox's sketch comedy show *MADtv* to lampoon the car in an on-air skit. As a marketer who had worked on a similar project—getting a cell phone company mentioned on Cartoon Network's culty *Aqua Teen Hunger Force* (a recent celeb in the viral marketing game themselves)— explained, "There's no better way to say 'you're it' than to have people parody you."[2]

That probably was true at one time, although what the popularity-equals-parody equation fails to recognize is that before culture jamming and copyfighting—two politically intentioned art mediums based on image reuse—parody was the primary domain of *Saturday Night Live*, *Mad Magazine*, and *National Lampoon*. All three started out as plucky and meaningful but eventually became status quo corporate entities that continued to wear the mantle of parody but increasingly allowed it not to be so funny anymore. Recently, a "parody" of a Burger King ad ran on the cover of the Warner Brothers–owned *Mad* that looked much like an actual ad for Burger King, except that Alfred E. Neuman peeking around from behind the king holding a barf bag makes it cooler, I guess, and the image appears on the cover of the magazine instead of the inside. While it's standard in some print publishing circles to sell ads on covers or use foldover ads, integrating falsely parodic content into the cover image of a youth-focused magazine that popularized satire for an entire generation goes a few steps beyond providing innovative advertising space. Years ago a *Mad* cover devoted to this same subject might have included a spoof name (Booger Queen comes to mind) and a disgusting rendering of the company's advertised product featuring, let's say, still-live animals, Grandpa's teeth, and unidentifiable ooze, all in Harvey Kurtzman's or maybe Wally Wood's monomaniacal attention to grody detail. Now, however, the "ad" and its "parody" are almost interchangeable, save the bag labeled barf. The Yaris sketch on *MADtv* aired when Toyota launched the car line, well before the name could have entered the national consciousness (if it ever would), and thus well before a natural parody would have had time to evolve. But it did coincide with the time the actual Yaris ad campaign kicked in.

In fact, the last few decades of marketing campaigns have increasingly embraced fun-poking, lighthearted mocking, belligerent teasing, and outright dissension into promotional strategies. *MADtv*'s Yaris sketch and similar campaigns prove the desire to turn negative commentary into promotions. These advancements in marketing may keep the industry edgy, but they also serve to mute criticism and rob image reuse of its unique power, thus rendering these acts of protest null and void.

Critics of representational strategies like culture jamming and copyfighting have always been aware of this confusion. Culture jamming has often been said to dismantle the master's house with the master's tools—and then provide the master with blueprints for a better house and better tools. Anticonsumerist books like *Culture Jam* and *No Logo* wind up inspiring new marketing strategies; a marketing manager at Pabst Brewing Company claimed that Klein's book "contained many good marketing ideas."[3] Even legendary ad man David Ogilvy seems to support the ideas behind culture jamming: "I have never seen [a landscape] which was improved by a billboard. . . . [M]an is at his vilest when he erects a billboard. When I retire from Madison Avenue, I am going to start a secret society of masked vigilantes who will travel the world on silent motor bicycles, chopping down posters at the dark of the moon. How many will convict us when we are caught in these acts of beneficent citizenship?"[4] Or place the GoGorilla Media handbook next to a copy of the zine how-to guide *Stolen Sharpie Revolution*:[5] Which is the marketing guidebook and which the underground, anticommercial, how-to manual? It can be hard to tell. Our political leaders have in recent decades incorporated dissent into promotional campaigns, too. Politicians place themselves regularly and happily on nighttime talk-show hosts' couches, from *Late Night with David Letterman* to the *Daily Show with Jon Stewart*, knowing that if they appear to be laughing at themselves, opposition to their campaigns will be more easily muted. Failing that, the politicians will at least come off as edgy, an evermore important quality to the increasingly targeted youth demographic.

It's all part of a technique *Brandweek* named "mocketing." The mechanism is simple: regardless of the message conveyed, mocketing capitalizes on the same name recognition that drives branding. "When brand awareness is the goal shared by all, repetition and visibility are the only true measures of success," Naomi Klein notes.[6] One research and marketing firm representative concurred: "If being remembered is good enough, and if recall is what the brand hopes to achieve, then [a mocketing] campaign would be a success."[7]

•   •   •

If we can look past the seeming ridiculousness of mocketing for a moment (and the awesome thought of Toyota and, earlier, Starbucks sponsoring DIY culture), we can begin to trace back how exactly dissent became an effective marketing strategy. Because the problem is not that marketing strategists have managed to convince dirty punks and radical activists the world over to shill for their products; it is that the way we experience marketing has changed so fundamentally that DIY enthusiasts *could* shill for corporate-made products. Marketers haven't finally come up with enough hot groupies, big checks, and sweet cars to woo over, say, that staunch defender of musical integrity Ian MacKaye. Instead, marketing has become so integral to everyday life at such an early age that supporters and fans of Ian MacKaye—or DIY crafters, or other members of the underground—don't question their own motivations or influences. They're just working with their pals, man, and now they're finally in positions of power and making enough money that the rest of the scene can get in on the action.

As they will, marketers blame us for the change. Tivo, the Internet, and unchecked multitasking, they say, have caused viewers to feel only impatience for TV commercials and print ads, forcing them to forge new advertising schemes. To some degree, this is true. We've not only become inured to, and bored by, traditional marketing campaigns to the degree that many of us would gladly pitch in to improve the form, but we've also allowed marketing to fully infiltrate every aspect of our lives. *Every* aspect. Ads appear in public restrooms and are laser-printed directly on our food. Marketing sponsorships bring us sporting, musical, fashion, and pet events. Companies send us e-mail and snail mail, bombarding us at home and at work and at play with posters and stickers and logos and product placement. Advertising's Kevin Roberts and *Adbusters*'s Kalle Lasn agree. Everywhere we go a sales pitch awaits.

Yet it's not as grand a plan as the ubiquity of ads might make it seem. Despite what the paranoid in the underground believe, clandestine marketing teams do not toil away by cover of night to concoct new, nefarious means of getting cultural producers and activists to give up their hard-won integrity for a couple of bucks, health insurance, or a sponsorship or two. Selling out, in the sense that members of the underground are willing and knowledgeable participants in the destruction of their community's culture in exchange for individual gain, is not the issue. Neither is co-optation, in the sense of the corporate world's assimilation of underground modes of production and communication. Marketing has simply become so diffuse as to be a social activity. Friends and acquaintances in the struggle to condemn the bad and support the good have simply gone into advertising. The infiltration is complete: there is no Us versus Them anymore. As Bonnie Burton, the zinester and Lucasfilm employee I'll discuss more thoroughly in the next chapter, put it, "I wanted to get some street culture into our promotions mainly because that's what I think is cool."[8] Other marketers today, whether working for PR firms like Faith Popcorn's BrainReserve, more traditional advertising firms like Weiden+Kennedy, or campaigns like Toyota YarisWorks DIY: Drive It Yourself, all want the same things the underground wants: wider appreciation of good music, art, and writing; enough compensation for the creators of good music, art, and writing to continue to do their work; and the elimination of tacky and dumb advertising from the world, forever.

But this recent subcultural appropriation didn't happen by accident. The hipsters at Weiden+Kennedy, for example, have been at the cutting edge of recruiting the underground since well before 1997, when they approached Negativland (inventers of the term "culture jam"), who were still recovering from several intellectual property rights infringement lawsuits, to do a Miller Genuine Draft commercial.[9]

An experimental art and music collective, Negativland has been together since 1980. Their 1992 album, *U2*, had not gone over as well as they had hoped—it only was available for a few days after its release but managed to kick off a pig pile of lawsuits that overwhelmed the band for years. A remix combining U2's "I Still Haven't Found What I'm Looking For," found sound, original recordings, and an unflattering clip of an angry Casey Kasem that a fan had passed to them after a show, the album was an intriguing, although sonically uneven, meditation on loss. The title was also a joke about loss. The cover image featured the letter U, the numeral 2, the band name Negativland, and a U2 fighter jet, whose historical significance they felt had lost cultural currency due to the commercial success of the band U2. That band didn't find the joke so funny, however, and neither did their record label, Island Records, or Casey Kasem, who all threatened the band with copyright infringement lawsuits. Negativland was forced to pull the album from store shelves within days of its release. Their own record label, SST, caved in to Island Records's demands that the band be held responsible for the price of the lawsuit; later, SST sued the band directly for reprinting a press release of theirs in the band's self-published book on the matter, *Fair Use*. So it took Negativland four years to release their next album, 1997's *Dispepsi*. This time they wanted to be better prepared.

Dispepsi is equally intriguing. It remixes Pepsi (and some Coke) advertisements to create a soundtrack to the cola wars, an effort to "obsessively and relentlessly focus on one product from beginning to end, to have this sort of ultimately insane product placement," explains Mark Hosler.[10] The entire length of the album plays as a series of meditations on cola and its (mostly negative) role in culture. Most concerning, the cover art for the album is a reworking of the Pepsi logo. Again the band used found sound and, although they claimed to actually like Pepsi, made no effort to portray the brand flatteringly, preferring instead to outright mock both it and competitor Coke. Attorneys were in contact even before the record's release to offer legal assistance—Negativland had achieved celebrity status among the copyfighting set—and the band began preparing its legal arguments preemptively. (Negativland's most recent release, 2005's *No Business*, goes a step further: it's entirely created from easily recognized music by high-profile former litigants in copyright cases and comes with a twelve-thousand-word essay defending the work as fair use.)

As Hosler told me a few years later, "The question that everyone had was, 'Why did you do this? You're taking this huge risk against the world's second largest soft-drink manufacturer, who's going to nail your ass.' . . . We had five volunteer lawyers lined up to help us out. . . . I was preparing some very basic legal briefs in response to Pepsi's attack on us, if it came. The lawyers were saying, 'If they go after you, you're going to have about ten days to reply to them. You'd better start thinking about it now.' So we were ready." [11]

The legal arguments the band prepared were never used in court; instead, they indicate precisely why Pepsi wouldn't—and ultimately didn't—sue for copyright infringement, despite the album's negative portrayal of the soda, using copyrighted, recognizable source material. Hosler's 1997 interview with Stephen Thompson of the *Onion* outlines the gist of the band's planned defense strategy: "When you finish listening to our record, the one thing that sticks in your mind is the one thing all companies want you to remember when you see their ads. They want you to remember the name of their product. That's all. Advertising is not intended to brainwash you and make you go out and buy something;

that's a real simple-minded way of criticizing it. . . . When Pepsi hears what we've done, if they're really smart, instead of getting upset about it, they should pay us a $50,000 licensing fee to use some of our record as an ad." [12]

Hosler himself pointed out later in the *Onion* interview that there was no need to use their record as an ad or pay them for their work: the record already *was* an ad, and the work on it was already complete. The album wasn't intended to serve as advertising, of course. The band had simply pursued their artistic desire to hear what it would sound like to go totally overboard ga-ga for one single product.

The resulting representations of soda, as well as the world of advertising and marketing, are not flattering to the companies who created them nor to the consumers who enjoy them. "Changing Coke is like God making the grass purple, or putting toes on our ears, or teeth on our knees / What about Pepsi? / The amount of money that Americans spend on Coca-Cola in one week will feed all of the poor children in all of the public schools in all fifty states for two years" are a few of the lines from the sample-heavy song "All She Called About." Remixed dialogue in the song "Humanitarian Effort" reports, "One technique to get prisoners to start saying things is to shake up a Coca-Cola and to put it up a prisoner's nose." [13] The album isn't just an unpleasant meditation on cola. It addresses our hypercommercial environment and mentions by name several beverages besides Coke that compete with Pepsi for almighty consumer dollars. Nonetheless, Hosler was right: the album (particularly its cover art) builds brand recognition for Pepsi and therefore functions as advertising.

At least, that's how the soda company also seemed to view it. When the company's response to the album came, it was quite literally not what the group had prepared for. A corporate spokesperson told the press it was "a pretty good listen," seemingly absolving the band from any possible litigation.[14] And that was the end of Negativland's Pepsi campaign.

It wasn't the end of their early foray into mocketing, however. Although the band has released approximately twenty albums, as well as works in other media, and gained a level of acclaim in the underground few dare to hope for, they've never been commercially successful. In fact, they're downright poor. Most of the members have day jobs—in fact, entire nonmusical careers. CD sales for experimental art noise collectives can be slow.

So when Weiden+Kennedy, the advertising firm best known for affixing the Nike brand upon the brain of every human alive in the First World, approached the band to do a Miller Genuine Draft commercial following the release of *Dispepsi*, they considered the proposal carefully. Weiden+Kennedy's thinking was sound: they were offering the band a risk-free opportunity to mine the beer company's back catalog of ads in the same way they had the soft-drink manufacturers', but this time for an enormous amount of money.

Ultimately the group turned down the offer and expressed surprise that their attempt at subversion had struck the ad firm as a great promotional ploy. In hindsight, however, it seemed inevitable that the album had appealed to the advertising firm. "They're fans," Hosler shrugged.

In some ways it all comes back to the pursuit of the "edge." The relentless chase for the next big thing is prized in our culture, particularly by the advertising community, which sees it as fundamental to winning over the youth demographic. "The edge gives us a special attitude," Kevin Roberts writes in *Lovemarks* (itself something of an edgy concept). "Cutting edge, leading edge, bleeding edge, the edge of inspiration, on the edge of our seats. It's a place to shake off conventions and worn-out formulas, and shake out ideas. New ideas. The edge is exciting and risky and extreme. I love it." [15]

Yet the love of edginess isn't universal; for example, my friend John Pierson recently took issue with it. Currently a member of the band Even in Blackouts, a former guitarist for pop punk legends Screeching Weasel, an actor, and a publisher, he has been involved in a lot of projects that might inspire someone like Roberts. Pierson's current band is fronted by a pretty blonde and plays acoustic pop punk. His former band, however, was a dirty, gritty, frequently naked group of boys who were as apt to write about TV character Peter Brady as they were the cute punk chick down the block, except you couldn't always make out the lyrics, and they didn't care. Screeching Weasel was a DIY punk mainstay from their founding in 1986, when the members were still in high school and inspired by the Ramones. This lasted until their breakup in 2001, following a flirtation with mainstream acceptance symbolized by a (rejected) major-label recording contract. In that fifteen-year period, the band had toured and then refused to tour. It had antagonized and challenged audiences physically as well as intellectually with songs like "I Wanna Be A Homosexual." Frontman Ben Weasel was aggressive and unpredictable. In short, Screeching Weasel was edgy. But this wasn't Pierson's doing, although he was a co-founder of the band; he's now more interested in exploring what's new to him than in challenging audiences. Even in Blackouts, as he will attest, is almost entirely devoid of edge.

"The thing about edginess," I remember him saying, "is that it never changes." [16] A February 19, 2007, *Brandweek* cover story called "The New Edgy" is proof: sex, rape, and suicide are all listed as possibilities under the new edgy, but seemed already to have been a part of the old edgy. [17] Edginess usually consists of some combination of the following elements: sexual content, political or social commentary, aggression, and humor. It serves to make viewers question their comfort with larger sociopolitical concerns, although perhaps not enough to change them. Edginess is urban, youth-focused, and distinctly masculine. It's hipper than hip, way more now than now, and uncomfortable in the most comforting way. And it likely always will be.

Yet edginess depends on context. Roberts's description of edginess implies a monocultural state with a correct and polite society when in fact we live in a mixed-up and contradictory culture. Most things labeled edgy are pretty safe, designed to irritate, but not truly upset, the middle class. It may be edgy, for example, to deal with sexual themes in one's work—unless one is a sex worker and it is a necessity. It may be edgy to point out unadulterated racism among law enforcement professionals if you are a popular black comedian, but to do the same if you are a black food-service worker and live next door to a white cop may just be a bad idea. It is central to the continued dominance of edginess in popular culture that no one actually abandons the comforts supposedly under attack in edgy ad campaigns or comedy sketches.[18]

Roberts points to this barely perceptible class structure as he continues his ode to edginess. "I believe 'edge cultures' will have even higher value in this millennium. Great ideas can come from anywhere, but most of them turn up on the edge. The places that are . . . resourceful."[19] That his language mimics that of the trend spotters and marketers we talk to in this book, who mine the "resourceful" underclass for great ideas in technology, fashion, and marketing, is no coincidence. Our consumer culture has been edging toward edginess ever since the youth demographic was identified as influential and desirable.

•   •   •

The acknowledgment that parody—whether paid for or not—is good, edgy advertising should not surprise the reader. Anyone dismayed by the easy assimilation of anticorporate sentiment into commercial endeavors may wish to consult accidental PBR marketing strategist Naomi Klein, who already explained it in *No Logo*: "ads co-opt out of reflex—they do so because consuming is what consumer culture does." [20]

What should cause alarm instead is that parody is an elementary act of nonconformity, one used often as a step toward more actively engaged dissent. It is accepted as given in contemporary activist communities that clever billboard alterations, subvertisements, and street theater open up a space for resistance. And sometimes culture jamming and copyfighting do draw attention to corporate wrongdoing or social injustice.

Rarely, however, does an antimarketing campaign directly contribute to effective change. This is because strategies that rely on parody or other forms of image reuse directly reproduce what is being rebelled against. They are intended as mocking, sure, but they still put a palatable message of Shell Oil or Apple or Calvin Klein in front of an audience raised on irony and advertising that, marketers hope, is learning to abandon reason entirely when faced with products. The differences between mocking and mocketing are negligible, if they exist at all.

Some would say the same thing about the differences between parody and politics. Consider the mission statement of one Canadian culture-jamming group, Guerrilla Media, whose work resembles a slightly less fictional *Onion*: "Using satire as our main political tool, we primarily create and widely distribute parodies of daily newspapers, and government and corporate promotional materials." [21] Their projects have included what they call "actions" on NAFTA, welfare reform, cuts to social programs, and environmental issues, all in the form of fake newspapers. "We use humor as a means to expose powerful interests," the group explains on its Web site.[22]

While the creation and dissemination of a newspaper of any kind, whether parodic in intent or not, is a difficult feat, *MADtv*'s Yaris sketch proves humor can be used to quell criticism as often as voice it. Somehow we seem to be confusing jokes with social change.

It's not the only confusion in play. Many cultural producers consider parody and satire synonymous, but in fact parody is merely the comedic imitation of a subject, while satire is an imitation of a subject intended both to amuse and to illustrate folly, and thus contains greater political possibilities. Clarifying these terms does not change their limitations, however. Both parody and satire narrow political response to two options: you "get it" and laugh or you do not—and enjoying a good chuckle is not a worthy stand-in for critically engaging with an issue. Moreover, parody and satire encourage more imitative responses—a more concise adbust, a funnier reworking of a logo—that can foster even more nasty, snarky responses to serious political matters. It can start to seem a viable act of political engagement to sit on the couch making snide comments while flipping back and forth between Fox News and the *Daily Show*.

The primary problem of parody and satire as political tools can be distilled thus: adbusting, subvertising, and many other activities employed by culture jammers and copyfighters alike, whether parodic or satiric, fundamentally reproduce, and reinforce, brands and the aims of branding. They not only reassert the icons they half-heartedly attempt to dismantle, they encourage their continued survival. Reverend Billy and the Church of Stop Shopping, as we saw in Chapter 3, need shopping to continue, whether of Billy's products or at a national coffee shop chain, to stay relevant. Negativland's *Dispepsi* relies heavily on Pepsi's continued status as the second most popular soft drink in the world in order to mock that status for its art. And the Toyota Yaris may have been the brunt of some edgy jokes, but it was the brunt of *something*. In other words, as the *New Yorker*'s Larissa MacFarquhar writes in an extended criticism of Michael Moore, "Satire doesn't unseat conventions; it reinforces them."[23]

The impervious logic of branding means criticism is becoming almost impossible to voice or hear. In some cases, criticism isn't going to matter anyway. "If you've got a fan base," Ed Keller, CEO of the brand management firm Keller Fay Group, told Rob Walker in an article on anticelebrity Web communities, "you can weather negative word of mouth." From the celebrity's (brand's) perspective, all publicity is good publicity. "Perhaps the real lesson of communities of disregard is that they're a sign of brand health," Walker postulates. "Nobody bothers to get together to hate an irrelevant entity."[24] The understanding that antifan Web sites may be an indication of healthy fandom isn't nearly as perverse as our consumer culture gets. As we've seen with mocketing, some companies are even willing to help create negative messages. In upcoming chapters, we'll find examples of outright criticism used as sales pitches.

Regardless of its positive or negative messages, work that mimics or quotes a known original "doesn't necessarily degrade or devalue the original. In cases of people like James Brown, [a frequently remixed artist] it actually is of great advertising value to the original," said John Oswald, the sound artist behind the 1989 all-appropriated album *Plunderphonic*, which was made entirely of found sound, in the documentary *Sonic Outlaws*.[25] That is, when certain mimicked figures or products have achieved iconic status—lovemarks, we might call them—parody no longer affects them negatively. It merely contributes further to their iconic status, brand integrity intact.

This may be the fault of consumerism. Because, in the end, consumers do not approach advertising *or* subvertising expecting to be challenged. They expect to be marketed to and will perceive even nonstandard messages in the way they have been trained to receive all messages: as a prompt for consumption. Because, if I may extrapolate from Klein's earlier statement, consuming is what consumers do in consumer culture.

Oswald, however, isn't posing an aesthetic concern. He's describing the defense copyright activists have adopted to argue for image reuse. And it's a good one, mindful of the profit-driven logic of the corporate world. Archivist and intellectual property rights activist Rick Prelinger describes the contribution of image reuse to iconic status on a larger scale in an interview with the alternative licensing organization Creative Commons.[26] When he asked an associate at Time Life what the highest revenue-producing image they owned was, she pointed to the ubiquitous image of the movie-theater crowd wearing 3-D glasses.[27] "You know this famous image," he described. "It's kind of emblematic of the fifties. [Time Life] makes a great deal of money selling that image. . . . It's also pirated. It's been shot over and over again by people. People have set up people in theaters and then shot it on film, so they have a movie version of it. Repetition and ubiquity haven't lessened the value of that image: they've increased it. . . . Ubiquity equals value."

In consumer culture, frequency of image quickly lends itself to greater consumption, and therefore to greater financial value. For parent company Time Warner, more legitimate sources will surely pay licensing fees for the 3-D crowd image even as it is pirated more frequently. Most defenses of image reuse look at Japan's *dojinshi*, one of the most influential if illegal forces in the hugely popular universe of *manga*, or Japanese comic books. *Dojinshi* are unlicensed Japanese comics that use characters, storylines, and drawing styles lifted directly from corporate-licensed books. Although Japanese copyright law is similar to U.S. law, a lax attitude toward crackdowns in Japan has made the creation and collection of illegal *manga* extremely easy and popular—and it only seems to bolster the status, and eventually the sales, of the original corporate-owned properties. *Dojinshi* is called either "homage" or flat-out "piracy," depending on the speaker, but all sides agree that unenforced intellectual property rights laws have led to more individuals investing personal time and energy in illegal comics, which has contributed to manga's now international ubiquity.

Dojinshi, pirated Time Life images, and mash-ups of James Brown songs all bolster the financial worth and cultural value of their originals. Although none were created to directly oppose consumerism, they were certainly made to skirt its standard operating procedures of getting permission, paying royalties, and granting attribution. These illegal forms may not be anticonsumerist, or even really nonconsumerist; in fact, they may contribute to consumerism.

So while a form of art that offers "great advertising value to the original" makes for an excellent reason to send the legal teams from the C&D department off on an extended vacation, it also points to the larger problem of reused corporate-created images, logos, phrases, and ideas representing (and re-*presenting*) those very images, logos, phrases, and ideas. Again. It is absolutely true that images, logos, phrases, and ideas considered intellectual property are elements of our shared cultural language; the corporations that aggressively put them into the world have no legal or moral right to control every aspect of their use. Sometimes, sure, they will try, often as a ham-fisted means of stifling criticism, yet to preserve democracy, activists must continue to fight them.

Other times, however, the underground naturally grows to love a corporate-created icon. At these times, the corporate copyright owner has no choice but to sit back and let the fans do what they will. Unfortunately, this love isn't always as natural as it seems.

6

THE FILMMAKERS

One spring day at *Punk Planet* in 2005 I received a messy envelope containing a stenciled T-shirt; several crappy, homemade stickers; some one-inch buttons; and a crumpled letter. This may be unusual at *Spin* or *Vibe*, where promo materials usually come in slick packages, but where I work most materials arrive crumpled. This package, however, was unusual. For one, it seemed deliberately, almost evenly, crumpled. Also, it was sent from the offices of Lucasfilm, Ltd.

The letter stated, in part:

This package of cool Star Wars swag was sent to you because you are:

[ ] Working at a cool, underground magazine.
[ ] In a band that might have a Star Wars fan in it.
[ ] An actor/writer/celeb who digs Star Wars—or I secretly hope loves droids, Wookies, and Vader.
[ ] Going to wear this rare Episode III shirt to all your paparazzi-infested events.

Be sure to wear this shirt with pride, sticker bomb your favorite hangout with these stickers, and decorate your favorite jacket with pinbacks. Yoda sure will appreciate the effort.

On my copy, boxes one and four were Xed off in lime-green crayon, and the package included a red shirt hand-stenciled with an image of Darth Vader, storm trooper buttons, and a handful of stickers. One of these depicted a sketchy outline of Yoda next to a digitized clip-art Mr. T, arm in arm above the slogan "Peace between the races." Another showed Yoda with a Mr. T hairdo flashing the devil horns. They were shabbily photocopied onto the same atomic-green sticker paper you can get at Kinko's, and I recognized the drawing style of MCA, a rock-poster artist whose work mixes heavy-metal imagery and pop iconography.

The crumpled letter invited readers to a Web site, Grrl.com, that featured no official markers of its creation by Lucasfilm employee Bonnie Burton. Although it has since morphed back into a standard personal Web site, during the lead-up to the release of *Star Wars: Episode III—Revenge of the Sith* it appeared at the time to be a wholly unofficial fan site for hipsters who grew up loving Luke Skywalker. That Burton is also the publisher of a zine called *Grrl*— she claims a direct connection to the early 1990s riot grrrl movement—only served to blur the line between what is genuinely DIY and what is done for the Man. Grrl.com, *Revenge of the Sith* edition, was an underground artist's dream: easy-to-follow directions for T-shirt stenciling, printable iron-ons, handmade sticker how-tos, wheat-paste recipes. Visitors to the site had to dig fairly deep to figure out that Burton works as a content developer for Lucasfilm's Web site, a job that requires "expertise in marketing Star Wars to teen girls," according to her posted résumé. Much of what the site described is not legal in public spaces, of course, but Grrl.com invited visi-tors to send in pictures of their *Star Wars*–inspired creations in situ anyway.

"*Episode III* ads and promos were easy to spot on TV, magazines, and in grocery stores," Burton explained via Starwars.com, the Lucasfilm news site she maintains. Then she goes on, deliberately obscuring her active role—both on and off the clock—in fostering the creation of less traditional advertising: "There also appeared a number of cool items tailored for teens and their interests including online community building, street art, underground fashion trends, and upcoming bands." The article's headline was "Underground Spawns Cool Swag and Avatars."[1]

It could have been synergy, except both parties are supposed to benefit from synergy. And although the "cool swag" may have been spawned by the underground, the distribution mechanism that got it into my hands came in a crumpled package from Lucasfilm, Ltd. From what I can tell, that's the only party that reaped any benefit from the supposed synergy. For artists who aspire to illustration gigs for major media, though, the opportunity to link one's work to Star Wars, however surreptitiously, fulfills the self-promotional demands these aspirations require.

"Were artists getting paid as well?" I asked Burton, who said she's familiar with *Punk Planet*—she had sent the crumpled letter—and expressed no concerns about talking to me on the record, originally for that no-major-media publication.

"No one was paid as far as participants that I know of," she responded via e-mail. "We just did it in an underground kind of way."

Her story doesn't entirely jibe with that of fellow Lucasfilm employee Carole Ambauen, however, whose job it was, she said, to conceptualize "an 'underground' youth campaign." For that campaign she made a Vader poster, stickers, avatars, and pins—some of which I received at *Punk Planet*, some of which were pictured on the Grrl.com Web site, and some of which looked suspiciously like stenciled images on the sidewalk I pass on my way to work every day. "I was a full-time employee and paid," Ambauen told me.[2]

Creative contributors to the campaign tell varying stories. Some say they sent work primarily to get their names out there; most just genuinely like the film series; and a few alluded to more tangible, financial compensation, yet I was unable to verify payment of artists even off the record. (I'll return to the uncomfortable issue of money in Chapter 11.) Had Burton's statement on the issue been a bit more concrete—"an underground kind of way" might mean anything from "I let their band crash on my couch and drink all my beer" to "I gave them money because I have a day job and they don't but do great work"—I could have written off all suggestions of financial reward. Instead, I was troubled by the fact that at least one artist involved later denied his participation entirely. Leaving open the possibility that his work had been included without his knowledge or his drawing style closely copied, it does seem that underground artists comfortable with promoting the series, officially or not, are not as comfortable discussing their work as marketing.

"It was very casual" was all MCA, the primary force behind the Boston area–based graphic design firm Evil Design, would say about the relationship that led to the inclusion of his Yoda/Mr. T stickers in the *Star Wars* promotional packet before declining to comment further. Besides displaying MCA's striking characters, the Star Wars promotional stickers listed his Web site, Evildesign.com. The early images shown there indicate that Yoda was probably in his drawing repertoire well before he was tapped by Lucasfilm.

After all, rock-poster artists, zinesters, and skateboarders alike all grew up with Yoda, Darth Vader, and Princess Leia. We claim Jedi Knight as our religious affiliation on our tax forms and use the *gzzzt* light-saber sound effect as if it were a synonym for combat. A meander through any DIY craft fair will route you past camo onesies decorated with wide-eyed baby storm troopers, or playful

1950s-era schoolchildren forever battling with light sabers on a felt skirt or the cover of a handmade blank book; a couple I know considered using the name Luke Skywalker for their new baby; girls I went to high school with wore pillowcases to be Princess Leia for Halloween in the 1970s, and felt betrayed by the golden bikini costume she wore in *Return of the Jedi*, since our own bodies would take years to catch up to that costume. Entire zines and tattoo Web sites are devoted to the film series' unique imagery; Star Wars references are common in hip-hop; "may the Force be with you" is a perfectly acceptable, if slightly out-of-date, salutation; an officemate's band is named Dianogah, after the garbage parasite monster in the original *Star Wars*; a former intern just named his band Darth Vader; and on my way to the *Punk Planet* offices I pass two Darth Vader stencils. A stroll in the opposite direction leads me past one of Yoda. The Star Wars series has produced some of the underground's most beloved icons.

Some of this is timing, and some runoff from our larger culture's obsession with the series. Or perhaps it's a seeming obsession that is actually just a suffocating ubiquity, the direct result of Lucasfilm's no-holds-barred licensing and merchandising campaign. Both punk and *Star Wars* were born in 1977, and achieved popularity through similar methods: Sharpied band lyrics on the backs of T-shirts marked fans of one and an ever-present deck of trading cards or Tie Fighter sketches marked fans of the other. Both relied, as dual fan and publisher of independent Love Bunni Press R. John Xerxes put it, on "the idea of rebellion against overwhelming odds."[3]

Inextricable from the movies were the licensing and marketing built into the fabric of the multipart Star Wars story as it wove its way into our culture. Even back in 1983, *Episode VI—Return of the Jedi* was accused of crass commercialization: the new Ewok characters were clearly made for toy stores, their sales bolstered by their central (and adorable!) roles in the film. Subsequent Star Wars films have each managed to achieve new echelons of hype. One critic memorably described *Episode I—The Phantom Menace* as "largely irrelevant after the marketing campaign that preceded it."[4] And as John Seabrook claims in *Nobrow: The Culture of Marketing, the Marketing of Culture,* "The marketing and the movie have become the same thing."[5] In fact, he writes, in his grocery store:

> Star Wars has taken over aisle 5, the dairy section. There are figurine mugs of Han Solo and Princess Leia, nine-inch collectibles featuring Emperor Palpatine, an R2-D2 dispenser filled with Phantom Menace Pepsis, and, down from that, another big display case filled with Star Wars–themed Frito-Lay potato chips. Pepsi has sunk over $2 billion into promoting the new trilogy. Each of Pepsi's three fast-food franchises—KFC, Taco Bell, and Pizza Hut—has licensed a different planet and festooned their containers with its characters.[6]

By *Episode III—Revenge of the Sith* series creator George Lucas had earned a reputation as "a Jedi master of merchandising."[7] With *Revenge of the Sith* characters hyping everything from cell phones to candy in TV commercials, and reappearing as action figures and toys for children as young as four (despite the film's PG-13 rating for violence), the marketing of the final Star Wars episode struck many as being as powerful as the Force itself. Perhaps, therefore, it was inevitable that the campaign would go underground. There just weren't very many other places for it to go.

• • •

While a vast network of spiky-haired, leather-clad social rejects doesn't seem the ideal marketing team for a multibillion-dollar entertainment empire, Lucasfilm doesn't seem to mind. In fact, Bonnie Burton—zinester, writer, punk-music fan, and Lucasfilm, Ltd., employee—saw no irony in the come-see-my-friend's-band, street-art style promotional campaign she helped organize for the big-budget, major-media event *Star Wars: Episode III—Revenge of the Sith*. Because there was none intended.

"We thought it would be a great way to reach out to our fans, especially ones that are into underground street culture and music," she told me. Like Tom Frank's sixties- and seventies-era revolutionary ad execs, she genuinely appreciates the subculture she borrowed from—but unlike those earlier men in gray flannel suits, Burton is an active participant in the underground. (Vote for her Jones Soda label photos: #0000036547 and #0000036546.) Although there may be more than a bit of opportunism in it— "I'm on a weird quest to be sort of famous, like an indie movie star that only the hip people like to chat about. . . . I want to be underground famous," she wrote on Grrl.com, before working on her *Sith* promotions—she's genuinely on "our side." She's a zinester; she just wants the culture to have a wider appeal.[8]

But at Lucasfilm Burton is not operating as an individual member of the underground. She's operating as part of a large and influential media corporation with a reach that most zinesters, punk bands, and graffiti artists would kill for. The posters, stencils, pinbacks, avatars, and stickers Burton helped distribute and popularize were an important—if cheap and easy—aspect of an extensive, multifront promotional campaign. As she herself concluded in an e-mail to me, "It's great to gain awareness from zines and such that usually get ignored by other film houses and media outlets."

There is, however, very little the zines, stencils, and wheat-pasted posters could have added to the marketing campaign that bus ads, action figures, and dairy-aisle takeovers at local grocery stores didn't accomplish. Even the usually elusive DIY punk demographic had been won over, practically since birth. Yet as ubiquitous as Star Wars may be, as forcibly crammed into every nook and cranny of our popular culture as it still is now, two years after the final film has left theaters,[9] there's still one thing the untrammeled merchandizing of the series couldn't plaster with a picture of Queen Amidala: integrity.

The integrity of a photocopied poster, messy and misspelled, staple-gunned to a signpost by a determined pilgrim is hard to ignore: born of raw passion, with concern for the message overriding those for conventions of grammar and graphic design. The accessibility and plain evidence of the simple tools behind stencils and zines demonstrate that at least one person found a certain something—a show, a joke, an image—worth his or her effort. That's the central thrust behind hand-created underground media: an individual likes a band, concept, or cause enough to devote a zine, button, or flyer to it. It's a charming sentiment, difficult to pass up. Yet when the forwarded "cause" is generic, mainstream media—created not by a single girl in her basement with a guitar but by film studios, professional actors, production teams, marketing strategists, hair and makeup stylists, and corporate licensee after corporate licensee—the message changes somewhat.

Perhaps more so in this case than in others. Feminists of my generation may be particularly upset by Burton's appropriation of riot grrrl, as a name and as an ethos, as a platform to sell the distinctly patriarchal message of the *Star Wars* series. The riot-grrrl movement was partially a reaction to the traditionally masculine punk-rock environments dominating Washington, D.C., and the

Pacific Northwest, and called for the creation of safe spaces for girls to explore sexual and artistic freedom, not to mention social justice. "You have to remember that a lot of girls weren't in bands, they were organizers, activists, and other types of artists," Allison Wolfe cautioned. Former Bratmobile frontwoman and *Riot Grrrl* zine contributor, Wolfe's now in the band Partyline and working at the *Washington Post*.

Fellow former contributor to *Riot Grrrl*, current member of Spider and the Webs, and an activist with the Feminist Action Brigade Tobi Vail underscored the political implications as well.

> For me, riot grrl was too identity-based and therefore sort of missed the point. The point being, what kind of feminist acts should we take, how can we change society. . . . As long as we are still working on stuff—building communities of resistance and politicizing culture and actively making meaning on our own terms—we are still powerful. The name riot grrl is not important or interesting. It's just a name. The interesting thing is young women coming together to resist male domination, and that is happening all the time; it's just not accurately represented in mainstream patriarchal media.[10]

Nonetheless, it's one thing to watch mainstream patriarchal media make common journalistic mistakes and fail to represent revolutionary ideas accurately; it's slightly different to take those ideas, divide them into flavors like Sporty, Posh, Baby, Scary, and Ginger, and sell them as "Girl Power." Even this, however, we almost expect. It's another matter entirely to *use* those revolutionary ideas to *sell* mainstream patriarchal media to, as Burton describes on her own Web site, "teen girls."

In fact, Wolfe agreed, it's "really weird. If you'd told me back in the seventies when I was a total Star Wars freak kid, I woulda been psyched!" But now, she said,

> obviously it's fucking lame and was never the intention of riot grrrl or anything I've been a part of. We never copyrighted the name, because we didn't want to be "corporate" about anything. So here we are now, with people being able to do whatever they want with the term, the ideas, the style. . . . It's a real bummer to have something that was meant to be about real ideas, real struggle, and totally DIY, be turned into this marketing tool.

But that's what happened in spring 2005, when Grrl.com became an underground marketing project of Lucasfilm, Ltd., employee Bonnie Burton. I asked Burton what was the agenda behind these DIY strategies.

She answered, "There was no agenda, other than to get fans— from all walks—excited about the *Episode III* film and DVD release."

Although it's creepy, we'd be hard-pressed to label Burton's blind enthusiasm for DIY punk Star Wars fans "corporate scum" or "evil." Then again, I, too, was raised on Star Wars and might find it unconscionable to call something I've loved since the age of seven so disparaging a phrase. Universal adoration of the film series, however, may not be the sole cause of our restraint. There may be some fear mixed in, too: some evidence suggests that Lucasfilm selectively pursues IP violators when they fail to be slavishly adoring.

In 1997, Star Wars fan and University of Vermont graduate

Steve Mount created the Web site www.tatooine.com. It wasn't a
fan site; it was mostly just a site to show off pictures of his kids;
a space to host fellow 1989 UV graduates' web pages; a résumé
of Mount's web design services; a message board devoted to discussing TV and film; and a list of local gas prices. It wasn't offensive
in any way; actually, according to Mount, it was "boring."[11] Regardless, in 2000 Lucasfilm threatened to sue Mount for copyright
and trademark violations.[12]

Aside from occasionally discussing the series on his message
board, alongside other sci-fi epics, the only connection between
Mount's site and Lucasfilm was the domain name. Tatooine is the
name of the planet the first film is initially set in; it's derived, as
Mount wrote in his response to Lucasfilm's C&D, from "a town
in Tunisia known as Foum Tataouine . . . the words Tataouine and
Tatooine are homonyms, both potential English spellings of a
Tunisian word. The ability to trademark the name of a foreign city
for all possible purposes is in doubt."[13]

"I wasn't using the site to disparage Lucasfilm or its properties
in any way," Mount told me via e-mail seven years later. "In fact, I
was and continue to be a fan of the Star Wars series and of Lucasfilm in general. . . . I had no idea it would cause a dustup."[14] But
Lucasfilm wanted the domain name. "I think Tatooine was special
to them, as the origin point for many of the major characters.
Frankly, I think they decided they wanted it, and they had the
means to take it, and they did."

Specifically, Lucasfilm wanted *his* domain name, or perhaps just
wanted him not to have it. "I did a search at some point and noted
that they had bought up a lot of the coms for the names they used.
But I note, today, that they did not do a complete sweep. Tatooine
.org and Tatooine.net are not Lucasfilm," Mount wrote. The first
links to a spamblocker and the second is currently available for

purchase. He pointed out, "They don't own Alderan.com (another prominent planet in the series)." [15]

Lucasfilm's charges of copyright violation are specious at best, as Mount himself makes clear in his initial response to the C&D. "I never claimed an affiliation with Lucasfilm, nor did I ever seek to profit in any way from any affiliation, express or implied. . . . The name 'Steve Mount' is prominently displayed." Just as hollow are the charges of trademark violation or dilution. "Lucasfilm and I are in totally different businesses. No one coming to my site is going to buy web design services from me instead of from Lucasfilm, because Lucasfilm does not offer web design services to the general public. Nor does Lucasfilm offer web programming services; nor do they generally post pictures of the Mount family. These are all services provided at Tatooine.com." [16]

Lucasfilm did not bow to these well-reasoned arguments, however, and a few days later Mount gave up the domain name under conditions he agreed not to disclose. Wondering if Lucasfilm might come to fear a fan backlash from such tactics, I asked Mount if the experience affected his feelings about—or interest in watching—Star Wars.

"It soured me on Lucasfilm a bit," he told me, "but that passed."

Given Mount's experience, it comes as no surprise that Lucasfilm is quick to punish actual copyright violators. In the fall of 2005, days before *Revenge of the Sith* was released, eight people in Los Angeles pled guilty to charges of copyright infringement for having distributed dupes of the film, including posting it online the day before its release. In a less clear-cut case decided a year later in U.S. courts, Lucasfilm won a $20 million settlement against a British costumer after the firm sold unlicensed Stormtrooper outfits and helmets and claimed that they were, in some way, "authentic." Yet the costumer, the London-based Shepperton Studios, had actually produced some of the first suits for the original Star Wars films. Lucasfilm successfully argued that the costumes were created as work-for-hire, which meant that the copyright for the designs belonged to the company and not the costumes' creator; the Shepperton proprietor denies signing any such work-for-hire agreement.[17] "Lucasfilm vigorously protects its intellectual property rights in Star Wars," president of licensing Howard Ruffman said in a release announcing its victory in court. "Infringers like Shepperton need to understand that we will pursue them."

Yet however ominous this sounds, the press release ends on a more friendly note, one that is far more telling of the Lucasfilm IP and marketing strategies. Star Wars is a beloved icon, the release claims, and fans are always producing at-home versions of their beloved film's costumes. Lucasfilm, Ltd., has no objection to this practice. "We appreciate that Star Wars has sparked the imaginations of fans around the world," Ruffman is quoted as saying. "We would never want to discourage fans from showcasing their enthusiasm for the movies."[18]

In fact, Lucasfilm has occasionally done far more than spark imaginations; sometimes it provides them a showcase. In 2002, the company devised an official Star Wars fan fiction film contest, judged by George Lucas himself. In another example, the company even defended the right of potential copyright infringers—"fans"—to post their work to the video-sharing Web site YouTube.

When, in August 2006, Lucasfilm discovered that some Star wars.com material had been posted to YouTube, they complained. YouTube quickly pulled all Star Wars–related material, possibly fearing litigation that could swiftly end their business forever. (Under the DMCA YouTube won't be held liable if everything potentially infringing is yanked without delay; thus, it immediately pulls any material that raises any ire, or any material related to material that raises any ire.) Lucasfilm, however, then asked YouTube to reinstate all the videos, except those using Starwars.com material. It backed up this request with an announcement on Starwars .com, underscoring their commitment to fans: "We would like the fan film community to know this was not done at our request. . . . We have asked YouTube to restore any works that were inadvertently removed," the announcement stated.[19]

Unfortunately, Lucasfilm's defense of the work of "fans" only goes so far, and hinges on their own fairly tight definition of fandom rather than the fair use statute. "We've been very clear all along on where we draw the line," Jim Ward, Lucasfilm's vice president of marketing, told the *New York Times*. "We love our fans. We want them to have fun. But if in fact somebody is using our characters to create a story unto itself, that's not in the spirit of what we think fandom is about. Fandom is about celebrating the story the way it is."[20]

So it makes sense that when the Official Star Wars Fan Film awards were announced in 2002, parodies, homages, and documentaries were eligible for judging, but dramatic reinterpretations of storylines and critically engaged comedies were not. In Lucasspeak this is called "a need to protect its copyright."[21] Yet the company is likely aware that the line they draw is not supported by IP laws, and so does not prosecute the creators of the latter types of works. Instead Lucasfilm limits their punishment to banishment from the contest. After all, a judge might interpret the fair use statute in a way that would allow for the creative comment forwarded in fan-made films, despite Ruffman's threats of "vigorous" protection following the Shepperton case.

The conversational environment that results is so restrictive that any and all participants must play directly into the narcissistic desires of the film series to be universally adored. It is an idealized brand environment that prohibits any potential negative, critical, or neutral comment. Reporters have noted this phenomenon as well. "Like the other journalists sent into the Death Star that is Star Wars, I was beginning to feel like I was part of the machine, too," John Seabrook commented, describing the parade of glad-handing and assurances of his respect for the series that opened the door to his interview with George Lucas. "In writing about Star Wars I had become a part of the Buzz industry." [22]

The line Lucasfilm draws between "fandom" and "infringement," if one exists, seems to be shakily traced along Lucas's own experiences as a "fan" of the work of Joseph Campbell, from whom the Star Wars creator claims he borrowed the plotlines and character attributes that formed the basis of the story line. [23] He's also acknowledged being influenced by Akiro Kurosawa's *The Hidden Fortress* and other independent films. The Lucasfilm IP strategy, therefore, might read something like this: imitation is the sincerest, and only allowable, form of flattery. Yet in practice, this narrow definition of fandom, while encouraging freedoms of certain speech, actively discourages others—in Steve Mount's innocuous case, even punishes them. The strategy begins to look like a legally enforced suspension of critical engagement.

However deeply human it may appear to encourage adoration and discourage ambivalence, George Lucas is not running for prom queen. He's running an extremely successful business enterprise instead. According to *Vanity Fair* it includes "1,700 employees and seven divisions that notches up some $1.2 billion in annual sales. It encompasses movies, visual effects, and lots of real estate." [24] And, of course, high profits for George Lucas.

These profits are not just derived from ticket sales to adoring fans; they also represent the savings made possible by the company's active engagement of adoring independent cultural producers. An enormous amount of unbillable marketing has come out of Lucasfilm's creative approach to IP preservation, some even from an unlikely source: self-professed fans who both eschew major media and no longer feel the franchise lives up to its hype. If any group of people were capable of avoiding the mainstream media quicksand ruled by Darth Vader, it would be underground media makers and artists. But Star Wars is so deeply woven into the mythology of the underground—and the rest of our culture at large—that it is genuinely unthinkable that we wouldn't attend and support every episode of the series. In this one case, the perfect formula for propaganda under democracy has been discovered: individuals may grumble mild criticisms but never question brand allegiance.

For example, I saw *Star Wars: Episode III—Revenge of the Sith* because I was raised in a media environment saturated with Star Wars imagery that dictated I care how the series concluded. In other words, I saw it because it seemed inevitable that I would. In a way, it *is* inevitable—it might be on at a friend's house one afternoon, background noise for some themed event, or just always already *on* somewhere, like the Beatles' "Yesterday." So I didn't *have* to run out within days of the film's release and watch it in theaters for nearly ten bucks. But I did, because when I received that package from Lucasfilm, I was both horrified and thrilled that *Punk Planet* was on the company's radar, and discovering other members of my community had contributed their work to the campaign brought an equal mix of negative and positive emotions. That I had any emotions about the new Star Wars film at all led directly to my suggestion that my friend Christa and I go see it, never mind the fact that I'd skipped the two previous films entirely. A quick poll of sixteen individuals, mostly friends, who have worked hard to create entertainment and distribution systems entirely separate from the corporate world's, and often under conditions of poverty, revealed a similar ambivalence. All but one had seen *Revenge of the Sith*—most in the theaters, and a shockingly large percentage on opening weekend. And they—we—went not with a sense of joy or anticipation but with a sense of resignation, knowing straight up that the movie was going to suck.

"I went against my better judgment, but had to finish what I started as a child with the original," Josh, a prominent street artist, told me. Roman, a radio producer, explained, "A lifetime of repeatedly watching the original series led me to it. It was inevitable." Independent publisher Joe declared that he went with "a moral sense of obligation to finish the job," while my own date for the film, zinester and visual artist Christa, wrongly remembered seeing it with her ex-boyfriend. When I corrected her, she responded, "Perhaps the ex-boyfriend memory I am recalling had to do with *Star Wars II*. They're all pretty much the same to me." Jon, a graphic designer, was less confused about the experience. "My expectations for *Episode III* couldn't possibly have been lower. Given how absolutely terrible the two 'prequels' that preceded *Revenge of the Sith* were, I was seeing this episode out of a sort of dreadful obligation," he told me. Still, he went to the midnight premiere.[25] Liz, zinester and manager of a popular independent bookstore, as well as the only one of my friends who had not yet seen the film, placed it "on her Netflix queue" because she said she wanted to "be a member of pop culture."[26]

All in all, roughly estimating ten dollars per ticket for fifteen of the sixteen respondents, that's a hundred and fifty dollars spent by people in my immediate social circle on *Revenge of the Sith*. In my rough-and-tumble, hot-dogs-or-health-insurance crew, this is a fair amount of money.

Admittedly, it's a small drop in the very large bucket that eventually contained all the *Revenge of the Sith* profits. "After starting the day with $16,912,367 from midnight shows alone," the online magazine *Box Office Mojo* reported, "*Star Wars: Episode III— Revenge of the Sith* closed Thursday with $50,013,859 from an estimated 9,400 screens at 3,661 theaters. That's the biggest day ever for a single movie in history." [27] As of October 2005, when the film had left theaters, worldwide box office grosses had amounted to almost $850 million, about seven and a half times the film's original budget of $113 million. The success of the movie helped put George Lucas at number four on *Forbes's* 2005 "Top 100 Celebrities" list—although he dropped to number fifteen in 2006—for earning $255 million between June 2004 and June 2005, and, according to the magazine, "nine figures on sales of episodes 4–6 from the box set alone" in 2004, twenty-seven years after the first film's release. [28]

Lucasfilm's corporate marketing agenda to get fans from all walks excited about the *Episode III* film and DVD release, as Burton put it, is not hidden, or evil, or even all that vile when you think about it. It's simply *capitalist*. But it's capitalism in overdrive. Like word-of-mouth agents, who volunteer their time to promote corporate products, members of the underground—filmmakers, zinesters, rock-poster artists—who helped build the *Star Wars* brand, trade on a noncommercial ethos for distinctly commercial ends they do not financially profit from. The work created is pointedly low-budget and tied to a community that values integrity; the aim is to sell movie tickets to their peers.

In fact, this may be how they justify their work as volunteer marketers among those same peers. While it originally struck me as odd that no illustrators whose work was sent to me in the crumpled package from Lucasfilm would go on record with a final accounting of the benefits, fiscal or otherwise, of their participation in the marketing of Star Wars, it is possible, if not likely, that such accounting might cheapen an otherwise natural appearing adoration of a beloved set of icons. The internal and public pressure to maintain the semblance of unadulterated passion for the childhood simplicity of Star Wars may outweigh the need to fully account for these influences.

Individual participants aside, it might be time to acknowledge that Star Wars resembles our ultimate advertising nightmare: that marketing can force us to act in a way that's antithetical to our own interests. The same fear first drove the scare over subliminal advertising that reared in the 1950s and again in the 1970s. The now-laughable notion that hidden images in ice cubes will cause us to associate gin with sex orgies was postulated in Vance Packard's 1957 book *The Hidden Persuaders*, which explored the so-called depth approach, a set of Freudian-derived marketing research strategies that supposedly uncovered and exploited our hidden desires to convince us to buy products we did not need. The depth approach and subliminal advertising have since been discounted, but the concerns that advertising can somehow control our behavior remain. Fifty years after *The Hidden Persuaders*, we read about people—good, smart, and not rich people—actively voicing displeasure with entertainment consumed seemingly of their own free will. They were convinced to consume not because their better judgment dictated they do so but because their emotional connection to the product and the mode in which it was marketed compelled them to. I know—I was one of them.

7

THE ATHLETIC SHOE COMPANY

Smack-dab in the middle of the summer of 2005, Nike SB, the three-year-old skateboard division of the athletic shoe company, unveiled a promotional campaign for its East Coast skateboarding tour, cleverly called Major Threat. They had even based the poster imagery on the album art from the eponymous 1981 Dischord Records album by Minor Threat, a band likely obscure to the average Nike shoe purchaser. It was, however, immediately recognizable to skateboarders.

Many came to view this as Nike's first mistake: the same demographic that happens to know about (and like) Minor Threat was the exact market whose respect (and money) the company hoped to gain with the promotional campaign. Nike soon found itself in the middle of what most companies would call a PR nightmare. The very demographic they wanted to attract was enraged, to put it mildly. Many felt the poster was too derivative of the album cover and the association with the devoutly underground band too jarring. Cyberspace was filled with immediate questions, accusations, and frustrations aimed at Nike.

Almost right away, to the relief (although not quite the admiration) of the skateboarding community, Nike SB pulled the campaign and issued an official apology on June 27, two days after the Major Threat 2005 East Coast Tour had begun and five days before it was due to end, on July 2. The campaign had been going for at least two weeks beforehand and had certainly done its job: every Minor Threat fan alive knew about the Major Threat 2005 East Coast Tour.

What came to be called Nike SB when it successfully launched in 2002 (after a few missteps) arose seemingly naturally from Nike's early reputation as the bratty little upstart in the world of sports-wear. An apocryphal story tells of a young Phil Knight selling shoes out of the back of his car, but the powerful brand image was carefully honed by Weiden+Kennedy. The marketing firm most associated with the company had made its name—and Nike's—through a barrage of brash stunts, smart ads, and creative associations with icons from a variety of fields. "The apostle of the image," Randall Rothenberg called the firm in his book *Where Suckers Moon*, which detailed an ad campaign they created for Subaru, noting that their appeal as marketers relied on their ability to "make you famous."[1]

Weiden+Kennedy's own corporate image was established in sharp contrast to the 1950s ad man, the man in the gray flannel suit. Rothenberg describes the in-house atmosphere as "T-shirts and jeans, long hair and insouciance, the meeting-was-supposed-to-start-an-hour-ago-where-are-they."[2] Legend tells of the moment Dan Weiden borrowed a typewriter from Phil Knight—the near-accidental birth of Weiden+Kennedy—and the truth is not too different. In fact the footwear company liked Weiden and David Kennedy's work at another firm so much that when the two struck out on their own in 1982, Nike followed, even lending office equipment to the agency start-up.[3]

The unconventional ad firm and the athletic-wear company made an unbeatable team, united in their desire for worldwide renown. That's a big omelet; eggshells were going to break. One crack occurred in the mid-1990s, when the firm decided to use the Beatles' "Revolution" for a TV ad announcing a new shoe line. After it first aired the resulting harangue of accusations from Michael Jackson (owner of the rights to the entire Beatles catalog), Yoko Ono, and the three surviving band members made it clear that unrestricted access to the copyrighted and closely monitored song had never been granted. But what were they gonna do? Weiden+Kennedy executive Kelley Stoutt told *Time*, "We never considered soundalikes. We're baby boomers too. This is our music. In our minds, it was the Beatles or no one."[4] It's a quote indicative of the company's attitude toward intellectual property: they felt entitled to the song, so they used it. Like Negativland did with Pepsi ads and U2's "I Still Haven't Found What I'm Looking For"—with results Weiden+Kennedy evidently admired—the ad agency viewed the popular cultural product as a part of their own history and felt no compunction about using it. The difference was that Nike was borrowing from the popularity of the Beatles's song to popularize their own product and Negativland was riffing on the popularity of Pepsi and U2 to comment on consumer culture.

The "Revolution" ad was also the commercial, as Nike's in-house ad director Scott Bedbury said, that "helped turn the company completely around."[5] Soon thereafter the shoe company's marketing strategy focused exclusively on stunts and Michael Jordan. One incident during the 1996 Olympics in Atlanta was dubbed "brash guerrilla" marketing, although others called the same event "ambush" marketing—in fact, the "ambush of all ambushes."[6] After a massive billboard campaign Nike handed out logoed banners to fans at all events and snuck "giant Swoosh signs into the arena. When the cameras panned the stands, TV audiences saw the Nike logo loud and clear." All without paying the $50 million for official Olympics sponsorship.[7] Actual sponsor

Champion went unnoticed; many believed Nike had been the official event sponsor.[8]

Such aggressive marketing didn't stop once Nike became the dominant brand either; it was just under less pressure to show results. In 2001, the company initiated an Astroturf campaign to highlight a certain athletic clothing manufacturer's shoes, purported to give Australian players an unfair advantage on the field. Closely resembling the antisweatshop actions that have plagued Nike for a decade and a half, the "Fans Fighting for a Fairer Football" action consisted of photocopied flyers, street protests, and stickers listing a Nike-sponsored Web site politicos were urged to visit for more information.[9] The "target" of the protest was, of course, Nike itself, and participants in the supposedly political action were the campaign's desired demographic. The company seemingly had done the impossible: turned anti-Nike sentiment into a selling proposition. You say you want a revolution, well, you know . . . we can have that ready for you by early next week.

However, marketing like this wasn't going to capture the hard-earned dollars of the mid-1990s skate-punk community. "Nike failed miserably in its first attempt to tackle the market," Jordan Robertson reported for CNN, "when poorly designed shoes and a glitzy, mass-market ad campaign resulted in a line that was pulled after just one year."[10] Skateboarders voiced suspicion instead of praise when they suddenly became a demographic sought after by monied fat cats, especially given that their sport had been considered a criminal activity just a few short years before. The new line prompted a relaunch of Don't Do It, a Nike boycott project headed by Birdo Guisinger, manager of Consolidated Skateboards. Nike had always been a rah-rah booster of teamwork and pure Olympic athleticism—things that don't have much to do with skateboarding. "It's not just a sport," one adherent, Ian MacKaye, told Dan Sinker in 1999. "Skateboarding was about redefinition. It was like putting on a pair of filtered glasses—every curb, every sidewalk, every street, every wall had a new definition." [11] But the athletic giant smelled money, and the late 1990s saw several more false starts, general fuckups, and outright failures before it managed to break into the underground sport.

By the time it did, the company had learned an important lesson: to "not behave like an $11 billion company." [12] (This number was from early 2004; more recent estimates put Nike revenues closer to $14 billion.) The lesson was learned shortly after Nike purchased skate- and surf-clothing manufacturer Hurley in 2002, thus acquiring both Hurley's expertise in the field and accumulated street cred. The sale upset surfers and skateboarders alike, but a compliant malaise soon prevailed. "Every company is huge now and skateboarding is huge, so it really doesn't matter anymore," one specialty shoe store manager explained. [13] Not behaving like a multibillion-dollar company also meant rethinking hiring practices. Sandy Bodecker, head of the nascent Nike SB, started hiring exclusively inside the field—and away from highly respected skate projects. First on board was Robbie Jeffers, former manager of the Southern California skateboarding team Stussy, who was followed by Kevin Imamura, former editor of skate magazines *Warp* and *Stance*. [14]

After all the failures one might wonder why Nike kept trying to break into the relatively small—and, at one point, resolutely anti-Nike—market. "I think Nike saw that if they weren't communicating to this segment of the population, there was gonna be a huge chunk of kids growing up not knowing about Nike," Imamura explained in an interview. "If you grow up skating and don't care too much about anything else, you're probably not gonna give

Nike too much mind space. And those were the consumers they didn't wanna lose out on." [15]

They certainly didn't. The individualistic and antiestablishment nature of the sport, as well as the comparatively low initial equipment costs, have always held an appeal for kids—boys, mostly. By the early days of the new millennium, however, video games, Tony Hawk, and the X Games gave skateboarding a healthy image boost. By 2002, the sport was gaining national popularity; by 2003 it would claim about thirteen million skaters. [16] It was certainly a "huge chunk," but, as Imamura's statement indicates, it might be quality not quantity that matters to the company: the specific qualities of Nike-hating skaters, that is. How to turn anti-Nike sentiment into footwear-branded mind space became Nike SB's central question.

Fortunately, the new staff had all the answers. With the input of insiders like Imamura, innovative plans were developed for limited-edition sneakers, graffiti artist–designed special editions, and lines exclusive to independent skate shops, all in emulation of the smaller companies Nike now knew how to compete with properly. Once Nike had mastered the look and feel of independently produced skate shoes, one manager found they started to "sell out the first few hours we get them." Another said "the phone calls start coming as soon as people hear we are getting a new shipment." But despite the popularity of the sport, a great bulk of the buyers were shoe collectors or eBay entrepreneurs. [17] The footwear giant had maximized demand for the skateboarding lifestyle and downplayed the importance of the actual sport. Skate shoes, with their long tongues and puffy exteriors, "are often bought by people who want to look the part," one reporter wrote. The president of another skate shoe company agreed. "The

14-year-old kid who doesn't ride a skateboard still wants to look like a skateboarder," he said.[18] "Sales are surging," another writer noted in 2005, "and skateboard footwear is gaining popularity even among kids who've never picked up a board. . . . Sales of skate shoes increased by more than 19 percent over the previous year."[19] The skate-punk lifestyle, it turns out, is something Nike could sell to a broad market.

But not too broad a market, Imamura maintains. At least not yet. "Everyone's perception of Nike is that we have tons of cash and can buy anything or anyone we want, but that's definitely not our modus operandi," Imamura told board sports magazine *Transworld Business*.[20] Not behaving like a multibillion-dollar company— perhaps behaving more like skateboarders—seems to mean not caring about profits above all else.

Compared to the potential of the market, Nike SB does lag, bringing in "less than 5 percent" of the annual $1.5 billion in skate shoe sales, which amounts to only 0.54 percent of Nike's annual profits.[21] Their sales may be growing—after all, they've barely begun to explore all that new skateboarding mind space—but Nike SB still values quality over quantity. "For now," one business writer tellingly wrote, "Nike is focused not on volume but on cachet."[22]

Dischord representatives felt fucked over by Nike SB's Major Threat campaign, a blatant appropriation of the label and the band's cachet, if not particularly put out by the fact that the campaign had already done its job promoting the tour by the time the official apology came. Fans had seen an immediate link between the tour poster and their album cover, and some wondered if an endorsement deal had been brokered. But devoted (and mostly older) fans knew better.

The Nike statement openly acknowledged the tour poster image had been "inspired by Minor Threat's album cover . . . an inspiration to countless skateboarders since the record came out in 1981," although it could not help realigning itself with the underground even here. "For the Nike Skateboarding staff"—remember, they're skateboarders, too—"this is no different." The poster's heavy reliance on the album cover art was, the company conceded, "a poor judgment call." Although the letter stopped short of admitting intellectual property rights infringement, it did admit that the poster "should not have been executed without consulting Minor Threat and Dischord Records. We . . . want to make very clear that we have no relationship with Minor Threat [or] Dischord Records and they have not endorsed our products." The apology concluded with another reminder that Nike is staffed by underground inside players: "We would also like to extend an apology to Susie Josephson Horgan, the photographer who took the original photo."[23]

When the admission of corporate wrongdoing appeared, Dischord's response came fast, in the form of a note posted on the label's Web site. Clearly, the acknowledgment that the sportswear giant had acted without permission was not substantial: there was more at stake here than hurt feelings. "It is disheartening to us to think that Nike may be successful in using this imagery to fool kids . . . into thinking that the general ethos of this label, and Minor Threat in particular, can somehow be linked to Nike's mission."

The label's continued insistence on distancing themselves from the campaign is understandable. The Major Threat poster image and Minor Threat album cover are nearly identical. Although one is blue and the other red, both are high-contrast images of a bald man seated in a stairway, his head resting on his arms crossed over his knees. Text runs down the right-hand side of the image in an all-caps, sans serif font: Major Threat / Minor Threat. Oh—but in the Major Threat poster image, the figure wears Nikes, cradles a Nike shoe box, and is seated next to another Nike logo stenciled onto the stairway.

Yet the photographic image in circulation around the time of the apology didn't capture the entirety of the poster's appropriation. The full image also includes, to the right of the photograph, the title in the same distinctive font used for the band's name on Minor Threat's 1981 album, *In My Eyes*, and 1984's *Out of Step*. Also, above the tour dates appears the insignia XXX, the symbol for the celibate, teetotaling, drug-free, straight-edge lifestyle attributed to the band. The term comes from the 1981 song "Straight Edge" and, while the original X symbol denoted underage (and therefore nondrinking) kids in clubs, the triple-X sign as it appears on the Major Threat poster can be traced back to band member Jeff Nelson's artwork.

When the Nike SB poster image first appeared online and in print along the East Coast tour route, Dischord's founder Ian MacKaye told me he was swamped with what he estimated to be "hundreds and hundreds" of e-mails, several from sympathetic lawyers. Dischord has militated against the capitalist world, and MacKaye is frequently the commander of these attacks. A former member of both Minor Threat and Fugazi (in Fugazi he once sang, "What could a businessman ever want more / Than to have us sucking in his store . . . You are not what you own"), his label has been a bedrock of independent music since its founding in 1980. Daniel Sinker writes that Fugazi "has never compromised its egalitarian ideals. Insisting on low door prices, independent venues (wherever possible), and low-priced, independently produced records, Fugazi has shown the world how to conduct business respectfully and honestly."[24] (The bands may have changed but the ethos remains the same; with little adjustment Sinker's statement could apply to MacKaye's current band, a collaboration with Amy Farina called the Evens.) Minor Threat's self-titled album was the third release from the D.C.-based label. Dischord's founders, in true indie style, only put out the music of their own, already dissolved band because it was good and not because it was profitable tour fodder for the now-scattered musicians. To many punks the label remains vital proof that independent culture can survive and even thrive in an ever-incorporating world.

So it's no surprise that MacKaye can't emphasize his distaste for the shoe company enough. "I never would put their fucking swoosh on anything I would do. Not for ironic reasons, not for cynical reasons, nothing," he told me within days of the Nike apology.

The label's official statement, however, was more reserved. Dischord's posting dismissed the experience as simply "another familiar example of mainstream corporations attempting to assimilate underground culture to turn a buck." The label felt their image and ethos had been co-opted but did not consider this a new or unusual experience. It wasn't. As a major force in underground culture, Dischord gets co-opted by peers all the time. Bigger players, too—short bursts of Fugazi songs have been used to hype everything from reality TV shows to NFL games, all without permission.

Nike's been at this game a long time, though, and it seems unlikely that such a savvy corporation could have committed a blunder so hopelessly doomed only to offend its audience. After all, if any company knows how to offend unapologetically, it's this one. Among its many enemies the shoe giant can count any number of antisweatshop groups, including United Students Against Sweatshops, *Adbusters*'s Blackspot alternative athletic shoe campaign ("designed," as one slogan put it, "for only one thing: kicking Phil [Knight]'s ass"), and individual activists like Jonah Peretti, who unsuccessfully attempted to order customized shoes emblazoned "Sweatshop" in 2001, and managed to reinvigorate criticism against the shoe manufacturer. Then, of course, there's Guisinger's Don't Do It campaign, a direct assault on Nike SB's repositioning of skater tag "Skate or Die" as "Skate and Buy." Given the company's history in ambush marketing, the Major Threat campaign seems a slightly smarter revisitation of the mid-1990s "Revolution" ad that did, after all, get an older, affluent, Beatles-loving audience talking passionately about a new line of shoes. This is a company that, often in consort with Weiden+Kennedy, identified cultural icons not as *symbols* but as signifiers of significance, markers of who or what may be important to the coming generation. In other words, the marketing strategy identified "sacred cows," in the words of one Weiden+Kennedy creative director, only in order to "make great steaks."[25]

So something more sophisticated is going on here than the brute assimilation of the underground by a nefarious corporation. As the Nike apology states, the poster was "designed, executed, and promoted by skateboarders, for skateboarders. All of the Nike employees responsible for the creation of the tour flyer are fans of both Minor Threat and Dischord Records and have nothing but respect for both." The blame, Nike insinuated in its apology, lay not with the $14 billion company but with the way skate culture worked. *We're all fans here*, the apology contended. *Surely you can understand.* And, to some degree, fans did. "Indie culture has long been appropriating corporate images and logos and twisting them for a laugh and to give the finger to the man," one Internet poster commiserated.[26]

Kevin Imamura, now communications manager of Nike SB

and the author of the apology, followed up his public mea culpa with an e-mail to *Punk Planet*. Knowing the magazine claimed a big part of the Dischord fan base among its readers and had always been a strong anti–Nike SB voice, Imamura (a *Punk Planet* reader himself) was eager to talk to me—but was constrained, he said, by an agreement with his company. He did explain that "the skate group's intentions in making the flyer were not malicious, as a parody, or even to rip off the band or the record label," and said that he was confident that Ian MacKaye and the label understood Nike's position. He then politely declined several interview requests and refused to comment further.

MacKaye, however, didn't seem to understand the situation as clearly as Imamura hoped. "It's such a fuckin' puzzler," he said. "And one that I never really asked for."[27]

Despite the many offers of legal help, though, label manager Alec Bourgeoise doubted Dischord would take any legal action. "Basically, Nike knows that they screwed up," he told me over the phone.[28] And that, at least for a while, seemed to be that.

Under any current interpretation of copyright law, the shoe giant stands on shaky ground. If Dischord had followed corporate logic on intellectual property rights issues, it would have hired a team of lawyers to teach Nike a lesson that would resound throughout boardroom culture. (Given the recent ruling in Tom Forsythe's case, the time was certainly ripe for such a message.) In acknowledging that the Major Threat poster was not parodic—that it was in fact done out of "respect," and "inspired by" the "iconographic album cover"—Nike admitted its aim to emulate the Dischord album in a manner intended to create the substantial similarity most frequently used to determine copyright violations. Moreover, the poster was commercial, intended to bolster ticket sales at an event and, eventually, sales of Nike merchandise. Commercial use is a major factor in many courts to determine the legitimacy of a fair use defense.

So Nike SB may have committed some sort of copyright infringement. And Nike's history, too, seems to indicate it is practically company policy to violate competitive decorum, as it did at the 1996 Olympics, and to blatantly steal the creative work of artists without regard for copyright. "This is our music," Weiden+Kennedy's Stoutt said of the Beatles' "Revolution," mimicking arguments made by copyfighting activists.[29] Their unusually liberal attitude goes the opposite direction too, and is more forgiving than Lucasfilm's policy: "Designers like Stussy, Hilfiger, Polo, DKNY, and Nike have refused to crack down on the pirating of their logos for T-shirts and baseball hats in the inner cities and several of them have clearly backed away from serious attempts to curb rampant shoplifting," Naomi Klein reported in No Logo.[30]

As an activist myself, I was left in something of a strange position when the news of Major Threat first hit Punk Planet: I defended the appropriation in print solely because I support unhindered freedom of speech and a relaxation of the crazily litigious system restricting our reuse of images and sounds in our culture. Yet I believe now that I made a mistake, and that Nike's use of the underground image is part of a larger project to which I object. Although the company claims the use wasn't a parody (and it would be difficult to imagine they would argue it was done for commentary or news reporting purposes), Nike also claims it wasn't a rip-off. (Anyway, it might not be wise to trust the corporation's defense of its own actions. Not only does Nike have a vested interest in soothing irked Dischord fans, but it also might prefer to let the matter die here, while the debate was about the photographic image used on the tour poster, and not the entire poster. The full poster's use of Minor Threat's signature font and triple-X insignia were far more blatant appropriations, and could constitute clear IP violations. Most never saw the full poster, however; it took me close to two years to track it down. The question, therefore, of who first circulated only the photographic image from it, and why, and whether or not its general release was planned to coincide with the tour's apex, remains open.) The company is essentially arguing the same kind of fair use defense that applies when Negativland sells a *Dispepsi* CD or Tom Forsythe sells a blendered Barbie. Nike agrees with the underground and copyfighting activists that, once created, cultural products have a life of their own, even excusing its own actions—committed "by skateboarders, for skateboarders"—as common, underground occurrences.

So while Nike may have wanted to appropriate Dischord's album cover art and street cred, it may also be embarking on a larger project to co-opt copyfighting itself. Because if the restrictions that govern image reuse in our culture are loosened or, as some activists would have it, abolished, there will be that many more sacred cows for Nike to sear—and more opportunities for activists to reproduce the Nike logo. This theory might be easy to dismiss if we hadn't already seen that Nike found political protests good marketing tools or if the underground's take on IP issues wasn't so very easy to decipher: skateboarders and other members of DIY punk communities prefer to stay away from lawyers; call for reduced or no copyright laws; actively support alternative copyright policies like copylefting, or the free, unattributed, reproduction of intellectual property; listen to sample-heavy music; and read appropriated zine content as vital educational and entertainment pursuits. All of which, even according to IP activists, benefit the sampled and appropriated brands. "It's all been fair game and talk of Creative Commons" in the underground, one commentator wrote on the art blog Movable Walls in response to the Minor Threat appropriation. "Now that a corporation turns around and returns the favor, everyone is up in arms. So where is the foul?"[31]

At least legally, the foul is impossible to call if no one's going to court. And anyway, that's not the way things are done in the underground. (I can't speak for MacKaye, but no one I know has ever personally registered their own creative work for legal copyright or trademark licenses.) And MacKaye stayed dedicated to keeping the matter underground. In an interview he began, "To get engaged in a legal struggle over any of this stuff . . ." and got quiet for a second. I've heard the same pause in the voices of everyone I've spoken to who's been tempted to go to court over intellectual property rights. No one who works in modes of underground cultural production wants to spend time and money battling for legal precedent from a court system to which they are basically opposed. And MacKaye's feelings on governmental systems are clear. In the Evens's song "All These Governors," he sings, "When things should work but don't work / That's the work of all these governors / Interfering by decree . . . / Shut up, shut up, shut up." Going to court, he told me, would leave "these decisions to be made by a deeply dysfunctional organization, namely the U.S. government."

In fact, MacKaye felt, any further engagement with the corporate shoe giant, whether in court or on the streets, "does their work for them." Nike desired an association with Dischord, and a court case would certainly provide an extended one. Yet with a legal battle off the table, the question of what to do—and who to hold accountable—remained.

Bourgeoise blamed, in part, corporate mentality. As evidence, he pointed to Nike's claim that the campaign was created "by skateboarders, for skateboarders." He didn't doubt the veracity of that statement. In fact, he said, "that's fine. But when your pay-check comes from Nike, you're no longer just representing yourself. If you belong to an independent company, then your company is a reflection of the workers." Yet when you work for a humongous megacorporation, like the $14 billion per year athletic clothing company, profits are an important issue. It may not be Nike SB's MO in the short term to accumulate "tons of cash"—and at 5 percent of $1.5 billion in annual skate shoe sales, it's debatable whether or not $75 million qualifies as a "ton"—but the company's focus on cachet over volume is still profit-minded.

Nike is "purely about the acquisition of capital," Bourgeoise contends. "The products they're making have nothing to do with the process." He's referring to the issues of integrity that arise when any mass of people abandon individual responsibility in favor of a common goal. The film *The Corporation* eloquently pointed out just how damaging mob mentality can be when financial profit becomes the fundamental intent of any group: the group adopts behaviors that our society labels criminally insane when performed by individuals.

Independent companies, however—particularly those as small as Dischord, *Punk Planet*, or any of the other tiny businesses that grew out of punk—are structured to minimize cost and maximize individual input; in other words, they aim both to be fiscally sustainable and to reflect the interests and personalities of the workers. This is as much an economic decision as it is rooted in the desire to maintain a respectful, appreciative, productive work environment when raises are rare: small independent businesses won't make employees rich, so they will try a bit harder to keep them happy.

And if anyone knows how to build a company that accurately mirrors its workers, it's Dischord. Members of bands on the label tend to work there, and employees tend to form bands. This is not usually the case at bigger labels, where playing, recording, producing, pressing, marketing, and selling music are all distinct and demanding jobs meted out to a variety of employees, divisions, and entirely separate companies. "I've always said that the difference between Dischord and major labels is that major labels produce plastic, and we produce music," Bourgeoise told me.

Combined, it all makes Dischord a crazy target for the shoe company's weird advertising appropriation, if a salacious one. Minor Threat and Dischord have long been respected for their indifference to merchandising opportunities and dedication to anticorporate values. It's proof that Nike SB wasn't just making a clever visual reference when they used the Minor Threat image; they were making a clever intellectual one as well, one that takes advantage of current marketing strategies to associate brands with pure passion. Moreover, because Dischord's skateboarder-influenced antiestablishment ethos runs so deep that the company prefers to avoid legal entanglements, the Major Threat East Coast Summer 2005 tour poster turned out to be a damn smart gambit, too.

Yet the question of how to right the wrongs outside the courts lingered long after the Internet furor. Although a financial settlement seemed possible, the label opposed the notion that its work, in this instance, could be sold. Even months after the fact, a settlement would imply that something had been purchased, however belatedly. And, while conventional wisdom might hold that forcing a payment hits companies in the only place they hurt, this essentially capitalistic response to a situation created by hypercapitalism in the first place struck Dischord as inherently wrong.

MacKaye eventually proposed an alternative plan, which Bourgeoise explained to me in an e-mail ten months after the Nike apology: "Ian was talking with them about making a donation of athletic equipment, privately and on Minor Threat's behalf, to D.C. public schools. Oddly enough it isn't Nike but the D.C. government that has failed to take an active interest." The issue had dropped off the agenda entirely by August 2006. Although Nike had verbally agreed to the terms, Bourgeoise explained, "dealing with the D.C. government and the Department of Education was *so frustrating* that the idea kind of stalled out. Ian has been so busy with recording, touring, and running the label that Nike became less and less of a priority."

There was an element of defeat in his note, and I asked him about it. "It sucks," he responded simply. "But then again, having an issue instigated by a company like Nike monopolize our time and distract our focus was beginning to feel like winning the battle and losing the war." [32]

8

THE MALE PERFUMERS

When Matt Malooly, a Chicago DJ and an editor at the local independent arts and politics magazine *Lumpen*, walked to work early one summer morning in 2005, he was struck by a stunning, multicolor, spray-painted cityscape featuring a well-endowed female figure on a public wall in a gentrified, moneyed—and well-patrolled—section of town. This was rare: the city's strict no-graffiti policy had been in place for more than a decade, and the hip neighborhood he lived in was always buffed clean of spray paint. In 1993 Mayor Richard M. Daly had made Chicago the first municipality to assume responsibility for removing tags from private property with his $4 million Graffiti Blasters program, which included sixteen vans equipped to repaint city walls and a fleet of nineteen portable "graffiti-blasting" machines that act like sandblasters but use baking soda to remove enamel.[1] There's even a twenty-four-hour emergency hotline number (311) to call and report graffiti. That morning on Milwaukee Avenue Malooly was excited that somehow someone had eluded both the law and the roaming cleanup crews and created a piece of what he considers public art.

Then he corrected me: "I wouldn't say excited. I would say *surprised*."[2]

He was understandably hesitant to assign any positive emotions to an experience that eventually started a citywide debate and nearly got a friend arrested. "The entire corner was covered in spray paint," he recalled. "You never see that on a Chicago street anymore. So your first instinct is, 'Oh, it's a permission wall . . . I didn't hear about that going up.'" A permission wall, an unusual exception to the strict vandalism laws, is a wall explicitly deemed safe for street artists to use as a canvas. There are only a few of them citywide, and Malooly would likely have heard about a new one. In addition to his independent media gigs, which give him access to a broad communications network of underground art events, performers, and supporters, he is an active street artist, although he generally keeps to a support position, serving as a lookout while friends install pieces in populated and watchful neighborhoods. He also pays keen attention to other local and national street-art scenes, rattling off movements and events in Paris subways as easily as those focused on the Chicago Housing Authority.

But that morning, Malooly realized that what he had seen was not graffiti. "There was nothing abstract about it. Just compare it to any real graf mural, [which] usually has a more collage composition, or calligraphy taken to M.C. Escher levels. This was just woman flesh and a brand name in some weak wildstyle." It was an ad. "That whole recognition process took a split second. Then it was just shock, like, 'Those motherfuckers!'" Seeing an ad styled as graffiti—called graffadi by those who differentiate it from noncommercial street art—in a city buffed clean of authentic artistic expression of the urban underclass heaped insult on injury. "It was like some Disneyland version of city living," Malooly recalled bitterly. "Here's some urban grit! Ooo!"

For a long time urban grit was the exact opposite image that marketing teams strove to create, preferring to associate products with luxury and sophistication instead. Yet on February 27, 2006, there it was again on the cover of the national ad-industry magazine *Adweek*. Here, though, the urban grit was even more Disneyfied than on the Chicago street corner. The cover featured the graffadi campaign for the Sony Playstation PSP recently undertaken on city streets throughout the country. The campaign was represented on the glossy's cover by a photograph of its four cute-kid characters as cardboard cutouts, held by the cultural creatives responsible.

The ad campaign itself, like the others described in this book, merely duplicated genuinely underground art practices. Like any good graffiti bombing, striking, high-contrast images appeared overnight in highly trafficked urban locales: the side of New York and Miami apartment buildings, the back of a deli in Atlanta, blank billboards in Chicago El stations, and along brick walls in Los Angeles and Philadelphia that rarely go a day without a new tag. When the country awoke the morning after this particularly widespread and well-coordinated act of vandalism, it was witness to a small cadre of spray-painted, wide-eyed, manga-style boys (and one girl) of various ethnic backgrounds clutching videogame consoles as if they were about to be used in active social games: as a skateboard, a puppet, a hobbyhorse. The paint dripped sloppily on some; a few were signed by well-known local street artists.

The *Adweek* cover, however, didn't picture the *artists* in their dirty pants, torn T-shirts, and bandannas; they were merely the instruments in this campaign. Instead the cover featured four portly older white men in impeccable black business getup and snappy ties. Suits. Professionals. Establishment. Employees of ad agency OMD Worldwide, just named the magazine's Global Media Agency of the Year. Juxtaposing their clean professionalism against their involvement in this street-based campaign, each clutched an ethnic street-art character cutout recently seen dripping paint on city walls yet here pristinely laser-printed and mounted on foam core.

Seeing the traditional-looking ad men next to the spruced-up versions of their urban grit campaign is a bit like visiting the Web site of Critical Massive, which the company claims offers graffadi-writing services as a "high impact form of outdoor advertising" in about twenty cities nationwide. "Utilizing our national network of the world's top graffiti artists and legal mural spaces," their Web site explains, Critical Massive "appeals to the core emotions of today's urban-style youth . . . creates word-of-mouth value and buzz, . . . enlivens local communities rather than exploiting them," and helps "employ local artists." All of which sounds grass-rootsy and authentic until you scroll across images of a local community enlivened by a straight-up ad for M&M's Candy or appealing to an urban-style youth's core emotions about US Cellular or White Castle.[3] This is, in fact, the use of underpaid artists and urban neighborhoods for the purposes of expanding product awareness and, hopefully, profit—or, in other words, exploitation.

Marketing world self-representations such as Critical Massive's Web site and the *Adweek* cover are jarring for their frustratingly naked assimilation of street-art techniques into the corporate ethos, but they're also indicative of a new climate. In recent years graffadi has become a legitimate advertising tactic, popularized by marketing for Sony, *Sex and the City*, Verizon, *Time*, Microsoft, Axe, Hummer, and Nike. Graffiti may be staunchly antiestablishment, but graffadi, at least, is now staunchly establishment.

And why wouldn't it be? The methods used by graffiti writers are cheap, effective, and easy to get right if you're using a stencil—and nobody bats an eye if the final results are kind of sloppy. "Subtle, stealthy marketing is popular among some advertisers right now, on the theory that young, trendy influentials are best pitched on the sly—they tune out traditional advertising, so you have to sneak up on them," Rob Walker writes of a 2003 Nissan campaign in which street posters depicting the cars were riddled with tags contributed by a hip-hop poet Nissan paid to travel around the country promoting the car.[4] Street art screams "authentic," "cred," and "underground," and by God it's fun. "It's all about hip-hop, urban and all that," one young adult graffadi target told USA Today. "They're just trying to get into the teenagers' minds. . . . I think it's sharp."[5]

Of course, it's also often illegal. In corporate culture, however, this doesn't always mean "wrong"; it just means "expensive." A few years ago IBM was forced to pay the city of San Francisco $120,000 in fines and cleanup costs for the Linux stencil campaign designed by Ogilvy & Mather, and later paid Chicago $180,000 for the same campaign in that city. On the other hand, sometimes it's a bargain: the Washington Post reported that Verizon only had to pay fines totaling slightly more than $1,000 for a campaign of chalked two-foot-by-three-foot ads in heavy traffic areas in the District of Columbia.[6] Police also have arrested the street-level perpetrators, who sometimes end up paying their own fines for implementing corporate graffadi campaigns. (While the street artists I've spoken to generally maintain that these costs aren't often covered by corporate project managers, one industry guide to graffadi suggests that advertisers stipulate in writing that they will reimburse artists for tickets and legal fees.[7]) This cavalier approach to criminal behavior has been called "brandalism," and even government agents aren't sure what to do about it. "My fines aren't going to scare Sony," acknowledged Philadelphia managing director Pedro Ramos, who oversees all major city departments.[8]

Such after-the-fact punitive costs are not the only ones associated with graffadi campaigns. Sony paid one San Francisco restaurant $100 up front for two weeks' use of its walls for the PSP campaign.[9] Of the businesses that went on record, this seems to be an average payment. In a hundred-venue campaign over six cities (I'm ballparking) the costs of space rental alone would quickly add up to $60,000. The pay rate for artists is harder to determine; none involved with the PSP campaign would go on the record. One article recommending finding accomplished artists to carry out the work (rather than going DIY with your graffadi campaign) suggests companies pay between $30 and $500 per piece, "or negotiate a day rate between $2,000 and $12,000."[10] The same hundred-venue, six-city campaign, assuming the low end of the day rate and that each artist would complete four pieces per "day" (although most would probably work at night), adds up to an additional $50,000 for the artists' labor.

This theoretical graffadi campaign (including wall rental, artists' rates, a $10,000 materials budget, a $100,000 agency fee, and an $80,000 slush fund for fines and cleanup costs) may end up running about $300,000. But even adding a fine or two and paying your genuine street artists on the higher end of the day-rate scale still doesn't compare to the costs of traditional ad campaigns: just a year before Sony's PSP campaign Chanel No. 5 released a two-minute TV commercial that cost $10 million just to shoot. Nicole Kidman was paid $12 million for the appearance (and wore $42 million in diamonds, although these were presumably on loan). Chanel showed some frugality by not buying notoriously expensive Super Bowl airtime (around $2.5 million per thirty-second spot in 2006), nor its runner-up, almost-as-expensive, year-round corollary, *American Idol* airtime (around $700,000 per thirty-second spot in 2006). Compared to $22 million, $300,000 is a negligible cost. "Comparatively speaking," former Tribal DDB

creative and *Ad Age* columnist Scott Johnson explained, speaking
of using graffadi in general, "something like this is much cheaper
than producing and running a national television commercial."[11]

Although the cost-saving aspects of graffadi campaigns are
perhaps not what most appeal to corporate benefactors. The real
attraction, as Critical Massive put it, is the ability to seed "word-
of-mouth value and buzz" in "local communities." Local communities, keep in mind, aren't devoting themselves to TV as wholly as
they used to. They're too busy sending each other links to viral
videos and texting each other on their cell phones. It's easy to
break into those kinds of communications if you're doing something newsworthy like, for example, getting fined by the city over
your new ad campaign. (A *Washington Post* story could be a pretty
effective way to seed a word-of-mouth campaign.) And despite the
criminal nature of any true graffadi blitz, the pluses may still outweigh the minuses. "If the fines are low," Johnson said, clients "may
decide it is worth it in light of the buzz the program will generate
for their products and services."

Johnson is hesitant, however, to acknowledge the advantages of
a wholly illegal ad campaign, and first points to the drawbacks.
"The negative publicity that comes with breaking the law is usually not good for a Fortune 500 company—especially if they're
breaking the law to market a product. It isn't exactly Gandhi and
passive resistance we're talking about. On occasion, however, I'm
sure that some corporations do a cost/benefit analysis of an illegal
marketing activity like unauthorized graffiti."[12]

The local community buzz the Sony graffadi campaign generated was extensive, especially among urban youth who correctly
read it as a co-optation of their own language. The images were, indeed, remarkable: youthful, fun, smart (or at least smart seeming),
and distinctly urban. And they *were* remarked on repeatedly, and

for several days, by many who saw them. Too cute to be street art, some thought, but too gritty to be advertising. Genuine street artists, though—those who actually work in the streets, making art in response to corporate creep, gentrification, and other local community issues—knew their practices were being exploited and sent out an immediate call to arms.

Jake Dobkin, the publisher of New York–focused Gothamist .com, was tired of the corporate usurpation of vandalism, a mode of art he'd grown accustomed to as a city dweller. He posted a quick response on the site titled "Corporate graffiti sucks. Sucks! Sucks! Sucks!" that detailed his objections. "It's like watching your dad trying to breakdance: it's just embarrassing, and you wish it would stop," Dobkin told me later.[13] More succinctly, graffadi is like watching your dad *get paid* to breakdance. It's embarrassing, you wish it would stop, and of all people your dad is the last person who deserves to make money doing it. "I hate seeing companies take a genuine grassroots cultural movement and turn it into another marketing vehicle for selling crap to young people," Dobkins said.

Other graffiti artists took graffadi campaigns slightly more in stride, at least at first. "The whole thing was not a big deal to me. I thought it was lame, but not surprising," graffiti artist eee from California told me.[14] But the Sony PSP campaign began intruding on the work of genuine graffiti artists. "They started going up over pieces here in San Francisco and covering up walls. That was just stupid," eee said. "First you try and co-opt a genre, then you destroy someone's work from that genre in the process. How did they think that would win over their target?"

Nonartists voiced opinions about the campaign, too. Albert Yee, a graff fan in Pennsylvania, liked the pieces, he told the Philadelphia *City Paper*, until he realized they were ads. "They were trying too hard to be cool," he said.[15] Other detractors emerged. "This 'urban' advertising does nothing for me (I find it quite annoying)," one Internet poster declared.[16] Engaged ambivalence was widespread: supporters of underground culture found it hard *not* to comment. "Don't get me wrong," a blogger known as Miss Typist wrote. "I completely love graffiti and street art, but not this sponsored, watered-down marketing gimmick graff that spreads over cities like a disease without any penalty." (Another poster responded to Miss Typist, hinting at the endless line of increasingly tacky imitators likely to follow the gaming behemoth, by asking, "What's next? Tagging for the sake of selling the newest Swiffer product?")[17] And while domestic cleaning products have yet to go urban grit with marketing campaigns, graffadi for TV shows, expensive cars, and personal hygiene products has only increased since Sony went guerrilla for the PSP.

People's frustrations with the Sony PSP campaign, however, were not limited to mild verbal rebukes, thoughtful comments, and funny retorts. People were already angry with the media giant for the recent inclusion of digital rights management software in a batch of Sony BMG CDs that had caused gaping security problems in consumers' computers. Dubbed the Sony rootkit disaster, it was a public relations nightmare and quickly became a potent symbol of the drive to protect corporate intellectual property at the expense of customers' rights.

Whether fury at the company or outrage over the invasiveness of the Sony PSP ads was the motivating factor, some community groups in Philadelphia responded by removing the ads on their own without hesitation.[18] In Queens, city councilmember Peter Vallone, Jr., felt the campaign encouraged vandalism and demanded Sony remove the ads and remit $20,000 to the borough's antigraffiti fund. (Hilariously, Vallone himself then became the target of a graffiti campaign by local street artists.)

In Los Angeles, one resident published a well-reasoned response to the PSP campaign on the women's technology Web site Popgadget.net encouraging organized action. "Is anyone else concerned that Sony PlayStation paid someone to vandalize our neighborhood to sell their latest toy, the PSP?" She detailed her attempts to have the city paint over one local ad, following up with a phone call to Sony's consumer services division. At first Sony denied any responsibility for the campaign, but she called back after word leaked out that Sony spokespeople were now acknowledging involvement. "If 'urban marketing' bugs you too, and you don't want PlayStation to set an example to other faceless corporations that take big consumer craps in our backyard, give them a call and ask them what their take on graffiti is," she wrote, listing Sony's customer service contact information.[19]

Although the actions were small and disparate, the Sony PSP graffadi campaign had fostered a widespread national backlash. This may be where the expansive scope of the multinational's campaign actually helped anticorporate activists: the only targeted cities where I was unable to locate antigraffadi actions were Atlanta and Miami. The other four cities where the ads were placed— Chicago, Los Angeles, New York, and Philadelphia—all saw organized responses during the campaign's two-week run.

When Matt Malooly told his friends—fellow artist Elisa Harkins and Edmar Marszewski, the founder of *Lumpen*—about the graffadi on Milwaukee Avenue, they got angry about the intrusion of commercialism into their subculture and neighborhood and wanted to do something about it. They decided "a city-style buff would be the best way to turn the tables," Malooly said, a simple cover-up in compliance with the city's zero-tolerance response to graffiti.

"So one afternoon when Ed, Elisa, and I all happened to be around, we grabbed some paint and long rollers from the storeroom and walked down the street," Malooly told me. It was pretty casual, he said, echoing Mark Hosler's "natural response to living in a mediated world" description of culture jamming. "This sort of thing is surprisingly often better done in the day when people aren't automatically suspicious of everything they see," he explained. "Just act like you're doing some boring job." Which, in a sense, they were: the boring job of buffing what appeared to be graffiti from a public Chicago street. The painting looked, after all, like graffiti, appeared overnight like graffiti, and was done in graffiti style. It just happened to be graffiti about Axe Body Spray.

The ongoing print and television ad campaign for the Unilever men's perfume was decidedly juvenile and widely criticized as tasteless at best. Salon critic Tracy Clark-Flory called the print ads "obnoxious"; they featured mobs of women pawing the shower drain of an Axe consumer; the fortified bedside supplies necessary for Axe users; and the best means of ditching the less attractive members of the throngs of women plaguing Axe wearers.[20] "They're not just sexist or politically incorrect. This 'Axe Effect' is violence against women," wrote a blogger on Feministing.com, a well-respected Web site devoted to women's issues.[21] Clark-Flory wrote that the Axe advertising strategy had "made quite an impression on young boys" after an April 3, 2006, Washington Post story reported increasing numbers of preteen male users of the body spray.[22] "The thing for today's discriminating middle-school boy," the Post called Axe; several such specimens agreed that the woman-magnetizing properties depicted in the ads had led them to the product. "There are days when I walk down the eighth-grade hall-way," one principal said, "and I am nearly asphyxiated." [23]

To our Chicago crew, eliminating the offensive ad publicly and openly, as if sanctioned by the city, seemed a natural act of civic pride. Harkins, a prolific street artist herself, had brought a video camera. ("People tend to control their tempers far better when they know it's on tape," Malooly said.) They laid plastic sheeting out to protect the sidewalk. And while the play on Graffiti Blasters was there in concept, the name by which their action would come to be known had not yet occurred to the group. "I don't think the words 'Ad Blasters' were uttered until Elisa had the camera rolling . . . that was all ad-libbed," Malooly remembered.

Once they started painting, though, the crew's action was not universally applauded. An angry man came by and became belligerent. Later it was discovered he was the artist who had executed the work; he signs his paintings WeAreSupervision.com. "He said he wanted to break our fingers for going over his piece," Marszewski told me.

"His *piece*?" I asked, surprised he would use the street term for the corporate project, which, it turns out, was a Critical Massive commission. "Did he call it that?"

But Harkins had taped the event and viewed it several times; after a pause to recollect, she confirmed that he had. Other passersby started yelling at them. Marszewski took an angry cell-phone call from a local underground artist demanding to know why the group was ruining his friend's work. The cops came by and busted up the scene in the middle of the cleanup, throwing Marszewski in the patrol car for a short time and threatening him with arrest. (Ultimately, they released him.) Yet the Ad Blasters had supporters, too. People walked by and exclaimed that they wished they'd thought of the action first, or had been wondering when someone would wipe out the ad. All in all, the group estimated, the approval rating for their action was about fifty-fifty. But Marszewski was quick to defend it. "Plus us," he said. "That puts us in the majority."

When Harkins's video was posted online soon afterward, the property owner and others wrote in with comments supporting the graffadi, citing such benefits as the ad's distinction from more common corporate billboards, the hired artist's financial straits, and the unsightly urban blight that usually afflicts the walls in the area; and excusing the ad because the owner claimed it was a short-term solution until windows could be installed in the building's wood façade (which two years later have yet to appear). Harkins responded with simple, unassailable logic. According to the zero-tolerance antigraffiti law, she wrote, "anyone is encouraged to eliminate graffiti in a public place if they feel that it is bothersome."

Regardless of the legal, moral, or ethical issues that were ultimately raised by their project, the Ad Blasters only got the mural partially painted over before the action was broken up, and Critical Massive did a major retouch job to reinstate it. But when the contract for the wall ended it was not renewed, and the two murals that appeared next in the space were decidedly noncommercial artworks by local graff heroes. "It felt like we had won," Harkins told me as we stood on Milwaukee Avenue, looking at the now-black wall decorated only with a "Please do not post" sign.

Malooly, despite the months of hubbub, only regrets not having been able to emulate the horrible hue the real Graffiti Blasters use to buff pieces away. "I just wish we'd had the right shit-brown color paint," he quipped.

Street artists responding to the Sony PSP campaign, however, formed eloquent in-kind responses to the graffadi, repurposing the imagery to draw out the inherent hypocrisy of the campaign. They vandalized the ads with phrases like "Directed at your counter culture," "enough already," and "I'll ride a Brompton Bicycle or I'll teabag a mime / before I'll give the Sony Corp another fuckin' dime." Some retooled the images to highlight corporate creep and gentrification, crossing out the images and demanding "Get out of my city!" and "Stop hawking corporate products and big business on our neighborhood walls." Others directly attacked the big business, painting out the offensive images in blood red and renaming the company Fony. One group that got started in the biz bombing New York's IRT in the 1980s, TATs Cru (for Top Artistic Talent), handled the graffadi campaign for Hummer in New York's East Village. The perceived hypocrisy led several artists to turn the signed PSP ads into commentary on graffadi and clever antiwar statements, in one instance manipulating three of the ads' characters into the "see no evil/hear no evil/speak no evil" monkeys, and adding the text "Impeach King George's War." [24]

To some outsiders it probably looked like the implosion of culture jamming, a strange, gentrified version of gang tag wars for control of neighborhood space. And it was—except the most powerful thug on the block, in all six cities, was always Sony. Street artists responding in kind to the ads soon discovered that the co-optation of their communication mode was only one reason to be alarmed. The hypocrisy of the campaign only multiplied when the most incisive in-kind responses were soon erased, thanks to the company's diligence in placing and maintaining the campaign. Not an hour after one Los Angeles ad had been thoroughly reworked by a street artist, eee told me, two artists—presumably hired by Sony—came by to clean the defacement and restore the company's pristine acts of brandalism.

"It's weird," eee agreed, after describing to me one painting he did "really late" one night in New York. "The next morning it was fixed. Sony's media company doesn't mess around."

It's no wonder such campaigns can be counted on to generate buzz. This particular mode of cultural production is contentious even in its most authentic form. When attempting to critically engage with the practice of graffadi, therefore, elements are easily confused, many mere runoffs from the confusion over the definition, and intent, of graffiti. Open debates rage whether or not graffiti is political, whether or not it is art.

Yet in the blind mania of late-stage capitalism, this is a selling point. *Time* magazine's graffadi project, implemented by legendary Bronx graffiti artist COPE2, capitalized on this confusion. For four weeks in June 2005 (around the same time as the Chicago Ad Blasters's action) the artist bombed a New York billboard with tags—one-word paintings of an artist's name or moniker, sometimes called throw-ups due to their quick, reactionary, and self-promotional nature—before a URL, the caption "Post-Modernism? Neo-Expressionism? Just Vandalism? Time. Know Why" and the magazine's famous red border appeared ringing the entire billboard.[25]

The debate over graffadi—and graffiti—rages within street-art communities as well. The TATs Cru Web site proudly proclaims its members' ability to make money doing street art, while detractors decry the group's consumerist content and abandonment of the street ethics member once personified. Made up of prolific taggers and bombers gone straight, the group does in fact sell out skills earned on the lam back to the establishment. More troubling, in doing so it encroaches on space that could otherwise be devoted to messages intended to communicate instead of sell. Some see the group and others like it as gaming the system, but this reading relies on an understanding of graffiti as purely self-promotional and not at all intended to provoke awareness of social injustice. Although the language varies, many practitioners don't agree on the intent of their practice.

In a panel discussion held shortly after the Ad Blasters's action Malooly and pals spoke alongside artists—including WeAreSupervision, who did the Axe ad in Chicago—who stated outright that "graffiti is not political." Malooly didn't agree. "The act of doing graffiti is political whether or not you intend it to be," he responded. Even throw-ups claim a spot in the city, marking graffitied space as monitored and protected by the tagger. Reminding viewers that the city is owned anonymously—is *public*—has inherent social value.

Eliot Rosewater, a street-art practitioner, concurred. A self-described "kid who didn't grow up in the Bronx and didn't grow up with graffiti," he helps maintain the Visual Resistance graffiti discussion Web site.[26] Even tagging, he said, which relies on the self-promotional impulses within the art practice, has always included innate political content. "It's not like someone wrote their name on the wall and were expecting to get a check from it," Rosewater explained. "Getting your name out there in the context of the 1970s Bronx is not an act of individualistic fame-grabbing. . . . They're saying, in a city that has completely neglected their peers, that they're still here and still talented." In other words, graffiti writers are expressing themselves in the same way writers of small, personal fanzines or home-recorded CDs do: by making tiny spaces to voice individual opinions within a culture predisposed to ignore them for reasons often tied to social injustice. To practice, in other words, freedom of speech as an act of self-preservation.

As proof, Rosewater cited a few little-discussed activities. "In the late 1970s and early '80s, people did try to set up their own mural commissions, their own legal walls; they were trying to build organizations and community, so it wasn't just an individualistic, let-me-get-fame [pursuit]. That's a big part of it, obviously, but it never was just that."

Now, though, it is more often an individualistic, let-me-get-fame pursuit. But to Rosewater, that doesn't simplify the debate. "Some of the people that took corporate money earned their stripes. You know, they earned it," he said. For the most part, he believes it's artistic intentions that have changed. "From what I can tell it's a different community than the Bronx in 1985," he said. "A bunch of [street artists] are designers or went to art school. They're not escaping desperate poverty with their art." The intent now seems to be less about social viability than financial sustainability, less self-preservation in an antagonistic society than creative exploration. "To some it's no different than if they'd gone the gallery route" to display work, he suggested.

Rosewater is referring to artists like COPE2 and the members of TATs Cru, who deliberately used their careers in street art to expand into commercial ventures, as well as people like Shepard Fairey, who work both for hire (for Levi's and Mountain Dew) and in the streets (bombing cities with his well-known Obey and Andre the Giant Has a Posse images).

And to people like Ad Blaster Elisa Harkins. By day, she makes Web animations for Chicago-based ad firm Leo Burnett's marketing-services partner, Arc Worldwide, but at night her work generally consists of very cute cardboard Eskimos—not unlike the charming Sony PSP character cutouts that appeared on the cover of *Adweek*, in fact. Her characters are a bit rougher edged, of course, each a bit more individualistic, and are meant to promote feelings of joy as opposed to the urge to shop. They are intended, in other words, to bring pleasure. When happened upon in an alleyway or perched atop a lamppost, her Eskimos often do. (In fact, rumor has it that her work is often removed not because it is illegal or offends, but to fill out the private collections of neighborhood residents.) Because her Eskimos are technically vandalism, however, their context gives them a renegade air—overtly political not in content but in form.

Harkins's two bodies of work, paid Web animations and unpaid cardboard Eskimos, delineate the differences between art and advertising. "Art is created for the love of the creative act," Jake Dobkin said. "Advertising is created to convince people to buy more crap that they don't need. Even though they sometimes look similar, they're totally different animals."[27]

Malooly agrees that the two can be confused. "It feels like you've been tricked," he told me, describing the frustrating experience of coming across a piece of graffadi. Then he adopted the sarcastic voice of a viewer sucked into thinking an ad was art. "Oh wait, there's no message? I'm just supposed to buy Nikes?"

Dobkin, whose sputtering rage was at one point limited to exclamation points, mild swears, and pathos-inducing allusions to breakdancing fathers, detailed exactly why graffadi sucks in a post about the Sony PSP campaign on Gothamist.com:

1. It's exploitive: the local street artists that are hired to paint these pieces risk arrest, and it's almost guaranteed that Sony's ad agency won't be bailing them out if they get popped.
2. It's fake. . . . Appropriating the authenticity of street art to promote a product is totally lame. The 24 to 36 year old demographic you covet so much knows the difference, and we are not fooled.
3. It's deceptive: if you are going to do this stuff, at least

>have the balls to sign the ads, Sony, so people know who
>to blame. . . .
>4. It's not positive brand association. . . .
>5. Neighborhoods don't like it. . . .
>6. It's illegal. . . .
>In conclusion: please cut this crap out.[28]

Although common utterances in this debate, these last three points are easy to dismiss. Coming from anyone who's ever done graffiti themselves (as Dobkin claims in the same post that he has), the charge that it's illegal and unwelcome doesn't hold water: if *you* didn't care about the legal issues or local reception, why on earth should one of the largest and most influential corporations in the world? Not to mention that the restaurants and building owners who rent out their property for graffadi campaigns make it explicitly welcome. While it's true that the Sony PSP campaign didn't generate uniformly positive brand associations (though it did generate some), it's equally true that in the new age of mocketing and multimedia saturation, marketers might not be looking for positive brand associations so much as *any* emotional associations with brands at all.

Dobkin's second point, that graffadi is fake, is a bit more complicated. When companies hire commercial artists who worked in the streets before establishing themselves as illustrators for hire, the question arises of who is doing the faking in the first place. Moreover, street-art methods are not the intellectual property of street artists: they are accessible to all by design. In order to preserve accessibility we cannot deny the use of these methods by any individual on the basis of income or social power. To hinge an argument against graffadi on inauthenticity establishes a hierarchy of access it would quickly prove impossible and fruitless to monitor. Anyway, fake or not, plenty believed the Sony PSP campaign was authentic street art. Fewer still could deny that no matter the identity of the creator, the ads were still there, stuck on the walls throughout the city, as authentic as they needed to be.

Accusations that graffadi is exploitive and deceptive, however (as well as the subaccusation that it is lame) hold up quite well. Eliot Rosewater agreed, calling the Sony PSP campaign, "So sneaky." Particularly egregious to him and the Visual Resistance Web site community at large was the form of the ad campaign. "It tried to pass itself off as legitimate street art. It was so deceptive."[29]

Dobkin's and Rosewater's accusations are bolstered by the *Adweek* cover depicting the forces behind the campaign, who only seemed to profit from its repercussions and backlashes, and who probably never got their hands dirty actually working on the paintings in the streets. This isn't so much an issue of whether or not they participated in the campaign or how. They did participate, but in the process they used a series of likely underclass street artists throughout the country to execute the work, thereby obscuring its marketing aims—which are, of course, its *only* aims.

A 2003 *Event Marketer* article titled "Guerilla Marketing: Street Graffiti" acknowledged exactly this fact: that the exploitive, deceptive nature of graffadi makes it the perfect advertising vehicle. Founded in 2002 to honor the work of agencies in what the mission statement called "face-to-face media" (aka word-of-mouth marketing), the magazine directly urged marketers to deceive the viewer. "The consumer may assume a brand is to blame for that soft drink tagline outside the pizza parlor, but they'll never be 100-percent sure," the article winked. The guide suggested companies consider leaving the logo off "undercover" ads, such as an obscure phrase ("Hello, is anybody out there?") that About.com had spray-painted in three cities and two thousand locations the previous year. Deceiving the ground-level players actually responsible for executing a project was also recommended. "Try not to tell the landlord what brand is involved," the article advised. It's a cost-saving measure: "Once they hear a major company's name they usually quadruple the amount they want."[30]

It may be too much to ask that marketers stop exploiting and deceiving the public: it is ingrained in what they do. But it is only natural, under capitalism, that if we are used in the course of a profit-making venture, we also be allowed to profit. Whether we cash in like TATs Cru and COPE2 or, like Dischord, do not, may remain a question of personal ethics. Yet the withholding of information that may allow us to proclaim our value seems a chilling abuse of power by an ever-more-monolithic system.

9

THE PHARMACEUTICAL MANUFACTURERS

A story.

In *Attack of the Suits*, the pseudonymous L. Vanderbilt's epic illustrated tale of underground co-optation, *you* star as a hipster parking garage attendant who happens to be the last bastion of defense against evil corporate interests intent on infiltrating, undermining, and destroying your lifestyle and culture. *You* will face several options while protecting the underground; each will allow *you* to change the path of the narrative *you* have chosen. The adventure *you* choose is the result of your choices. *You are responsible because you choose!*

Fortunately, you are aided by seven friends: lethally good breakdancer Asia One; BMX racer Dave Young, whose bike contains a secret weapon; matter-manipulating filmmakers Rick and Buddy; Janna Meyen and her shape-shifting snowboard; surfboarder supreme Joel Tudor; and Tony Trujillo and his flying skateboard, all staunch defenders of independent culture. This savvy team of eight (including your bad-ass self, their chosen leader) is charged with the task of outwitting greedy developer Conrad Constructus, whose land-grabbing schemes have given him control over most of the city. Now he's after the Caverns, the underground maze of rooms devoted to the exploration of extreme break-dancing, extreme surfboarding, and extreme underground art-making (according to drawings supplied by pseudonymous illustrator Floyd Eces).You must defend the Caverns at all costs.Your integrity is at stake.

When Constructus drives his SUV into your parking garage one day, you are faced with two options: let him in, which might allow him to discover the secret entryway to the Caverns, or turn him away. If you turn him away—and you know he won't like that—you will gather your friends together to prepare for his angry return. Secret handshakes will be shaken, passwords will be passed, and thrilling extreme sports maneuvers will be discussed in thrilling, extreme detail.You could try the Arial Assault on Constructus, Rick's silly plan, ultimately guaranteed to scatter the bodies of your extreme pals around the room as if dead, leaving the Caverns destroyed and you permanently stuck in the dead-end job of parking garage attendant with, the text suggests, little to no reason to go on living. Or there's the Manatee Maneuver, some crazy scheme of Joel's you suspect will drown you all. Turning Constructus away thus seems pointless: he's bound to discover the Caverns one of these days, you rationalize, and after that it's just a matter of time before he owns them, too.

So you let Constructus in, sure that your awesome friends and their insanely cool powers will trump his evil corporate ways, even with a million zombies in suits set to do his bidding. But you're proved wrong. It does not take the suits long to overpower you, gaining control of every aspect of the city, including the sky and everything underground, even though they are not actually wearing suits because it is casual Friday.Your team will not, however, go down without a final fight: you all leap up in a rage, Dave's bike releases an electrical shock that scatters the suits, and Asia One break-dances them into submission.The suits cower and await their leader Constructus, who arrives and, surprisingly, delivers a lengthy speech filled with praise for you and your totally rad friends.

"Your extreme abilities . . . have impressed me. Join us," he begins. "We could use more creative types, and you kids are just the ticket. I'll fix you up right with health care, dental, 401K, and you can even bring your dog with you to work." Constructus is evil but convincing, and you consider his offer. After all, you're tired of being poor. You're not sure if you're ever going to make it big like you always wanted to and, hell, your dad is right: you just can't fuck around in the underground forever.

Of course, there's a catch. It's not zombification, but Constructus does want to keep his carpets looking good. Pretty much all you have to do to join up and start paying down your debts is wear a pair of comfy leather clogs while you're at work. That seems pretty reasonable. These negotiations put Constructus in a new light. His kinder side is exposed, and you begin to appreciate his unique charms. Suddenly, you realize that all of your past contempt for him was nothing but jealousy over his power and money.

You smile at your friends, and they smile back. Together, all of you take off your shoes in exchange for some decent heat, lighting, AC, and benefits. You become a suit. And this is how the story ends.[1]

It's a story McNeil Consumer and Specialty Pharmaceuticals doesn't want you to read. Which is weird, because it's fiction, although it happens to parallel the true-life story of all the extreme people in the underground who really did sign up to join McNeil's Team Ouch! Moreover, McNeil paid for it to be written in the first place, and the company's reasons for not wanting you to hear it aren't typical: McNeil is not suppressing negative facts about a product. McNeil doesn't want you to read it because it's just not believable.

Team Ouch! would never sell out like that. For health care?

• • •

The Ouch! campaign serves as a primer for much that is hip in underground culture: comics by acclaimed underground cartoonists Ron Regé, Jr. (also the guitarist in the band Lavender Diamond), David Heatley, and Leslie Stein; films by hot up-and-comer Tim Greenberg; a free CD featuring Texas-born independent musicians American Analog Set and Drag City recording artists White Magic; a staff including is-he-a-musician-or-a-motivational-speaker BARR and skate journalist Jocko Weyland; zines by photographer and filmmaker Tobin Yelland; writing and consulting by *Arthur* founder Laris Kreslins; plus extreme sportiness by snowboarder Janna Meyen, surfboarder Joel Tudor, and skateboarder Tony Trujillo. Ouch! was conceived as a sponsor of events, like underground film fests and athletic competitions, which "relate to modern day lifestyles that involve pain," according to Ouchthe website.com. Announced with advertisements in cool magazines like *Giant Robot* and *Spin*, Ouch! appeared to many to be a simple organic offshoot of underground culture. But wait, there's more: Ouch! is "brought to you by the good people who make Tylenol®."

Apparently the drugmaker, McNeil Consumer and Specialty Pharmaceuticals, a subsidiary of Johnson & Johnson, had tired of the reputation of its main product as a stodgy old over-the-counter painkiller in an age when sales of newer medications like Aleve and Advil were booming. So they brought in Faith Popcorn and her BrainReserve for some brand revitalization. BrainReservists specialize in invisible marketing, an area of guerrilla marketing that enlists consumers in corporate decision making in order to conceal the fact that those consumers are spreading word of mouth about specific products. These consumers resemble BzzAgents in that they are engaged with a product and encouraged to talk it up based on limited information and for little or no compensation. Calling herself a "futurist" instead of a PR person or an advertising expert, and dubbed the "Nostradamus of marketing" by *Fortune*, Popcorn is credited with predicting (and helping advance) the fast-food backlash that led to McDonald's salad options and the safety concerns that supposedly underlie the demand for four-wheel drive vehicles.[2] One of her pioneering techniques in foreseeing and then nurturing trends goes by the name "co-parenting," a Popcornism meant to describe the ideal relationships consumers can have with brands. "Without emotional attachment," Popcorn wrote, "it's too easy" for consumers to "dump your brand." She lists the M&Ms promotion in which fans were asked to pick a new candy color and the Zagat's Survey Restaurant Guides ("100,000-plus co-parents") as examples of successful co-parenting campaigns.[3]

Popcorn's a visionary, to be sure—but of sales techniques and not cultural trends, although working with her sounds like an experience in cultural immersion. She prohibits visible brand names on her employees' clothing, recommending instead logo-free blacks and grays. It's described (or ridiculed, or honored) in William Gibson's novel *Pattern Recognition*, a dystopic vision of a future driven by ad companies.

BrainReservists might find it a little odd at first but grow to appreciate the uniform. "Being so intimately involved in evaluating and carrying out guerrilla marketing campaigns made [one employee] appreciate the purity of clothes that hadn't been marketed to her," the *New York Observer* reported.[4]

While it may seem strange that a company made up of people strongly resistant to brand associations—not to mention the mantel of marketing—would spearhead a product-repositioning campaign, these very factors gave the BrainReserve significant insight into Tylenol's target market: the antiestablishment *No Logo* generation skeptical of the Man, selling out, and bogusness, and devoted to authenticity, integrity, and passion—even if they have to suffer for it. "To do anything meaningful, you're going to have to deal with pain," the Ouch! Web site confided to its pierced and tattooed target demographic.[5] Thus, despite David Ogilvy's warning— "Advertising drugs is a special art. . . . [P]hysical discomfort is no joking matter to the sufferer"—the BrainReserve placed pain at the center of Tylenol's new campaign.[6] It was a bold strategy intended to address what Popcorn saw as the "consistent masochistic streak" in those who shunned Tylenol at an increasing rate of 10.2 percent per year.[7] "The single most sought-after demographic in marketing, 18- to 34-year-olds, actually thinks pain is cool," one writer claimed.[8]

The BrainReserve's bold strategy quickly paid off—at least for underground artists. The "youth culture branding initiative,"[9] as one writer called it, meant real money fast for struggling cultural producers. "I got paid what I usually make in a year," said Ron Regé, Jr., who designed a set of three dolls (the Ouch! Twins and the Wizard) with the toy company Critterbox in a matter of weeks.[10] Regé was excited to do it, despite the fact that he hadn't done anything "that corporate before." He was interested in seeing how his weird graphic language would translate into mass-produced three-dimensional objects. His combination of cute figures, uniquely grotesque elements, and heartfelt sentiments with an accessible line-drawing style and distinctive panel compositions earned him a healthy following in the small world of underground comics. But he had never made toys out of his characters.

"It was part of the whole concept that they get someone that was not that well known and that hadn't done toys before," he said. When they were done, all three thousand five hundred figures were snapped up in a matter of hours, despite extremely limited distribution through only eight comic-book and toy stores located in Los Angeles, New York, and San Francisco. And although they likely could have retailed for around $40 each, Ouch! gave them away for free, in exchange for coupons downloadable from the Web site or clipped out of *Tokion*, *Giant Robot*, *Arthur*, or other independent publications. "I am sure that making the dolls and all the other stuff that was involved with it was more costly than paying me," he added. (Although he wouldn't go on the record with exactly how much he earned, I'd estimate it was in the $15,000 range, give or take $3,000, based on the annual income of other cartoonists I know.)

"A commercial haven for funding art," *Print* magazine called Ouch! The article postulated that the campaign was over, having been abandoned as a failure ("a bad dream," as one designer called it to the magazine) by BrainReservists and McNeil alike; neither would discuss it with *Print* for this reason. Ads, however, continued to run for several months thereafter in *Tokion* and other publications.[11] (Still, neither the BrainReserve or McNeil got back to me for my original *Punk Planet* article or this book.)

Yet the Ouch! campaign wasn't much of a failure, as at least one of the goals of the campaign seems to have been fulfilled: to have the drug "talked about in different types of conversations," as BrainReservist Sophie Wong explained to the *Chicago Reader*.[12] Not conversations about OTC painkillers, either. Conversations about culture.

One remarkable Ouch! project offered health insurance to the winner of the King of Zine contest cosponsored by *Tokion*. Shortly after the contest was announced, I had a conversation that would have pleased Wong with three thoroughly independent artists: Sam Gould of the Portland, Oregon–based arts group Red76; Bonnie Fortune of Free Walking, a Chicago-based organization devoted to the exploration of walking as entertainment and education; and Mike Wolf, founder of the Network of Casual Art, an information and funding resource for local artists, and a member of the Chicago noncommercial art space Mess Hall.

We had gathered for beers late one night during an arts festival in Chicago. So I could tape a roundtable discussion with participants in collaborative art groups. I was particularly interested in the work of Red76; I had started following it when I lived in Seattle a few years earlier and was intrigued by the extremely small-scale projects that Gould and his cohorts had put up throughout the cities in which they traveled. Mess Hall has a similar group-project mentality; none of their acclaimed members gets any more attention or credit than any of the others. I felt that these projects—secretive, anonymous, and yet ever present—provided an interesting antidote to our increasingly branded culture.

My plan had been to tape-record our conversation, but we began talking before I'd unwrapped the first cassette. Gould had launched into a story about his morning shower, when he had enjoyed a "spiritual moment" after popping a new CD into the player. The experience, he said, was so moving, so profound, such a superlative listening experience, that he'd been talking and thinking about it all day.

Our conversation moved on to less transcendental matters, like making a living in a collaborative arts group in an age when hopes for national health care had been dashed. I was reminded of the Ouch! campaign and asked the group, "Have you heard about Tylenol's King of Zine contest?"

"I know Ouch!" Gould responded. "Tylenol is putting out little art things and they're putting out CDs. . . . That was the CD I was talking about—when I had that very spiritual shower moment!"

"Sponsored by Tylenol," I joked.

Gould laughed. "Sponsored by Tylenol! I have very mixed emotions about that. I think it's both a really interesting thing, like, 'Maybe that's a really great thing! Way to go, Tylenol!' Or, maybe that's a really horrible thing. Like, 'I don't want you involved, however. Get out of my spiritual knowingness.'"

"Well, check this out," I leaned in to explain. Everyone at that table had been involved in self-publishing at one point or another. "They're doing a contest where zinesters send in copies of their publications to win a year of health insurance."

Gould's reaction was straightforward: "Whoa!"

Fortune was no less shocked: "Shut up! I got to send that in! I need health insurance hardcore! But that's terrible! And it's those people who need health insurance!"

"I can't wrap my head around it—I need some aspirin," Gould quipped.

I'm sure hundreds, if not thousands, of similar conversations took place across the United States around that time. In fact, after an early version of this story was published in *Punk Planet*, I got mail from all over the country that confirmed it. After all, the contest had been promoted through zine listservs and artistic social networks. Ads had appeared in *Tokion*, which boasts a national circulation of 89,000, and other magazines associated with creative culture. I'd even personally been asked to submit, as had several other people I know. Our conversation wasn't particularly sparkling or witty, and we had no more knowledge about the subjects of zines, health care, or Ouch! than anyone else. It is simply remarkable that four dedicated independent cultural producers had a conversation about Tylenol at all, and it made me realize that, evidently, my attention *can* be bought.

Wolf finally weighed in on the health-insurance prize: "That's crap!" Usually a subdued man, he was nearly spitting his beer. "I mean, what PR genius came up with that?"

The PR genius is none other than *Arthur* founder Kreslins, a "pain partner" in BrainReserve parlance, who judged accurately that Tylenol would be willing to spend its money on a cool idea even if it had to overlook the glaring fact that it was downright weird to offer health insurance to someone the rest of the corporate world would probably deem an undesirable. Zinesters were, after all, notorious for repurposing day jobs or national chain stores into spaces for the creation of anticorporate screeds (*Temp Slave!*, *Dishwasher*, and many others), a practice at least partially fueled by the lack of benefits (health insurance included) available at such jobs. Not to mention how downright bogus it is to have to compete for health care.

"I didn't come up with the zine idea. Just the idea for a prize," Kreslins told me.[13] There was no cynicism to the suggestion, either; it was born purely from self-interest. "At the time I didn't really have health care. I just thought, if you're going to throw money at something, do something useful. Don't give away cash prizes!"

Tokion publisher Adam Glickman loved the suggestion. "We had the idea for the King of Zine contest before presenting it to the Ouch! campaign for sponsorship consideration," he said. The magazine is known for its Creativity Now! conference, which annually gathers the most cutting-edge artists (or, as some critics note, the most cutting-edge *male* artists) in New York and Tokyo for discussions of contemporary art trends. A self-publishing contest doesn't seem out of place in a magazine that claims a 58 percent creative professional readership; nor, for that matter, does the notion of *Tokion* seeking sponsorship for it from Tylenol, which, with Ouch!, had recently made inroads into edgy arts funding.[14]

"Our original idea was to offer a cash prize, but they suggested the free health insurance," he said. I considered correcting him about who should be credited, but then remembered that Kreslins was on the Ouch! payroll when he came up with the idea.

For Glickman, the prize cinched the deal, however ambivalent he felt about partnering with a drug manufacturer. "I could talk for hours about the goods and not so goods of U.S. pharmaceutical companies," Glickman told me. "But I thought the prize they offered was a great idea. We all know how expensive health insurance has become, especially for artists."

And few probably know as well as McNeil Consumer and Specialty Pharmaceuticals's parent company Johnson & Johnson. The unseen although likely myriad links between the high costs of preventive health care and the affordability and popularity of medications give the prize a very weird context indeed.

But it's not so much about the contest prizes, Ouchthewebsite .com explained. Nor is it about the cool free stuff. "We don't just showcase the talent, we get them to do the work too. To get an inside look into the pain of living, we're letting the stories come directly from an inspirational collection of artists, writers, illustrators, musicians, and photographers who bring their own piece of artistic vision to this project." [15]

Allowing stories to flow directly from the artists' visions is the core principle of corporate arts sponsorship, and the lack of editorial meddling implied is one major reason artists do the deal. The well-known Absolut Vodka campaign is one famous example. Started in 1980, the campaign features artists' renderings of the no-nonsense liquor bottle both run as ads and displayed as art. In 1997, the company helped promote *Wired* magazine editor Kevin Kelly's book *Out of Control* on a Web site named AbsolutKelly.com that featured nothing more than an excerpt of the illustrated book. No banner ads or overt product placement here: Absolut was merely the content provider. It was a breakthrough in corporate arts sponsorship. As Naomi Klein writes, the site had achieved "what the brand managers had aspired to all along: for their brands to become integrated into the heart of culture. . . . What they really want is for the right to be accepted, not just as advertising art, but simply as art."[16]

The reasons that underlie this desire go beyond the simple jealousy the ad man was rumored to hold for the highbrow creator of fine art. For a corporation to be accepted as a producer of art and culture means it has earned a place as an agenda setter, a tastemaker. And these, as Sophie Wong hinted, set the tone for different types of conversations than mere products do.

In the case of the Ouch! campaign, going beyond simply showcasing the talent meant becoming the impetus for the work. This isn't just Pepsi sponsoring a concert series. It's not even Jones Soda's seemingly organic appearance at an extreme sports event. Instead, Tylenol claimed to be the motivation to participation in the concert or extreme sports event. *We get them to do the work too.* The artistic visionaries of Team Ouch! are doing what they normally do, just contributing their creations to the Ouch! campaign. But they're doing what *they* do as an integral part of what Tylenol does. Tylenol's commercial interest in visionary work isn't tacked on after the fact. It is integral to its creation. Although the works aren't overtly branded—indeed, maybe because they aren't—they were created entirely at the behest of Tylenol and distributed exclusively through its networks. In other words, Tylenol hints, we *own* a part of this scene. "Though the branding of Ouch! is up-front—Tylenol isn't trying to conceal its hand—it's also low-key," wrote Bob Mehr in the *Chicago Reader*. And the artists seemed to agree.

Pain partner Leslie Stein, who won the 2003 Xeric Grant, the annual award given to outstanding self-published comics creators, described her relationship with Tylenol as "really organic, which made it a very easy and uncomplicated job situation. . . . Throughout this process I had no contact with anyone from Tylenol and only talked to Jerry [Lim of Plastic Enigma, a multimedia duo hired by Ouch! to create their Web site], who was basically just trying to use his friends' bands, artists, and writers to give them a bit of money and exposure, or at least that's what it seemed like to me." Stein's drawings are undulating and emotional, almost the opposite of Regé's, although popular with the same underground comics crowd. "Aside from the style in which the cartoon was drawn, it's not really much like my other work, and I purposely made some characters up I knew I wouldn't really care to use again."

As to the organic process, Stein explained, "I didn't really feel a part of the whole corporate advertising machine. It's not like I drew a picture of a guy holding a bottle of Tylenol and smiling; I basically just did what I wanted. And Tylenol and Ouch! put their name next to it." Specifically, Tylenol published her comic on Ouchthewebsite.com, branding both the distribution of her work and the concept behind it: "They had had some idea that the cartoon should be something wacky and threw out ideas like 'The Pain Brothers,' so I just kinda went with that."

Whether or not Stein *felt* a part of the corporate advertising machine, however, it would be difficult to argue that she wasn't a part of it—an integral part, in fact. She and the other participants made the campaign possible; their participation, in fact, *was* the campaign. Although the explicit aim of Ouch! was most likely not to mine the integrity of Stein, Regé, Lim, Kreslins, and the rest, the expanse of the project points to an intent to insert itself into the independent production underground. Yet, in agreeing to create commissioned work, the artists left the realm of independent production. That in many cases they failed to realize this—due to the casual nature of the business relationships, the self-directed projects, and the whiff of authenticity Tylenol insisted on maintaining throughout the campaign—may not be surprising. But for those of us interested in maintaining a corporate-free sphere in our culture, it should be cause for concern.

Unfortunately, Tylenol's behavior during the Ouch! campaign was neither as above reproach nor as hands-off as many in the underground would like to believe. Regé, for example, was commissioned to create three comics to run as ads to publicize the release of his Ouch! dolls, yet the company failed to place the complete run of strips and neglected to provide other promised marketing support.[17] Although the campaign explicitly claimed that all works would "come directly" from Team Ouch! participants, cartoonist David Heatley was asked for an editorial change before publication. Heatley's work combines autobiography and dream sequences in a multipaneled, brightly colored, black-outlined style well suited to his large-format self-published books (although he also does illustration work, including a recent New Yorker cover). The content for his Ouch! project was also to be autobiographical. "I was doing three strips about pain—physical and emotional," he began.

> The strips I did were called "Paralyzed," "Disillusioned," and "Heartbroken." Or something like that. The disillusioned one had to do with a superlefty political group I had

been involved with in New York around 1995. The text was taken from a journal entry where I was going off about how corny everyone was. I think I said something about "corny ass white people." That's the phrase they objected to. It was a funny situation, since I'm white, and Jerry, the guy editing me, is Asian. He was just flagging it because he thought someone would object in the meeting when they presented it. They didn't want to alienate anybody coming to the site who was white, I guess. It was strange. I bristled at first, but then was fine with changing it. I think it became "whitebread" instead. And just "corny" instead of "corny ass." Not too far off the original.

Admittedly it was a minor concession, and probably made for the best. Having to make it, though, was new to Heatley, who had never before undergone such a process. "It was one of my first experiences of having my comics edited for content," he said. "I've only ever done my own comics exactly as I want them to be done with zero input. But as I'm maturing as an artist, I realize that it's been a nice bubble to live in, but if I want to really engage with a wider audience, there may be some compromising down the road."

We can probably all agree that a suggestion to tone down racial epithets is a worthwhile editorial concession (although the reasons Heatley would prefer not to alienate white people as distinguished from the reasons McNeil would not are worth considering). The point is not that Heatley was in the wrong for agreeing to this change, only that he agreed to it because the requested concessions did not seem unreasonable. Neither, from a certain distance away, does agreeing to wear clogs at work to avoid mussing carpets.

Yet Ouch! claimed to be a hands-off distributor of underground art, when it was not. It turns out this was only one of several changes the pain partners were asked to make in revising their artistic visions for corporate sponsorship. One particular request seemed more intended to position the campaign falsely than decrease potential offense among viewers. An early draft of a Choose-Your-Own-Adventure zine-style pamphlet originally traced the Team Ouch! story as I described it in the beginning of this chapter. It was at the time called *Attack of the Suits*, although it was eventually published in an edition of "hundreds of thousands" and inserted into skateboard and independent art and culture magazines under the name *The Cave of Pain*.[18]

Originally BrainReservist Sophie Wong objected, as she wrote in an e-mail, to "the ending on page 12." She's referring to two sentences that end the storyline described earlier: "Yes the shoe thing is annoying, but you've been waiting for a chance to trade in the caves for some decent heat, lighting, AC, and benefits. You and the team lay down your weapons and take off your shoes."[19] She found the text unacceptable because:

> Tylenol sponsors Team Ouch! because they choose to take the path not taken. Because they're committed to their life of pain, and refuse to sell out to the corporate world. Therefore, when they happily decide to join Conrad's crew, it's such a cop out. It doesn't have to be entirely re-written. Maybe we should approach it as a bad tragic ending, like "Look at the horrible place Team Ouch! has ended up because of your choices," as opposed to "A 401k and health insurance actually sounds good."[20]

Wong is of course overlooking the fact that Team Ouch!, in the words of one anonymous pain partner, had *already* "sold out to the corporate world by accepting sponsorship from McNeil."[21] To her the Ouch! campaign is not an act of "sell[ing] out to the corporate world . . . a cop out . . . a bad tragic ending." She associates the Ouch! campaign—despite its $2.5 million dollar budget bankrolled by Big Pharma—with "the path not taken."[22] Or perhaps she, personally, doesn't, and is merely using the chance to underscore the authenticity of the project. Nonetheless, her comments indicate a confusion shared by more than one pain partner about the integrity of the work they did for Tylenol.

In its final version, the ending of *The Cave of Pain* reads:

Yes the shoe thing is annoying, but you've been waiting for the chance to trade in the Caverns for some decent heat, lighting, and A.C.

But wait! Is this a trap? Yes! What to do but devise a trap of your own? You glance around at the team. Silently, the plan is set.

You and the team lay down your weapons and take off your shoes. Constructus and his suits close in, ready to initiate you into their bland family. Their guard is down. "Now!" You scream, laying a mighty blow into Constructus' ample stomach. The team joins in the ambush. A few minutes later, the remnants of the suit army have fled. Their lesson has been learned. They will not be back.

The new ending varies dramatically from its real-life parallels: Team Ouch! participants took the health insurance (or at least the money that would have enabled them to pay for insurance) in exchange for some very minor concessions. About on par, actually, with wearing comfy clogs in the office.

Simply labeling this change "editing" elides the fact that it significantly altered the content and scope of the story. Editing is supposed to help authors clarify their vision (such as that done at a book publisher).[23] Yet the content changes requested here were made not to aid comprehension of the work but to limit it. Once changes are required that do not elucidate original artistic vision but instead force its conformation to outside policies, I suggest we call it "censorship."

Editing and minor censorship may be par for the course in a culture overrun with commercialism, but the drugmaker caused even more damage when it got involved in a 2003 indoor skate park project. A $30,000 seed grant from McNeil helped initiate construction of the Autumn Bowl in Brooklyn. When it was completed, with no signage identifying the space as funded by Tylenol or McNeil, as Wong told the *Chicago Reader*, the skating community still miraculously picked up on the connection and started calling it the Tylenol Bowl. "You can't purchase that," Wong said. "The audience took it themselves and they're marketing it without a dollar being spent."[24]

She seems to be announcing the accomplishment of her stated goal of making Tylenol a part of "different types of conversations" while overlooking the initial $30,000 donation. (The *Reader* reported that Tylenol had helped fund the skate park but did not seem to consider this marketing.) If true, her claims would stand as irrefutable proof that the Ouch! campaign fulfilled even Wong's *unstated* goals for it: that the underground had grown to love Tylenol all by itself, based solely on the affection hipsters genuinely felt for their favored headache remedy. But it wasn't true. In fact, it was an Ouch! announcement that nicknamed the Autumn Bowl after its corporate sponsor.[25] David Mimms, owner of the Autumn Skateshop, the New York skateboard store behind the Autumn Bowl, explains that this renaming and other incidents of dishonesty and secret strings attached to his no-strings-attached agreement led to the end of his relationship with Tylenol.

It had all started with a basic idea Mimms had talked about with a few other friends. Building a skate park was a simple, small-scale plan that they hoped would grow organically. After some discussion they slowly began looking at spaces and planning their schedules around building a skate community. One of Mimms's friends was working on the Ouch! campaign and thought the pharmaceutical manufacturer might throw in some money if Ouch! could hold an opening party there. A $30,000 donation arrived shortly thereafter. "It was way too easy," Mimms said.

Suddenly, the small group had money to make their project happen, so it happened fast. In fact, it happened so fast that the $30,000 was gone in no time. Tylenol offered another donation and urged Mimms and company to spend whatever they needed, promising to kick in more cash down the road.

Mimms was already overworked, and the accelerated timetable didn't help. "I was really in trouble," he admitted. He could barely manage to keep both the skate shop and the park open. And expenses kept accruing. Soon they were in debt for another $25,000 on the Autumn Bowl. It was finally completed, but the group was exhausted. "We were losing more every month," he said dejectedly. "We hardly ever had any staff there."

Despite Tylenol's pledges, no more money ever appeared. Realizing the drug company had ended up "promising more than they delivered," Mimms cut his ties with them and tried to figure out how to pay down the debt on the skate park, which wouldn't have been so pricey if the corporate sponsor had not urged a speedy completion requiring needlessly expensive materials. But at least Tylenol's influence would no longer be felt.

It was infuriating, then, when Mimms later heard from a friend in publishing that Wong had purchased an ad in a hip magazine for a new Ouch! contest to "win a trip to the Tylenol Bowl." The skateshop owner couldn't have been more frustrated. Mimms snapped, "It should be called the Pat Smith Bowl" in honor of a friend who worked to keep the space open after further Tylenol money failed to come through. "The ad cost more than they'd spent on us," Mimms noted drily. After he complained to Wong, it was pulled before the issue hit the stands, but somehow the name stuck. The most frustrating part of his experience on the Tylenol Bowl project? "They still call it that!" Mimms exclaimed.

Mimms's frustrations are mirrored by some who experienced the "underground" Star Wars campaign or the Sony PSP and Axe graffadi and are described (albeit in veiled, contradictory language) in Nike Skateboarding's Major Threat apology. The story often goes like this: a sudden spate of work emerges, seemingly organically, from the underground, and any ties to its origins in corporate sponsorship, however loose, are buried deep. Participants may balk—Dischord did, Chicago street artists did, Mimms did—but the damage is essentially already done. To at least some audiences, the underground has been marked as corporate-owned. In some cases, genuinely independent cultural production is branded; in others, corporate-sponsored projects are described as independent, their branding labeled accidental, authentic, passion-driven. It is true that the lines between corporately derived and autonomously created work are blurring constantly—but in not one instance is the independent sector responsible for blurring them.

The individual artists involved may have seen the corporate sponsorship as an easy way to make a buck, get a leg up in a tough market for creatives, or as concessions necessary to join the distribution network guaranteeing a large audience. By joining up, these artists, extreme sportspeople, writers, musicians, publishers, and filmmakers—pain partners—did not precisely follow the Conrad Constructus storyline that starts this chapter. There was never a moment they weighed the options: integrity or clogs? Regardless, they allowed the integrity inherent to their status in the underground to be bought. And it will prove mighty hard to buy back.

10

I LOVE MONKEY

Love Monkey, the most amazing show in the entire universe that has been or ever will be on TV, is the story of a tall, quirky, dark-haired guy with a wide smile, a quick wit, and a cool-ass job as an A&R rep at a major record label. His name is Tom Farrell, and he is played by the lovable guy last seen in the cornball feel-good show *Ed*. In the first episode, Tom bops around the club scene (because that is part of his cool-ass job) until he finds a hot new talent: Wayne! Wayne is awesome. Wayne is like Jeff Buckley, but very young and not at all reclusive. Also: alive. He is like Fiona Apple except not as strange, like Good Charlotte except actually alternative, and like *NSync except that he likes girls and is not fake, really. Although he is better than all of the above because he is un-signed! Raw! Virginal! And Tom wants Wayne to sign with his major label, Goliath.

Unfortunately, Tom is an idealist. One day at his major-label job, where he bops around an office filled with attractive cowork-ers having witty conversations, Tom stands steadfast behind his ideals. Goliath, it seems, has called a meeting to remind employees of its mission. And Tom is there to help. "It's about the *music*," he says to a roomful of his colleagues. (At least I think he said that. Well, it was either him or one of my stoned friends back in high school.) Tom then looks around the room, knowing he has just spoken the truth. Even though so many record labels out there don't understand what it's really about (answer: the music), he is sure that here he is adored for his quick wit, wide smile, and height, and therefore is safe to speak this truth without fear of losing his job.

But he is wrong. In a plot twist straight out of *Jerry Maguire* but *way awesomer*, Tom gets fired because the major label just doesn't agree. It's not about the music, they tell him. It's a business. A business his idealistic, music-loving ways just don't fit into anymore. It isn't about the music; it's about the money.

This is a pretty weird message for the show's executive producers, record label Sony BMG, to be putting out in the world. Clearly they were trying to paint *this* major label as a bunch of baddies, but in terms of being a major label, Sony BMG is one of the most major—and, many would say, baddest. The months leading up to the appearance of January 2006's *Love Monkey* saw profits of $178 million for the music division. (It was a relief to the company, which had recently suffered a massive PR backlash over the infamous Sony rootkit disaster, and whose previous quarter was a mere seventh of this amount.[1]) Within a year, by January 2007, Sony BMG was pulling in profits of $288 million.[2]

So *Love Monkey*'s central narrative theme, that no one in the music industry understands what it's really about (answer: the music), is not to be confused with *Love Monkey* executive producer Sony BMG's metanarrative: claiming it's about the music is a great way of making money.

Radio's been in a slump lately. With corporate giants like Clear Channel taking over, wherever we tune in we hear mandated playlists, boring major-label groups peddling brand-name products, and cookie-cutter pop stars promoting their latest movie release with anodyne soundtracks. The same stations dispense the same songs and the same robot DJs blare the same robot bullshit from cars in markets thousands of miles away from each other. Too many stations spew "right-wing rhetoric dispensed at toxic levels," in the words of a DJ at the midwestern pirate station Radio Free Ohio. Most offer nothing more than "corporate-mandated opinions," the microbroadcaster charged. Certainly, the DJ lamented, "gone are the days when we could hear a newsman deliver the news about what was happening in my town."[3] The fact is, radio needs to change. Thank God at least one outlet is sending that message loud and clear—a lone pirate radio station in the heart of Ohio.

Radio Free Ohio: a May 2005 marketing campaign from Clear Channel Communications.

No one likes Wal-Mart. There are movies and books devoted to this subject, anti–big box protests and city ordinances, Web sites you can look at, funds you can donate to, and organizations you can join. There are several resource lists available that you can visit online or in person that helpfully provide the names and addresses of independent alternatives that can meet your shopping needs. These small-business retailers may involve slightly higher costs, but most assuredly operate under a stronger system of ethics, and definitely pay their workers better, than the big-box giants.

One of the places you can go for such a list is your local Wal-Mart store. Just look for what the company calls its Small Business Spotlight, which features an advertisement for an independent store in your neighborhood that you could patronize if you weren't already in the Wal-Mart.

I don't know why I feel uncomfortable about lying on an application to become an unpaid promoter of brand-name goods and services to my friends and colleagues, but I truly regret the dishonesty. The company I am signing up to volunteer for is evil, sure, but some of the people that work there are probably *really nice*. Also, I am scared. I feel sure they will catch me, discover that I write negative things about marketing and corporations, and that I strive to eliminate brand names from my writing, neighborhood, and culture, and for these reasons will deny my application to bring up Al Fresco Chicken Sausage in workplace conversation or note the wonders of Glad Sandwich Bags at company picnics. But I am compelled to commit the dishonesty because the Web site offers no information about what promotional campaign materials look like, who can join, or how it all works. And this I need to know.

So I click the boxes (I have, like, a zillion friends), fill out my address (I supposedly live at my office), proclaim my expertise in the areas of films, books, cooking (I do like food), and, impulsively, in the write-in box, claim to hold quite a bit of sway over the political leanings of my friends (not true, but who knows what kind of campaign it might involve?).

Mere moments later, I get an e-mail: "Welcome to BzzAgent!," it says. "You have joined a growing community of talented communicators." I am urged to attend boot camp immediately, which I do because I am excited. I cannot believe they allowed me to join their ranks. This sudden thrilling rush of total acceptance may partially explain how BzzAgent has gotten over two hundred thousand people to sign up for their volunteer marketing corps, including some staunch anticorporate activists like me, BzzAgent AEM.

Boot camp goes something like this: as an education on the tenets of building buzz, I read through case studies of real-live reports from the field. At one point I am given a half-page personal essay describing two office workers' conversation about the merits of a certain motor oil, and it is so riveting and hilarious and represents by far the longest time I have ever spent reading about motor oil that I mention the product, by brand name, to a friend later that night. Next in boot camp I read the most boring description of a woman serving soup to her officemates that I can possibly imagine, and then reread it just to try to find the brand name she was supposedly buzzing: the chicken sausage I already mentioned. After reading each case study I am told why the reports are good examples of word of mouth, and note a growing affinity in my heart for both chicken sausage and motor oil. My time at boot camp ends, and I am awarded a seemingly arbitrary number of points. I feel conned: I don't think I actually learned anything, but clearly I have undergone some sort of change. Most remarkably, I am now deliriously enchanted with the phrase "chicken sausage."

It is notable that the BzzAgent corps also functions as part of the target audience for the products it claims to promote. While the building of buzz is celebrated with astounding frequency and volume—it is, after all, just talking—the instances where agents expressed such enthusiasm for to-be-buzzed products that they ran right out and bought them instead of waiting to receive them for free are held up as praiseworthy models. Bzz-Agents evidently thrive on positive feedback—after all, it is their only compensation—and being distinguished as a case study is the highest praise possible in the BzzAgent world. Although no financial transactions take place on the site, BzzAgents are rewarded when they personally conduct them to purchase the buzzed products. To this same audience, the marketing of each product is relentless: campaign descriptions are frighteningly, maniacally positive, and even confirmation e-mails manage to work in glowing reviews of products or services the recipient has already agreed to buzz. It is an exhausting funhouse where everything is venerated simply because it has been granted entry into the BzzAgent world, and this enthusiasm is easy to emulate. And I am a part of it! Bzz-Agent AEM!

The BzzAgent welcome kit I receive in the mail a few days later poses the helpful query "What is word of mouth (WOM)?" It also provides the answer: "Honest—Real—Powerful. It's something we do every day—it's the way we communicate. It's part of our social fabric. WOM is the shared opinion about a product or service between two or more people. Share your honest opinion, and you're creating WOM."[4]

"In a world where products are screaming for attention," marketing strategist Seth Godin writes, "the most precious commodity is attention. And attention is harder and harder to achieve." This oddly meditative quote closes out my BzzAgent welcome kit, and presents an unassailable logic. Its inclusion is also a clever bit of buzz building: Godin is a frequent client, and his books often find their way into the hands of BzzAgents, who seem to really connect with his message. Buzz!

Word-of-mouth agencies, then, when they do not act as pure advertising to members, are not intended to get friends to buy certain products or services as much as they are intended to get them to formulate opinions about them: more succinctly, to connect *emotionally* to them. On its face, this is not offensive. In fact, although there is something repugnant about word-of-mouth marketing, it's nearly impossible to locate what, partially because it does rely to some degree on honest and real communication. However, members are urged to articulate their heartfelt opinions, yes, but only about Al Fresco Chicken Sausage. And they are convinced to do so by people who have a vested interest in increasing sales of Al Fresco Chicken Sausage. At no point, true, is chicken sausage actually transacted in the BzzAgent world. Still, something is: the question is, what and among whom?

Compare this world to Neopets, a creepy online fantasy universe run by Dohring Marketing Research where young people sign up to create fanciful characters in outrageous outfits, and then buy them virtual versions of already existing brand-name products. Neopets is a space almost beyond both marketing and research, where kids go to let their imagination run free and conceive of a . . . Burger King. In that space their reactions to the appearances of Whoppers are carefully recorded. It is an interactive consumer playground not unlike American Girl Place, where all potential creative engagement is precommodified. But here, real-world money is unnecessary. The economy is based on Neopoints, which are awarded for completing in-world tasks or filling out surveys.

Approximately thirty million people worldwide are Neopets members, only 21 percent of whom are legal adults. (The remaining 79 percent is split almost evenly between twelve-and-unders and thirteen- to seventeen-year-olds; as with BzzAgents, there are more female members than male.[5]) Users of the site create pets and then buy them goods or services with Neopoints. Membership is free, yet the company remains profitable. In its own words, it generates revenue "through the use of User-Initiated Brand-Integrated Advertising. . . . Similar to product placement, [this] directly integrates a sponsor's product or service into the activities available on the site." Neopets also conducts market research. Its "unparalleled access to young people, coupled with the company's highly sophisticated, proprietary market research system, enables Neopets to conduct detailed consumer studies for companies that target young people."[6] It's a well-respected source for demographic research, cited frequently by *Advertising Age* and, the company claims, several Fortune 1000 companies. But does the blatant product placement result in increased sales of integrated products?

One survey indicates that it does. Conducted over the course of two months, the survey tested a juice drink on approximately five thousand members. While product awareness, preference, and usage frequency all rose by around 5 percent, a more remarkable increase was seen in the average number of the juice drinks consumed per week: 25 percent. In other words, those who were already aware of the product consumed more of it over the course of the campaign. Additionally, 43.5 percent of respondents stated that they were more likely to drink this brand of juice after seeing it on Neopets. Even more amazing were the BzzReportlike write-in responses provided by members when asked how they feel about having the juice drink on the site. "It [makes] me as a person feel good to drink that drink and to give my Neopets that same kind of drink—well that makes [me] feel so happy it almost makes me cry."[7] (As much as I'd like to chalk this up to some clever kid's response to the poll, this was only one of twenty-two overwhelmingly positive responses reprinted verbatim in the report.)

While the BzzAgent world integrates product placement into its content about as seamlessly as, say, a store does, it does offer a remarkably similar experience to the Neopets site, as all brand interactions are positive and monitored (although, OK, the friends on Neopets are merely virtual). As such, BzzAgent retains the potential to be a similarly duplicitous experience. You may think you sign up to receive information to convey elsewhere; really, you are providing it. The terms and conditions for membership make this explicit:

> Any material, information, or other communication you transmit, upload, or post to this site ("BzzReports") will be considered non-confidential and non-proprietary. . . . BzzAgent and its designees will be free to copy, disclose,

distribute, incorporate, and otherwise use the communications and all data, images, sounds, text, and other things
embodied therein for any and all commercial or noncommercial purposes. . . . Any comments, ideas, notes, messages, suggestions, or other communications sent to the site
shall be and remain the exclusive property of BzzAgent,
and we may use all such communications in any manner,
including reproducing, disclosing, and publishing such
communications, all without compensation to you.[8]

Such language, even if never fully exploited, grants the company ownership of whatever intellectual property users submit in
the process of recording their experiences buzzing products, and
these reports aren't so much a required aspect of participation as
they are the only means of interaction in the BzzAgent world.
Clauses like this aren't unusual in employee contracts but, in most
work environments, employees demand compensation for their
contributions. It's like a work-for-hire contract, except no one is
hired but everyone works anyway.

And works relentlessly. "Every time you take a poll on Bzz
Agent.com, you're telling us a little bit more about yourself," the
welcome kit explains, then assures participants, "We certainly don't
sell or use the information for anything other than our own purposes." The purposes of BzzAgent, however, are ultimately to sell
more products to more people. But don't worry, the booklet offers,
"We're not doing market research here. We're trying to find great
matches between the behaviors and preferences of our BzzAgents
and the 'target' audience of our clients." This actually turns out to
match the definition of the phrase "market research" fairly well:
"The systematic gathering, recording, and analyzing of data with
respect to a particular market, where market refers to a specific

customer group in a specific geographic area," according to the American Marketing Association's online "Dictionary of Marketing Terms." [9] Anyway, by the time members have received welcome kits, they've already agreed to the terms and conditions, which state unequivocally, "Using the site means you're taking part in campaigns, polls, surveys and other word-of-mouth (WOM) activity. We can offer any/all of this to whomever we want." [10]

BzzAgent (and it seems safe to assume other word-of-mouth agencies) has created a strange social space where every communication reflects a sales pitch and is preowned; where labor is called "sharing" and remuneration is not an option; and where your initial acceptance of these terms is the essential transaction. So although you may sign up with BzzAgent thinking you can game the system—I certainly did—perhaps by selling the free stuff, using the site only socially, or failing somehow to spread buzz, the rules of engagement prevent subversion. You will be subject to a barrage of messages telling you what you should buy—I certainly was—and you will spread word of mouth to your friends—I certainly did. Most important, any response you provide will be preowned and available for sale to whomever BzzAgent wants. You will have sold out for no compensation at all.

Back to Wayne—nobody owns Wayne. He's a free agent. He's independent.

And Tom's a free agent, too, at least for a little while. While he considered starting up his own label at the end of the first episode—a diversion that lent the show just the aura of authenticity it needed but never went anywhere except to reemphasize that Wayne is *really just that good* and would be *totally worth starting a whole label over*—independent True Vinyl Records swoops in and offers Tom a job as an A&R rep.

Forget for a moment that A&R reps don't usually work at independent music labels. They can't pay 'em and don't need 'em anyway. A&R reps at the majors are generally charged with seeking out great new bands, which every independent label I know is flooded with already. A&R reps are also tasked with hand-holding musicians through recording albums, touring, and managing their image; independent labels tend to choose bands they can trust to complete these tasks on their own. Forget also that True Vinyl gives Tom a fancy office and immediately starts throwing big money and big decisions his way, never questioning whether his judgment might have been influenced by his years at the corporate label Goliath, where, as we have already learned, it was about the money. And forget that Tom seems to have nothing going for him but his height and his quirkiness and his smiliness and Wayne. But: oh! Wayne!

Wayne has a dulcimer voice and heavy-lidded, pale blue eyes, and long-ish messy hair, and he plays his acoustic guitar as if he were singing each song directly to his girlfriend, which, when you hear him play, you pretend to be. Wayne is seventeen. Wayne loves his girlfriend. Also, he loves his family. And his guitar. Wayne is everything the music industry lacks right now: heartfelt talent, genuine sincerity, untrammeled authenticity.

Wayne is so good that True Vinyl enters into a bidding war with Goliath over him. But Tom of True Vinyl is the forerunner. "You're Wayne and we'll try to keep your Wayneness," he tells the young musician. Everyone wants Wayne because he really is that good, which is awesome for the viewer because it turns out Wayne is played by Sony recording artist Teddy Geiger, whose CDs are readily available at your local music store.

"So if I get this right," Internet critic Brian Del Vecchio theorized, "we'll meet a new 'unsigned artist' in each episode, only those artists will all actually be signed to Sony. . . . In order to sell us music, Sony must pretend to be the opposite of what it really is. And that, my friends, is fraud. It's the opposite of indie cred: it's Goliath Records, a soulless media corporation, exercising its ability to appropriate culture for profit. . . . And it's all constructed to sell me corrupt and toxic CDs." [11]

Canceled from CBS after only three episodes, revived on VH1, and then quickly canceled again, *Love Monkey* brought product placement on television to entirely new highs or lows, depending on how you feel about product placement and television. Viewers, apparently, failed to engage with the show's time slot, characters, dialogue, storylines, actors, constant brand mentions, and the silly parade of hats Tom wore in the opening credit montage to symbolize his quirkiness. Not to mention the outrage that was expressed over the central conceit of the show, for it was not merely a program that presented major-label recording artists *as independent*, it was a fictional environment in which *independence was owned outright* by Sony BMG. (We get them to do the work, too, as the Ouch! campaign put it.) It's the fictional environment that Clear Channel presented by forcing a pirate radio–style break into its own programming, and the same one Wal-Mart claims its Small Business Spotlight promotional campaign inhabits. The space constructed is designed to appeal on a purely emotional level. One which, as Kevin Roberts put it, "lies beyond reason." Or better, contradicts reason entirely.

As media endeavors, these projects were all miserable failures. *Love Monkey* the television program was immediately exposed as inauthentic, misguided, deceitful, stupid, and downright weird by the very independent-label-loving fans it intended to attract. Over only three episodes viewership dropped like a stone: from 8.6 million to 6.2 million viewers, few of whom expressed any desire to watch again.[12]

Radio Free Ohio's on-air, anticorporate spots led listeners to a Web site, radiofreeohio.org, that radio wonks discovered was registered to Clear Channel Communications in San Antonio, Texas.[13] The truly independent Internet radio station WOXY and *Stay Free!* magazine's blog publicized the deception, which Clear Channel admitted was merely a prerecorded break-in into regular programming designed to draw attention to Akron, Ohio's 1350 AM station format change to moderate progressive talk radio. "Once we determined we were going to change the format, we tried to get into the mind-set of people who would listen to this new station," said the company's Akron vice president and market manager. "Clear Channel, as I see it, is dedicated to entertaining radio and to getting results for our advertisers."[14] The company's means of doing so was unacceptable to the moderate progressives the format change was designed to court; they complained about the deception on the fake station's Web site and to the *New York Times*.

And when Wal-Mart first announced its Jobs and Opportunity Zones Initiative, of which the Small Business Spotlight is only a part, it was described by CEO H. Lee Scott, Jr., as intended to "develop business opportunities" in "economically challenged" urban areas "with high crime or unemployment rates"—in other words, as a way to open new Wal-Marts.[15] The initiative was decried by the activist community, who correctly read it as a hollow campaign intended to defeat the big-box ordinances that had grown out of legitimate concerns over the low-wage work that would flood already depressed urban areas. (In fact, they were right. The proposal—as well as some politicking, clever PR, and payments to local politicians—was enough to convince Chicago's mayor,

Richard M. Daley, to veto their big-box ordinance and allow Wal-
Mart to move into town.[16])

Yet these campaigns were miserable failures on a level it wasn't
possible to achieve some years ago. An entire television program
devoted to hyping the underselling bands on Sony's recording
docket? Viewers in legions as strong as 8.6—or, hell, even 6.2—
million, willing to sit through an hourlong dramatic interpretation
of why they should buy a Teddy Geiger album? If we call it an ad
campaign, *Love Monkey* was a breakthrough success. The program's
aim was clearly not to create a popular or award-winning series.
It was to sell Teddy Geiger records—and it succeeded. The show's
theme song, "For You I Will (Confidence)," from the album *Underage Thinking* (Sony BMG), topped the Billboard Hot 100 at 29 and
was nominated in the Best Love Song category of the 2006 Teen
Choice Awards. It may be more precise to say the aim was to sell
Teddy Geiger, the first man in five years to appear on the cover of
Seventeen magazine. The failure of the television program seems to
have had no impact on his career at all, save frequent MySpace
postings from devoted, youthful fans who still miss the show. The
program's demise probably didn't bother Sony's marketing division either, which in the heady days leading up to the show's premiere did not mention the actors' talents, the program's narrative
themes, nor indeed any reason whatsoever to watch it. "It's an
amazing opportunity to get to a much bigger audience," one executive told *Rolling Stone*.[17] During a year in which the company suf-
fered nearly constant criticism for the rootkit fiasco yet still raised
profits by $110 million over the previous year, Sony seems to have
found a much bigger audience indeed.

Clear Channel, too, like Nike SB, seems to have found an in
with their traditional enemy, political progressives. While the company may not have actually gotten "into the mind-set of people

who would listen to this new station," they certainly found a way, as BrainReservist Sophie Wong described the Ouch! campaign, to get talked about in different types of conversations.

And when, finally, the first Wal-Mart Jobs and Opportunity Zone opened in January 2007 in Chicago, it was heralded with press conferences, welcoming stories in neighborhood papers, and the open arms of independent retailers in the area. Perks of the new store were frequently touted: beyond the increased numbers of jobs in the region, $300,000 seed grants would go to local chambers of commerce, and "support to local businesses" was offered to certain independent retailers in the form of the Small Business Spotlight, which included "advertising inside Wal-Mart's store and in local newspapers."[18] It would not be too much to say that local small-business owners were thrilled. "This will be a great boost to my business," enthused the first Small Business Spotlight designee, Active Auto Parts owner Chris Prayer. "Having a Wal-Mart in the neighborhood will probably generate consumer traffic and will hopefully bring more business to my store."[19]

Unfortunately for Prayer—and Wal-Mart—a February 2007 trip to the same store found that an hourlong search, the assistance of two cashiers, the entire customer service department, consultation with two of the store's assistant managers, and a series of unreturned phone calls to the Wal-Mart division headquarters yielded no evidence of the Small Business Spotlight. "I don't know anything about that," one of the customer service assistants, an employee of the store listed in two local papers as having promised Active Auto Parts in-store radio and print ads, told me.[20]

The problem is this: the messages are all true. The music industry is, to a great degree, about money. Corporate radio does suck. And independent stores remain viable alternatives to big-box stores.

But when broadcast by the music industry, corporate radio, and big-box stores, these messages are not intended to be heard so much as to be felt. We are positioned to respond to them emotionally, yet still react in opposition to them. In a world where mocketing is marketing, dissent is buzz. Like the essential transactions BzzAgents agree to, if we participate at all we are already doing the work.

Yet these examples also illustrate something a little more interesting to those of us who wish to strategize a future that is not wholly owned and managed for profit. These campaigns and media projects, along with all the others we've discussed in this book, indicate a renewed interest in naturally autonomous cultural products. Under capitalism, power comes not from having a voice but by being recognized as a market; clearly there is a market even for shoddy imitations of independent culture.

The task ahead of us will be to acknowledge the strength of that market without succumbing to its potential as a marketing tool.

11

TAKING DISSENT OFF THE MARKET

"I'm not disputing doing work for Tylenol is selling out," Laris Kreslins, a longtime self-publisher, told me when I asked about his participation in the Ouch! campaign. I'm pretty sure I hadn't used those words myself; I merely wanted some insight into how someone used to doing things on his own terms and for his own reasons decided to do them for a pharmaceutical company. I was building an argument, I told him, that the integrity that had grounded punk and DIY culture for so long was shifting, maybe even eroding away. I intended to compare Nike's appropriation of the Minor Threat image to the more cooperative arrangements between independent cultural producers like himself and companies like Tylenol, Starbucks, Axe, and Sony. But Kreslins saw no similarity. "Nike is a different situation. It's not like [Tylenol] said, 'We like Ron Regé, Jr.'s work; let's totally copy it and send it to the public.' The Nike thing was totally disgusting."

Ian MacKaye agreed. "The Nike business differs [from the Ouch! and Star Wars promotions] in that it wasn't an authorized campaign, nor was it national—though the Internet made it worldwide. I suppose there is an undeniable co-opting of revolutionary or rebellious images or ideas in play here, but at least in this case it wasn't one with which the band/artist collaborated."

Although Minor Threat themselves didn't collaborate with Nike SB, a group of corporate-sponsored skateboarders in the marketing department who felt a strong allegiance to the long-defunct punk band did—one at least as strong as the one they felt for their employer, the shoe giant. Their deep emotional connection to the corporation somehow trumped the anticorporate ethos at the heart of their culture. The question is how—and why the rest of the underground cannot articulate its objections. In this case, some answers can be found in the history of Nike SB and in the renegade branding work of Weiden+Kennedy (both described in Chapter 6), as well as in the company's acquisition of Converse in July 2003, which finally granted the Nike brand the full indie cred that had eluded it to that point.

Beloved among hipsters and skateboarders in particular, Converse started making basketball shoes in 1917, and since then has been associated with the first African American pro basketball team, the Harlem Renaissance, and Nirvana's Kurt Cobain. The high-top was practically a required uniform for my 1980s-era adolescence, only replaced in the 1990s by the low-top. But in 2001, primarily due to growing competition from Nike and other athletic clothing companies, Converse announced it had accumulated insurmountable financial losses and filed for bankruptcy. Two and a half years later Nike bought the company for $305 million. It turned out to be a sound investment. "Nike doesn't break out results for each sub-brand, but the group's sales grew 51 percent to $1.4 billion [in 2004, the fiscal year following the acquisition]. With nearly a quarter of the sales growth, Converse was the star," *Business Week* reported in September 2004.[1]

That an athletic-shoe manufacturer long criticized by activists for its labor practices now owned a beloved icon didn't mitigate the underground's love for Converse, even under new management. Some fans who had always wanted to work for the iconic brand actually got the chance, thanks to Nike.

Chicago rock-poster artist Jay Ryan had been creating hand-silk-screened posters for Shellac, Fugazi, Hum, Guided by Voices, and other bands at his studio, the Bird Machine, for close to ten years when he got a call from the shoe company. His illustration style is unique, and his dedication to hand-pulling each poster with his team of Bird Machine faithfuls would seem to make his method impossible to mass-market. Still, Converse approached him "with a very open project," Ryan explained. He's a ridiculously tall man, and just as jarringly soft-spoken. "[They were] basically saying 'Draw anything you want for us, and we'll make a billboard and pay you some money, and send you a pair of shoes.' I knew Converse was owned by Nike, and had Nike proper called, I would not have taken the job. I won't wear Nike shoes, and don't want my name on their ads. I have, however, worn Converse pretty much my whole life."

Ryan and I work closely together. The Bird Machine shares studio space with *Punk Planet*; joke breaks during days we are both in the office are frequent and long. He has done work with the magazine for years, and released his first monograph with Punk Planet Books. I watched him struggle with the offer, unsure whether or not he would lend his vastly praised underground postering talents to the megacorporation. Ultimately the artist most famous for his Shellac gig posters did end up working for Nike. "Since the image didn't even have to have shoes in it—which it doesn't—I felt I could justify taking this job," he told me. The image includes a number of undifferentiated orange mammals hanging by ropes from rotating conveyers; one lone dude (shoeless) flies free from a loose strand. It's printed on a canvas one hundred feet tall that was hung from a building in downtown Chicago in early 2005. And suddenly—although Ryan hadn't granted his approval to include his name on the final image [2]—there it was, his work and his name, on a really big poster proclaiming his endorsement of Nike-owned Converse.

As cartoonist Leslie Stein commented, becoming a part of the corporate advertising machine feels "really organic." I know; I once took a paycheck from Starbucks to plan the first-ever InkSpot for Seattle's annual Bumbershoot Arts Festival, a three-day music and culture festival at the Seattle Center. The InkSpot was a free zine-making creative area and workshop space for all attendees (although the Bumbershoot admission price was hefty; a three-day pass cost around $80). Several weeks after the contracts were signed, and days before the festival started, my two co-organizers and I were given a single, bizarre, and ultimately unacceptable requirement: the logo of Starbucks, a last-minute sponsor of the workshop space, would be placed on the back of each zine. Following our protests the stipulation was dropped, but the logo of the company infamous for preying on the independent coffee shops that are the homes-away-from-homes of many zinesters did appear on the programming guide, in all promotional materials, and in several locations within the venue. And the free coffee was plentiful. The zine-making space was branded, even if the zines themselves were not. *I* had done that. My compulsion to explain what I did with the money—hold free-candy workshops throughout the country—was echoed by Ron Regé, Jr., and Jay Ryan, who listed the groceries and cross-country move that wouldn't have been possible without the corporate paycheck. Still, I could not shake the realization that Starbucks had wanted an in with my people, and I had provided it.

Like Jay Ryan, Christen Carter has been a key figure in DIY communities for the past decade. She runs the Busy Beaver Button Company in Chicago, a business making pinbacks for bands, fashion designers, and visual artists. Also like Ryan, she is a part of my social network. When we were at a birthday party together recently, I complained that I couldn't get anyone to go on the record about their involvement in the Toyota YarisWorks DIY: Drive It Yourself campaign. (Yes, I am a boring party guest.) I was shocked when she told me she had been involved. Extremely involved—she had been one of the local organizers. A blunt, intelligent woman, she harbored no delusions about her role in the campaign. "They wanted access to my people," she told me straightforwardly.

I sent her a follow-up e-mail a few days after the party. "When did you realize they wanted access to your people? Do you think you provided it?" I asked her. As an organizer her job had been to enlist approximately fifteen craft artists, self-published comics creators, and independent musicians over a four-month period to join the summer 2006 promotional campaign. By giving Carter the job instead of approaching local underground artists directly, Toyota was not only saving itself time reading rejection notes, but also tapping directly into Carter's leadership role in the Chicago independent community.

"Pretty immediately," she answered. "I was a little reluctant to do it. But it seemed like a good chance to get my friends some easy money, and for me, too. Partly because I had all these hospital bills and other big expenses, but really $1,800 just made a tiny dent. And I was curious about the experience. When I asked people to do it, I said, 'They're trying to get to our people,' and thought that we were smart enough to make our own decisions about cars or other products for that matter, and couldn't be romanced by their 'DIY' approach."

Her description of the experience mirrored mine with Starbucks. I'd also given ambivalent warnings to the InkSpot workshop leaders. Despite the similar campaigns, however, she felt immune to the lure of the Yaris, as the $11,000 price tag was well out of her budget and that of most of the people she approached to lead workshops. But Carter soon realized, "It's not really about my friends buying the cars, it's more about us selling the cars. Great, now I'm a car salesperson. I'll add that on my résumé."

Automobile salespeople usually make a decent commission, though, and she didn't seem to be rolling in the dough. "Were you properly compensated, in your opinion?" I asked her.

"At the time I thought the pay was fair," she responded via e-mail. "Now I'm thinking it's a little low. Not outrageously low, though, but I don't have a grasp at all on the value of this sorta thing. . . . [T]hey were also paying for the trust that my friends who contributed had in me and my decision to participate when I asked them to teach classes. I know when I was asked to do it by Laris, I was definitely more into it because he contacted me than if Toyota or someone I didn't know [had] asked me."

When Carter first mentioned Laris's name at the birthday party, I was physically taken aback. It was the second time his work has almost caused the spilling of beer in my presence. "Laris Kreslins?"

Yup, she confirmed—later, he did so himself, although he failed to respond to a follow-up interview request. In fact, most participants in the Toyota YarisWorks DIY: Drive It Yourself campaign, like BzzAgents and those involved in the *Star Wars Episode III* underground-style promotion, weren't interested in discussing their marketing work.

Overall Carter deemed the experience not "too unpleasant." Toyota may have been, as she described, "not very organized" and "sorta lackadaisical," but she didn't feel she'd given up anything significant, particularly not her own claims to authenticity. "I do think the DIY theme was done sorta lazily and not with the care that I've seen at the DIY craft fairs. Since doing them is really a labor of love and based on community, a marketing campaign [that makes use of crafters' efforts] can't really do that well, maybe unless you get a real crafter doing it all, but even then, it's questionable."[3]

That, however, is the remarkable fact of the matter. "Real crafters" and other members of the DIY/punk underground *had* just done a marketing campaign for the Toyota Yaris. The campaign helped win the company acclaim from *Advertising Age*, who gave Toyota their 2006 Marketer of the Year Award (the *MADtv* mocketing segment is called out for special praise). "With sales of 51,748 units, the Yaris has actually grabbed 34% of the segment and 40% of Yaris buyers are 34 years old or younger," the announcement read.[4]

The fact is, our relationships to these corporations are not unambiguous. Some members of Negativland genuinely liked Pepsi products. MCA grew up loving Star Wars and didn't mind having his work sent all over the United States to all the "cool, underground magazines" they were marketing to—why would he? Sam Gould had a spiritual moment in the shower listening to a CD created, according to Sophie Wong, so that he would talk about Tylenol with his independent artist friends—and he did. Many of my friends' daughters will be getting American Girl dolls and books as gifts well into the foreseeable future. Some skateboarders in Washington, D.C., were asked to create an ad campaign for the East Coast Summer Tour, and they all love Minor Threat—why not use its famous album cover? How about shilling for Converse? I would have been happy to ten years ago. So what's really changed?

The answer is that two important things have changed: who is ultimately accountable for veiled corporate campaigns that occasionally strive to obfuscate their sponsorship and who is requesting our participation in such campaigns. Behind Converse and Nike SB is Nike, a company that uses shit-poor labor policies and predatory marketing that effectively glosses over their shit-poor labor policies, even to an audience that used to know better. Behind Team Ouch! was an underground-savvy BrainReservist on the payroll of Big Pharma; behind the recent wave of street art in hip urban areas near you was OMD Worldwide on behalf of Sony; behind your cool hand-stenciled Vader shirt was Lucasfilm; and behind a recent cool crafting event was Toyota. No matter how you participated in these events, whether as a contributor, cultural producer, viewer, or even critic, these are the companies that profited from your attention.

All of which helps to explain MacKaye's anger when he says he won't deliberately associate with Nike's "fucking swoosh." I argued it might be impossible to disassociate after being linked to the shoe giant against his will, but MacKaye remained steadfast. "There was a mistake made. The mistake was acknowledged and a public apology was made," he answered.

In marketing terms, however, the athletic clothing company may have already won, as I told MacKaye. Nike's message—Major Threat is happening—got to more people partially because of the controversy the campaign elicited. The link to Minor Threat was implicit, and the apology may not have erased it. He conceded this: "There may be some people who don't get the memo." Because of the perceived association, some may no longer pledge allegiance to Dischord Records, MacKaye agreed. But, he suggested, there may also be some "who will never buy Nike shoes again."

And that's a distinct possibility—unless the company can find a way into the Nike-hating demographic. Again.

Because MacKaye is overlooking the more significant change

that's happened in the world of marketing: who is creating it. In his case, it was corporate-paid skateboarders who genuinely loved Minor Threat. Over at Toyota, it was Laris Kreslins and at Tylenol, Sophie Wong. At Lucasfilm, it was Bonnie Burton. A few years ago in Seattle, on behalf of Starbucks, it was me. Word-of-mouth agencies are thought to be successful because certain key figures build buzz for certain products; this held true in all of the above cases.

Acknowledging these two important changes—who is ultimately accountable for underground-themed marketing campaigns and who is enlisting the aid of the underground—allows us to understand that the problem isn't a lack of commitment to integrity in punk and DIY culture: it's that structures have been put in place to deliberately erode that integrity. In fact, the dawning awareness of the scope of these structures helped fuel the rage behind the underground's response to these campaigns.

"The reason it became such a big story," MacKaye told me, "is that people are justifiably upset by the totality of the marketing world. People's uproar and outrage [seems to be] an indication of their spiritual frustration with a society that has such total and complete marketing . . . it's everywhere, at all times."

And because we live in a consumerist society, where we are trained to read image appropriation as straightforward advertising, where mocketing exists and is not a joke, where DIY is a sales pitch, and where companies named Anti-Marketing, GoGorilla Media, and Critical Massive are all available to give any campaign that anticorporate edge so hot with the youth demographic, far more of us are culpable for the totalizing experience of marketing than will readily admit to it.

"It's easy for someone from my generation to say, 'I can't believe these kids are working for Toyota,'" Rob Walker said to me, citing the Yaris campaign as emblematic of the others in this book.

"On a personal level I find it a little strange. . . . I think sometimes they're not as smart as they think they are. They think they're putting one over on the Man, and that sort of works both ways."

He wasn't claiming he's any smarter than the perhaps unwitting marketers involved; Walker's just pointing out that it's a difficult game to play, and it may be impossible to win. In fact, if the BzzAgent experience is any indication, participants may accede victory by simply agreeing to play.

This is one of the rules MacKaye realized early on. In attempting to find a solution to the Minor Threat image theft, the label was given to understand pretty quickly that it could ask for money and the point would be made: Nike had done something wrong and would pay for it. It wouldn't be an unheard-of deal, and, if Internet message boards were any indication, fans would have approved. But a secondary and more resonant point would have been made as well: integrity can be purchased, even if it was never put up for sale. "Everything has a price," MacKaye concluded. By refusing to name one for Dischord, Mackaye acknowledged the rules of this new marketing game but refused to play by them. Placing any price on labor that was never offered for sale—not just art, but the work that goes into community-building, maintaining friendships, and family relationships, for example—might just be naming the terms of your own defeat.

Let's pretend for a moment, however, that money is our primary concern. Assuming that the companies using small-media tactics and DIY-inspired techniques as marketing strategies are doing so partially as cost-saving measures (something that insiders Scott Johnson and *Event Marketer* agree is possible), let's attempt to approximate, as Christen Carter put it, "the value of this sorta thing."

Although most participants wouldn't discuss money on the

record, two did, and their earnings do not seem out of line when compared to the off-the-record conversations I had with other participants. Christen Carter made $1,800 for four months of work with Toyota in 2006. She got $300 for preparing and teaching a button-making workshop (a three-hour commitment), and $1,500 covered the period when she enlisted her cool pals to lead other classes. In 2002 I was paid $2,400 for a similar, although larger-scale, project for Starbucks. We prepared for six months, and I was contracted to be on hand during the festivities, which ran for three consecutive twelve-hour days.

One of the artists (who asked to be anonymous) involved in one of these campaigns created a commissioned piece over a six-month period, and was originally offered a very low five figures for his efforts. He responded with a request for 150 percent of the original offer and was granted it without hesitation. He accepted before he realized they would likely have doubled the offer.

His payment averaged out to around $300 per week. Let's assume (for the sake of defining an hourly rate) that this creative work could take up around twenty hours per week. This gives us a combined total for these three underground marketing campaigns of sixty-four workweeks—1,280 hours—and the payment averages around $15 per hour. This is not terribly low for creative work, considering how notoriously underpaid creatives are in Western culture. It is, however, significantly lower than what is paid to employees of marketing departments. *Promo*, a magazine for marketing professionals, reported in 2005 such employees make an average annual salary of $74,145, or around $35.64 per hour, assuming a forty-hour work week.[5] This doesn't include the employer's portion of income taxes, health insurance, paid sick and vacation days, however, which we'll estimate at around one-quarter this total, making our hourly wage estimate for marketers around $44.55.

If we put aside the hands-on hours and look exclusively at the social networking duties Carter and I took on in enlisting our friends as fellow marketers, however, we uncover a different picture. Subtracting my thirty-six hands-on hours at that $15 per hour (it's low for managing a workshop space, but if I were to charge that $300-for-three-hours workshop fee Carter was paid, Starbucks would still owe me $1,200 for those three days), Carter and I worked a combined total of approximately eight hundred hours and made a combined total of $3,360. Word-of-mouth agencies don't pay for friend enlistment and therefore must value it less than creative production; it doesn't surprise me too much that we averaged only around $4.20 per hour for putting our integrity behind Starbucks and Toyota and convincing our friends to do the same. For comparison, the federal minimum wage is $5.15, although in Chicago it was recently increased to $7.

Note to self: if you're going to sell out again, try to hold out for minimum wage.

Financial matters played a role in two Washington, D.C., street-stencil cases, and the discrepancy between the corporate and individual punishments highlighted some of the legal biases underlying these issues. When some graffadi touting Verizon appeared in D.C. and the company was required to pay a relatively minor fine, local graff fans were livid that just a few months earlier, a prolific graffiti writer named John Tsombikos had been punished with substantial fines, jail time, community service, and a lengthy parole for a similar (although noncommercial) offense.

Tsombikos's creation, a character named Borf, was almost omnipresent in the city when the graff writer was caught in November 2005; his tags, one D.C. Department of Public Works employee told the *Washington Post*, "prompted almost daily calls to the city call center."[6] Tsombikos pled guilty on December 12, 2005, and was fined $12,000; initially sentenced to eighteen months in jail, although this was later reduced to a single month; charged with two hundred hours of graffiti-cleaning community service; and put on parole for three years, during which time he would not be allowed to own or use art supplies.

Verizon had chalked approximately 135 two-foot-by-three-foot ads in an orange-red color loudly proclaiming the name of the company: "Looking for Something? Find it in the Verizon Yellow Pages." Since most were washed off or worn away by the time cleanup crews came around, the city fined Verizon $150 for each of only seven of the ads throughout the city, a total of $1,050. Company spokesperson Vanessa Banks did not admit outright that Verizon knew the campaign was a criminal act, yet apologized nonetheless. "We regret that this was outside of the city's code," she told the *Washington Post*, explaining, "It's harder and harder to catch consumers' attention, so many companies, including us, are turning to nontraditional advertisements. At this point, of course, I don't think we'll be trying it again."[7]

Tsombikos's messages, in comparison, were nonsensical: "Borf is good for your liver," one said. "Your investments are our playground," and "Borf doesn't fit in . . . at all," proclaimed others. My favorite: "Borf is in general." These sayings were artistic, intended to prompt in viewers insight into their own lives and their urban environment. Although it was part of his project to appear as if he had a vast entourage of coconspirators, Tsombikos had no multinational enterprise to help shoulder his punishment.

The differences between the messages of the Borf and the Verizon campaigns are obvious: Borf intended to make art, and Verizon intended to advertise. From a legal perspective, however, their crimes were the same, even given the different materials used in each. While it's possible to mount a logical argument that each individual involved in the Verizon campaign—the contractors who executed the pieces, the marketing team who designed them, the campaign manager, the company spokesperson, and whichever executive signed off on the project—deserved a fate similar to Tsombikos, the artist ended up with the stricter punishment. Paradoxically, it's the corporation that gets a lighter fine, while the individual acting on artistic and political motivations gets the heavier fine and is prohibited from expressing himself in his chosen medium for several years.

Still, some see positives. "That graffiti is used in advertising is a sign of it being mainstreamed," said Eliot Rosewater of the Visual Resistance Web site, implying that a wider social acceptance of his art form might help its practitioners. Yet the benefits promised by mainstreaming haven't hit graffiti culture. He says, "It's still not legal. The Vandal Squad [in New York] has seen its budget go up by 50 or 60 percent, and arrests have doubled in the last two or three years. There's no one to protect those kids. But there are still hundreds of kids going to jail for this, every year." Not a single piece of graffadi, meanwhile, has resulted in jail time—and certainly none have led to stipulations barring further advertising for any period of time.

It's not just that businesses co-opting his medium of communication are let off easy, Rosewater added. It's that they are making it harder for individuals to use it. Increasingly, there are "no nonadvertising venues for artists to create work that is not corporate." Few permission walls or commissioned murals mean few legal outlets for the art form, making graffiti a criminal activity unless sanctioned by marketers, a concern echoed by the Chicago Ad Blasters. This contradicts conventional arguments in support of the mainstreaming of fringe cultures—that economic benefits trickle down and ultimately find their way even to the fringe culture's purists. Here, no such benefits are in evidence for anyone but big business.

The tingly paranoia settling into the back of your mind was aptly described in William Gibson's *Pattern Recognition* during a conversation between Magda, a paid viral marketer, and Cayce Pollard, a brand strategist. Magda's job is standard word-of-mouth product-awareness raising: go out, start a conversation, build buzz. The reactions of those she markets to come as a surprise, though. The targets of her buzz campaign lie, she complains to Pollard. They pretend they have heard of a product that has not yet been released.

Pollard, a freelance marketer with an overwhelming mistrust of all advertising, says, "That's why it works. They don't buy the product: they recycle the information. They use it to try to impress the next person they meet."

Yet Magda has a deeper concern, and it's not about the marketing industry. "It's starting to do something to me," she says. "I'll be out on my own, with friends, say, not working, and I'll meet someone, and we'll be talking, and they'll mention something. . . . Something they like. A film. A designer. And something in me stops. . . . I'm devaluing something. In others. In myself. And I'm starting to distrust the most casual exchange." [8]

The fictional Magda isn't the only one to voice this concern. Matt Malooly alluded to an increasing disaffection when he described the corporatization of street art, commenting that it is getting harder and harder to trust the origins and intent of more and more forms of communication. Other interview subjects made similar comments. Before we write this off as delusional, it may be worth noting that *Pattern Recognition* was offered as one of BzzAgent's prizes for building excellent buzz, and Rob Walker's overwhelmingly disturbing portrayal of that same company generated buzz of its own, causing a sudden recognizable boost in the number of volunteer marketers. More and more people seem not to care how creepy this all is. Instead, they want in.

Yet as much as our ability to rely on the integrity of those we communicate with is being destroyed, it's still unclear what benefits can come from passion-reliant and authentic-seeming marketing.

Rob Walker, for one, isn't sure that underground marketing techniques like zines and stencils will be used for much longer. "The funny thing about that stuff is, I'm not actually convinced that it's that effective. . . . At some point it seems like it would just pollute things to the point were people would get upset." And in Chicago, Philadelphia, Los Angeles, New York—all over the United States, actually, and on Internet message boards and in newspaper articles and on the streets—people are voicing frustration. Yet marketers remain desperate to catch viewers' attentions. "Right now the advertising industry is in such a state of fear that they're kind of willing to try everything," Walker continued. "At some point they're going to want evidence of how this pays off."

Likely true, but the damage may already be done. The underground-themed marketing campaigns discussed in this book have taken place over a time period, from 2003 to 2007, that has concurrently seen a dramatic reduction in the number of independently supported cultural projects coming out of punk and DIY culture. The list of independent music labels that come and go on a regular basis is always long; in recent years, however, the volume of them has decreased dramatically, requiring *Punk Planet* and other music magazines to reduce the number of ad pages devoted to them (in 2003 the magazine averaged 109 total ads; in 2007 we're averaging 68). Some of the labels have decreased their ad budgets; many have simply gone under. Independently produced comics are in a slightly different boat; their numbers are dwindling in part because the creators are busy procuring book deals at major publishing house conglomerates. The crafting community, always an uncomfortable hybrid of DIY and consumer cultures, is expanding—although predominantly through sponsorships and licensing deals. And independent magazines—at least, the wave of them that grew directly out of mid-1990s zine culture—are releasing staff, closing doors, and going on extended hiatus at a shocking pace. Since late 2005, *Stay Free!, Clamor, Rockpile, Kitchen Sink, Law of Inertia, Herbivore, Grooves, Women Who Rock, Rock N Rap Confidential, HeartAttack, Rockrgrl,* and, by the time you read this, *Punk Planet* all have ceased publishing print periodicals.

Those who remain unswayed by this staggeringly long list will note that these represent more than mere cultural artifacts. Each of these publications, releases, and creations documented, bolstered, and existed as separate (and often youth-led) spaces of resistance against corporate and political power. Others will argue that because marketing exists mainly in the realm of representation it has little impact on the real world. Yet we know, because we have read Kevin Roberts's version of it and have traced its evolution in this book, that marketing doesn't really deal in representation anymore. It now focuses on emotion. At the exact same moment the authenticity, sincerity, honor, and personal vision of autonomously produced media and cultural products are being emulated for the purposes of increasing sales of corporate goods and services, we begin to feel that our need for these crucial noncommodities has been satisfied. Our desire for integrity has been slaked. Meanwhile, as Rosewater pointed out, genuinely independent media and cultural products—made out of passion and not in pursuit of profit—are unable to compete.

So while I cannot say whether or not emotion-based marketing, slaked with integrity, works to increase sales, as Walker wonders, I do not care. It has had the effect of strip-mining a naturally occurring field of independent modes of communication through the toxicity of branding, the appropriation of image and media, the exploitation of labor, and strategies that repurpose dissent as marketing. Roberts's lovemarks may do nothing whatsoever for sales of corporate-produced goods and services—perhaps the Toyota Yaris is a fluke—but they are successfully clearing away our desire to create, support, demand, and envision other options.

The spiritual frustration MacKaye noted earlier, along with our distrust of casual conversation, street art, and small media, are all growing, to be sure, but the backlash that's building to preserve the integrity of independent cultural communication has not yet cohered. Frustratingly, misgivings only manifest when viewers—target audience members—are confronted with traditional, identifiable advertising campaigns: when they *feel* marketed to. No sense of frustration has seemed to affect the growing number of people who work for Tremor or BzzAgent, nor did qualms impede the artists who worked for Lucasfilm, Toyota, or Tylenol, the skateboarders who created the Major Threat campaign for Nike, or any of the street artists employed by Axe or Sony. I didn't harbor any concerns about working for Starbucks—until the company's plan to brand the work produced began to resemble advertising.

We know it's because it feels organic to become a part of the corporate advertising machine. "Organic" not in the sense of natural, untrammeled, and sustainable, of course, but in its use as a promotional tool. Participants in word-of-mouth campaigns never question their own motivation when they contribute to the awareness of product availability, as Rob Walker made clear in his story on BzzAgent, and neither do many of the people who have worked on the campaigns described in this book.[9] Few tell friends they work in marketing because they know it will limit their credibility among peers; certainly this holds true for underground cultural producers. Their friendships and community relationships thus *feel* natural, untrammeled, and sustainable—but in fact they are promotional tools. Word-of-mouth marketers, who work on a volunteer basis in exchange for points they can (but most often don't) exchange for more products, or hired employees who are simply paid poorly, do not feel they are forwarding a hidden agenda. They know better than anyone else that they are not a part of the corporate advertising machine. They can see it in their (lack of) paychecks.

But if our sense that we have sold out relies only on how much we sold out *for*, it is no wonder that marketers themselves seem to remain unaware of their work promoting corporate goods and services. And if they are unaware, why would their target audience be wiser?

Culture jammers—and their situationist international heroes before them—are right about one thing: a disconnect needs to be made manifest. It's not going to come from a cleverly reworked ad, however, because ads are for products—and no one sells those anymore. It's not going to come from a subverted logo, either, because these signify brand images. Further, working with corporations' ads and logos, as MacKaye put it, "does their work for them." Marketing now is about making an emotional connection, so if a disconnect between marketing and the marketed is going to occur, it's going to have to be based in emotion.

One emotional disconnect was captured in the PBS *Frontline* documentary *The Persuaders* during a segment shot at a market research firm outside Boston. A perky researcher questions a subject about a product. "I'm going to read you some different emotions," the researcher begins. "For each one of them I just want you to tell me yes or no as to whether or not you think you feel that emotion when you're eating white bread. The first one is accepting."

The subject, a reasonable-looking man in a gray cardigan, looks slightly baffled, and rolls his eyes over the room. After a lengthy pause, he haltingly responds, "Yeah, I would say accepting." It's clear that it had never occurred to him that he might feel accepting of such a meal, but the suggestion that he might was persuasive. The researcher continues as if nothing is amiss. "Affectionate," "lonely," "disappointed," "afraid," and "trusting" all get negative responses, however, and it is not until "uncertain" is called out that our subject seems to clue back in to what is going on.

"Yeah," he responds. "A little uncertain—I've got a question," he hurriedly adds, knowing this is breaking the rules established for the survey. "Can I ask a question? The question was, 'When you eat bread do you feel lonely?' Have you found people to feel, to say yes, they feel lonely when they eat bread?'"

The researcher's response is lost to the viewer, but the question is the important moment anyway. For that's the moment when the subject voices his emotional distance from the process of emotion-based marketing. He's just realized that he's not sure what the connection is between bread and loneliness, really, and he might not even *care*.

If emotion-based marketing—lovemarks—is an attempt to

subvert our integrity, to work in the realm that Roberts believes "lies beyond reason," then realizing we might not care—about specific types of bread, or athletic shoes, or chicken sausage—may give our reason a chance to return. There *is* a great flaw in the plan, a stain on the blueprint of emotion-based marketing, but it only becomes visible when we remember that there are things in which we cannot emotionally invest.

This is, however, only an initial step toward preserving a corporate free space in our culture, whether physical or emotional. We must also, for example, acknowledge that such campaigns *are* marketing, if not straightforward advertising. We must fully admit to our participation in them and acknowledge when we have been paid or otherwise urged to back corporate products, by whom, and what we received as compensation. We must not pretend to take these projects on as autonomous agents. When asked to join such campaigns, we cannot do so lightly, thinking we'll be able to bring our friends in on the windfall, but only after consideration and discussion with others about the exact benefits of participation, financial or otherwise. And if we are not offered proper compensation for our work as marketers—$44.55 per hour is the industry standard—we should refuse.

After all, none of the strategies presented in this book, the small ways independent cultural producers have attempted to resist the increased corporatization of independent art and media, have stopped the successful machinations of this process. Not the Church of Stop Shopping's anti-Starbucks action, Negativland's pure artistic reenvisioning of a world gone mad for Pepsi, the Chicago Ad Blasters or Sony PSP graffiti responses, or Christen Carter's warnings to her friends that Toyota was on the hunt for her people.

These strategies have, however, helped us identify an effective language of dissent. That language does not include brand names or corporate funding, and must not take place within spaces that are already owned. Some things must remain unmarketable, and our ability to speak for ourselves, in the modes of communication we have developed to register dissent, should be one of them.

Yet the new mash media arises anyway, a hybrid culture created from the corporate adoption of the trappings of independent culture, perhaps best represented by MySpace.

On MySpace, some argue, we are all equal. And this is true, unless you don't have access to computers or the Internet, find the graphics of the site intolerable, aren't in a band, or prefer to do your social networking in public and therefore aren't on MySpace at all. The site is, in fact, privatized public space, like American Girl Place, Sony's *Love Monkey*, Wal-Mart's Small Business Spotlight, Clear Channel's Radio Free Ohio, Dohring Market research's Neopets, and the BzzAgent Web Site, because MySpace is owned by NewsCorp.

The lesson of MySpace—in fact, of all this mash media—is that you have a choice to participate or not. You are responsible because you choose. You can allow your future to look like the wonderful wacky world of *Love Monkey*, where everything is awesome all the time, except that you only get to see those things you are expected to love and then purchase. This world will be filled with Tylenol-sponsored independence, Nike-commandeered dissent, Sony-approved rebellion, and Lucasfilm-inspired creativity—customizable, courtesy of Toyota. You will be free in this world to speak out about anything, you may protest or mock to your heart's content—go ahead! Culture Jam!—but the content of what you say is already owned, and the effect of its voicing is always promotional. And anyway, why would you ever have anything negative to say? When everything is so awesome?

Or you can choose to explore this messy, unfunded, strange, creative world that will continue to exist with or without your support. It will soon be hidden and hard to find, gone deep underground once again, but if you know to look for it, you will be able to make out its outline.

Strategies that do not play directly into the maniacal logic of consumerism are difficult to locate and describe, mostly because doing so plays directly into the maniacal logic of consumerism. One previously favored strategy, celebrating spaces of resistance, seems to have only made them easier to identify, co-opt, and destroy. See, for example, the lengthening list of independent magazines, bookstores, labels, publishers, and projects now defunct. These spaces are resistant no longer. (Remember, this is the system that mined *No Logo* for marketing ideas, spawning brandalism and mocketing as a result.)

The challenge is to describe a strategy for conducting ourselves under consumerism's new rules that does not rely on location and states our refusal to play more resolute than resistant.

The model I propose—although others have stated it before me—is perfectly appropriate for our dirty, messy underground: a stain. A slight flaw. A little failure. A mark imperceptible to most, and difficult to locate but impossible to remove, a stain looks very much like everything that surrounds it, until you notice its fundamental difference. And by then you can't get rid of it.

One such mark is created by HeWhoCorrupts, Incorporated, a megacorporate entertainment empire run out of the Chicagoland basements and bedrooms of CEO Ryan Durkin and label manager

Andy Slania. HeWhoCorrupts is a music label and a band, and although they may sound a lot like hard-core punk, their goals are pure profit. The band plays loud and they play fast because, as Durkin explained in the calm demeanor appropriate to the boardroom, "If we played any slower we would have less time to concentrate on our profit margin."[10] While the audience may find the consumerist message of songs like "Ride the Limo" and "Baby, You're So Worth the Investment" confusing given band members' frequent onstage nudity, Durkin is patient with their marketing plan. "Let's face it: when you look at the demographics of our core audience you are dealing with fourteen- to twenty-two-year-olds, many in high school or lacking a GED. So can I really blame them if they don't know what positive cash flow is?" Durkin asked.

"And that target audience," I asked Slania in an interview, "who, exactly, are they?"

"The type of people who purchase audio recordings from our artists," he told me via e-mail. "We typically like to stay away from creative people like bloggers, critics, and people genuinely caught up in the music world because these types of people generally do not purchase music from any record label, including ours."

The label's blatant moneygrubbing, scorn for audience, and ever-ready willingness to strip off their business drag, however, isn't exactly a parody of a top-five media conglomerate. It is also authentic. HeWhoCorrupts, Inc., is a struggling label in a rough environment, competing directly with companies like Sony for survival. Forced to compete, they are also forced to engage in and emulate the corporate model. Luckily, the corporate model has a lot in common with how a bunch of white boys would prefer to spend time with friends. Which leads the viewer to some pretty weird realizations about how that model operates, some concerns about how power is distributed in it, and some questions about why it works at all. I was prompted to ask Slania, "Honestly, does your profit-minded approach to entertainment pay off?"

Slania, who reminds me of no one as much as the tall and quirky Tom Farrell of *Love Monkey*, responded, "To put it simply, yes. Yes, it does. I don't think you can be truly independent and profitable. Some of these losers will twirl around in the flowers and have candy cane dreams and all that fruity shit and think they're really making a difference in this world. . . . This world is controlled by corporations and creatively fueled by the independents; it's only a matter of time before both entities walk hand in hand in harmony."

HeWhoCorrupts, Inc., and their roster of other hard-core bands, videos, live shows, and releases—not to mention their ridiculously well-conceived merch, which includes wallets, ties, and credit cards—is simply mirroring an approach to culture that we are all familiar with. In fact, we have traced the expansion of this approach throughout this book. Like the Yes Men, who occasionally present themselves not as the independent artists, hackers, and pranksters they are but as business professionals and members of the World Trade Organization, HeWhoCorrupts is as difficult to digest as the model they emulate. Their hypermasculine posturing, while intended to be read as (ahem) nakedly profit-minded, is offensive in every conceivable way. On purpose. (If they played sets that lasted any longer than twenty minutes I probably couldn't stomach them at all.)

Admittedly, this does not make them immune. It's an unfortunate truth that HeWhoCorrupts, Inc.—their blatantly ridiculous procorporate stance, their silly merch, their nakedness, and their genuine desire to make a living in this culture—could easily be co-opted and marketed in support of some other corporate product. Or, in a few years, Ryan and Andy's youthful desire to participate in the joke may fade, and HeWhoCorrupts, Inc. will become at last nothing more than what it pretends to be.

In the meantime, however, they are an independent music label claiming to be its opposite. HeWhoCorrupts, Incorporated, may look like what we are expected to consume from corporate entertainment media, but it is different in a fundamental way. It fails to fulfill the single mandate of a corporation: pursue profits over passion.

We've already discussed a few models that show us how failure can operate successfully. Most particularly, Dischord's fight with Nike SB over the shoe giant's image appropriation. After all, MacKaye's final plan, to have Nike donate branded athletic equipment to the D.C. public schools, looks a lot like the company's current inner-city marketing strategy, which revitalizes urban basketball courts and slathers them with logos, fostering an intense association with the brand among inner-city youth. The failure of this plan to get off the ground, given MacKaye's "spiritual frustration with a society that has such total and complete marketing," is, in fact, a success worthy of emulation. It's a model that will be useful if we wish some things—our emotion, our relationships, our ability to voice dissent, our integrity—to remain unmarketable.

NOTES

1. Free Candy

1. Zines, if you're unfamiliar with them, are self-published booklets that got their start in the 1940s when several individuals simultaneously became entranced by certain science-fiction writers, stories, and movements. These individuals—many of whom had tired of not seeing their own work in print due to rampant sexism and their feminine names—wrote and published their own responses to and elaborations on this work. Although originally called "fanzines" to distinguish them from their mainstream counterparts, magazines, the term was shortened to "'zine" by the mass media, which covered them extensively in the early 1990s, and then was shortened again to "zine."

2. Daniel Sinker, *We Owe You Nothing: Punk Planet, the Collected Interviews* (New York: Akashic, 2001), 10.

3. Steven Shapin, "Paradise Sold," *New Yorker*, May 15, 2006, 85.

4. Ibid.

5. Naomi Klein, *No Logo* (New York: Picador, 2002), 67.

6. *The New American Webster Handy College Dictionary*, 3rd ed. (New York: Signet, 1995). For comparison, please see the definition below, provided by the dictionary that comes along with my computer's word-processing software, Encarta World English Dictionary (Copyright 1999 Microsoft Corp. All rights reserved. Developed for Microsoft by Bloomsbury Publishing Plc.).

> punk n
> 1. a youth movement of the late 1970s, characterized by loud aggressive rock music, confrontational attitudes, body piercing, and unconventional hairstyles, makeup, and clothing

2. a member of the punk movement

3. See punk rock

4. an offensive term referring to a young man regarded as worthless, lazy, or arrogant (insult)

5. a young homosexual partner of an older man (archaic slang) (sometimes considered offensive)

6. a prostitute (archaic)

7. dried or decayed wood used as tinder (archaic)

adj

1. feeling bad, depressed, or ill

2. inferior in quality or condition (informal)

I invite you to draw your own conclusions as to why a college dictionary would define "punk" as unappealing, and why a corporate-produced dictionary might describe it as unconventional, worthless, gay, and inferior in quality or condition.

7. Dischord Records, http://www.dischord.com/about/page05.shtml (accessed August 22, 2006).

8. A stellar postmortem of this time period called "The Crash" was written by Kyle Ryan and published in *Punk Planet* number 39. It's highly recommended reading, and covers the satisfying major-label experiences of Girls Against Boys and Green Day as well as the bands that went on to major-label deals but didn't ever seem to cash in— Jawbreaker, Jawbox, and The Smoking Popes—as well as bands like San Francisco's J Church, who were offered the chance to jump but didn't.

9. Alison Wolfe interview, September 2006.

10. Nina Malkin, "It's a Grrrl Thing," *Seventeen*, May 1993, 80–82, available at www.cs.xu.edu/~tankgirl/twelvelittlegrrrls/articles/seventeen.html (accessed August 23, 2006).

11. Ann Japenga, "Riot Acts," *New York Times*, November 15, 1992, sec. 2, p. 30, available at www.cs.xu.edu/~tankgirl/twelvelittlegrrrls/articles/newyorktimes.html (accessed August 23, 2006).

12. Emily White, "Revolution Girl-Style Now!" *Chicago Reader*, September 25, 1992, 8–9, 16, 18–21, available at www.cs.xu.edu/~tank

girl/twelvelittlegrrrls/articles/chicagoreader.html (accessed August 23, 2006).

13. Kerri Koch pointed out the male surcharge in the riot grrrl documentary film *Don't Need You* (New York: Urban Cowgirl Productions, 2006).

14. Lauren Spencer, "Grrrls Only," *Washington Post*, January 3, 1993, available at www.cs.xu.edu/~tankgirl/twelvelittlegrrrls/articles/washingtonpost.html (accessed August 23, 2006).

15. Alison Wolfe, ibid.

16. Sinker, 113.

17. Alissa Quart, *Branded: The Buying and Selling of Teenagers* (Cambridge, MA: Perseus, 2003), 208, 212.

18. Ann Powers, *Weird Like Us* (New York: Da Capo Press, 2000), 230.

19. Klein, 61.

2. Scene for Sale

1. Kevin Roberts, *Lovemarks: The Future Beyond Brands* (New York: Powerhouse Books, 2004), 15.

2. Ibid., 26.

3. Ibid., 30.

4. Naomi Klein, *No Logo* (New York: Picador, 2002), 21.

5. I visited a high school in early 2007 and asked the students what "branding" meant: about half mentioned corporate logos, and the other half mentioned ranches, cows, and searing flesh. Just for fun, let's remind ourselves—using my doubly branded computer dictionary software—the entire scope of what the noun *brand* means in our culture.

    brand n
    1. a name, usually a trademark, of a manufacturer or product, or the product identified by this name
    2. a distinctive type or kind of something
    3. a mark burned into the hide of a range animal to identify it as the property of a particular ranch, farm, or owner

See also branding iron
4. in the past, a mark made on the skin of a criminal or an en-
   slaved [sic], especially to identify the owner
5. a sign or mark of disgrace, infamy, or notoriety
6. a piece of wood that is burned or smoldering (archaic)
7. a flaming torch (literary)
See also firebrand
8. a sword (literary)
9. a fungal disease that affects garden plants by causing brown
   spots to appear on leaves

Encarta World English Dictionary (copyright 1999 Microsoft Corporation. All rights reserved. Developed for Microsoft by Bloomsbury Publishing Plc.)

6. Klein, *No Logo*, 66.
7. Stephen Duncombe, *Dream: Re-imagining Progressive Politics in an Age of Fantasy* (New York: The New Press, 2007), 93.
8. Roberts, *Lovemarks*, 35.
9. Located online at www.anti-marketing.com.
10. Kevin Roberts interview, *Frontline: The Persuaders*, PBS, 2004; transcript available at www.pbs.org/wgbh/pages/frontline/shows/persuaders/interviews/roberts.html.
11. For more on vending deals, see Melanie Warner, "Lines Are Drawn for Big Suit Over Sodas," *New York Times*, December 7, 2005; David Nakamura, "Pushers: US Schools Hooked on Junk Food Proceeds," *Washington Post*, February 27, 2001; and Verne G. Kopytoff, "Now, Brought to You by Coke (or Pepsi): Your City Hall," *New York Times*, November 29, 1999.
12. Roberts, *Lovemarks*, 52
13. Ibid., 57.
14. Ibid., 132.
15. Alissa Quart, *Branded: The Buying and Selling of Teenagers* (Cambridge, MA: Perseus, 2003), 42.
16. Ibid., 43.
17. Ibid., 44.

18. Roberts, *Lovemarks*, 132.

19. And why is no one tracking the actual sales of hotcakes online?

20. Rob Walker, "Pabst Unsold," www.robwalker.net. A similar version of the story appeared in the June 22, 2003, issue of the *New York Times Magazine*, although I found the version available on his site under the category "Journal of Murketing" (accessed August 4, 2006).

21. Yes, in theory. In practice, the mistrustful attitude toward the privileges and tastes of mainstream culture, and the deliberately outsider stance of punk and DIY communities, left more than one scared kid out in the cold.

22. Ryan Underwood, "Jonesing for Soda," *Fast Company*, March 2005.

23. Andrew Kaplan and Heather Todd, "The Art of Innovation," *Beverage World*, March 15, 2004. For more on van Stolk's past in the beverage distribution industry, see "Keep Up with the Jones, Dude!" *Business-Week*, October 26, 2005, available at www.businessweek.com/innovate/content/oct2005/id20051026_869180.htm?chan=sb (accessed December 13, 2006); and Anne Marie Borrego, "Big Plans: Anatomy of a Start-up Collection," *Inc.*, January 2001.

24. "Keep Up with the Jones, Dude!"

25. Underwood, "Jonesing for Soda."

26. "Jones Soda Co. Announces 2006 Third Quarter Financial Results," Jones Soda Company news release, November 1, 2006, available at www.jonessoda.com (accessed December 13, 2006).

27. Lloyd Sakazaki, "Jones Soda: Close Look at the Premium Hip-Pop Brand (JDSA)," *Seeking Alpha*, February 8, 2006, available at retail.seekingalpha.com/article/11720 (accessed December 12, 2006).

28. "Keep Up with the Jones, Dude!"

29. Ibid.

30. Bruce Horovitz, "Gen Y: A Tough Crowd to Sell," *USA Today*, April 21, 2002, available at www.usatoday.com/money/mlead.htm (accessed December 19, 2006).

31. Though appealingly alarming, I doubt the veracity of this 250,000-member claim. Of the kids I've known who've joined Tremor, many played around with it for a while before abandoning it altogether. Even the free stuff, I'm told, got pretty lame. Were it not for Walker's

experiences, in fact, I'd wonder if buzz marketers might not be doing buzz marketing on their own behalf.

32. Marian Salzman from JWT Worldwide, quoted by Bruce Horovitz, "P&G 'Buzz Marketing' Unit Hit With Complaint," *USA Today*, October 19, 2005.

33. Ibid.

34. It is interesting to note that at last estimate 75 percent of buzz marketing agents were female. This may be explained by an enthusiastic quote that flashed on the screen when I visited BzzAgent's Web site: "Women tend to be the biggest viral forwarders of content." And while women are frequently reputed to be more reliant on social networking and interaction than men for business purposes, one also wonders if perhaps the economic disparity in wages between men and women isn't driving some toward volunteer work that may result in small, free luxury items or bolstered social standing among their peers.

35. Shannon, "Bzzing," *Tales from the Fairy Blogmother*, available at shanrev.blogspot.com/2006/05/bzzing.html (accessed December 19, 2006).

36. Rob Walker, "The Hidden (in Plain Sight) Persuaders," *New York Times Magazine*, December 5, 2004.

37. OK, it was my BzzReport. The full text—a lie patterned after a sample BzzReport—read:

> I was out last night at a friend's house and we were talking about holiday drinks. Someone mentioned [the crème liqueur] as an ingredient in a really amazing-sounding minty drink, and I'd tried a sample a few weeks ago and then heard (from you) that it sounded great, so we decided to experiment with it for our holiday party on Wednesday! Two of my friends are also very successful private chefs here in Chicago and were thrilled by the recommendation—even suggested bringing it into their holiday menus at the parties they're catering for clients. So, already we've got three different holiday plans for [the crème liqueur]. I just hope that my chef friends come up

with a good recipe before I'm forced to start experimenting!
I'm terrible at mixing drinks.

See Chapter 11 for full details on my experiences with
BzzAgent. (Although please note: this was my only campaign.)

38. Jeff Gelles, "New Buzz Tactic: Manipulating Teens," *Philadelphia
Inquirer*, October 31, 2005, reprinted on the Commercial Alert
Web site, www.commercialalert.org/issues/culture/buzz-marketing/
new-buzz-tactic-manipulating-teens (accessed March 1, 2007).

39. Rob Walker, author interview, August 2006.

40. Taeho Yoh, "Parent, Peer, and TV Influences in Teen Athletic
Shoe Purchasing," *Sport Journal* 8, no. 1 (Winter 2005), available
at www.thesportjournal.org/2005Journal/Vol8-No1/taeho_yo.asp
(accessed December 13, 2006).

41. Thomas Frank, *The Conquest of Cool: Business Culture, Counterculture,
and the Rise of Hip Consumerism* (Chicago: University of Chicago
Press, 1997), 9.

42. GoGorilla, 2001 GoCard LLC, New York. The booklet further
warns that it is "intended to be viewed by mature marketing professionals" and underscores the secrecy of its contents by contending,
under the copyright symbol, "Reproduction in whole or in part
without written permission is prohibited." This will seem a little
funny once we get to a discussion of intellectual property rights law
in Chapter 4.

43. Ibid.

44. Ibid.

45. From an author interview in August 2006.

46. "By the way," Johnson further offered, "please know that I have answered your questions with the understanding that there is a greater
than zero chance I will be held up as a symbol of all that is wrong
with global marketing and commerce." It is not my intention to do
so with Johnson, just as it is not with any of the personal friends, acquaintances, and compatriots I write about in this book. The logic
that underlies global marketing and commerce, in fact, seems to de-

serve the most blame. Some of us have just assimilated to it more easily than others.

3. Preaching to the Converted

1. Bill Talen, *What Should I Do if Reverend Billy Is in My Store?* (New
   York: The New Press, 2003), 9.
2. The term "adbusting" combines "advertisement" and, well, "bust-
   ing" to describe a straightforward manipulation of existing corporate
   or governmental propaganda. It's a practice that's been around for
   decades, although it's unclear when the term itself came into use.
   Regardless, it's now branded and essentially owned by Kalle Lasn,
   who named his magazine for it. The term "subvertising" was also
   popularized by Lasn, a combination of "subversion" and "advertising" that describes a specific type of adbusting. A subvertisement
   may be a television commercial, for example, promoting the notion
   of recycling rather than a specific environmental product. Yet as Lasn
   himself agrees, all work in the end to promote the *Adbusters* name.
   When used on a global scale, the phrase "cultural intervention" generally refers to some sort of forced imperialist conformity; when
   used in culture-jamming circles it refers more to the situations supposedly created by adbusting—in other words, the situationist de-
   tournement. The technique of creating new language to describe
   your activist practices in rapid response to the changing meanings of
   existing language of dissent has been used extremely successfully by
   both the marketing industry and the *Adbusters* crew, and goes a long
   way toward showing how much you can control the debate if you're
   making up the words with which to have it.
3. Talen, *What Should I Do*, 2.
4. "'Shopocalypse' Coming?" *RedEye*, December 9, 2005.
5. While Stephen Duncombe quotes him in *Dream*, it's a joke I've
   heard Talen use in other contexts as well. And it's a funny one!
   Stephen Duncombe, *Dream: Re-imagining Progressive Politics in an Age
   of Fantasy* (New York: The New Press, 2007), 65.
6. Naomi Klein, *No Logo* (New York: Picador, 2002), 349.

7. Connie Murtagh and Carla Lukehart, *Co-op America's Boycott Organizer's Guide* (Washington, DC: Co-op America, 2001), available at www.coopamerica.org (accessed November 29, 2006).

8. "Conscientious Consuming: Keys to a Successful Organized Boycott," available at www.con-suming.com/keys_of_succesful_boycott.htm (accessed November 29, 2006).

9. David Oglivy, *Confessions of an Advertising Man* (London: Southbank Publishing, 2004), 136.

10. "While still devoted to ad parodies and TV bashing, [*Adbusters* has] adopted the strategies of its opponents, dumbing everything down to the lowest common (eyecatching!) denominator. It's become an advertisement for anti-advertising. . . . *Adbusters* makes the perfect brand—a fun, do-good, hip image with a unique selling proposition," McLaren wrote in "Advertising the Uncommercial," Matador Records's *Escandalo*! number 3, formerly available at www.matadorrec.com/escandalo/3/adbusters.htm (accessed December 12, 2003, although the link appears to have been removed now).

11. In fact, culture jamming and adbusting appear to be quite a healthy business, if we estimate combined revenue from sales of *Adbusters* magazine and Lasn's book *Culture Jam*; donations to the 501(C)(3) Adbusters Media Fountation; and workshop and speakers' fees charged by the slew of organizations that provide more hands-on lessons.

12. Kalle Lasn, *Culture Jam: The Uncooling of America* (New York: HarperCollins, 2000).

13. *Sonic Outlaws*, Other Cinema DVD, 1995–2005.

14. Klein, *No Logo*, 287.

15. For a more complete discussion of this process, see my essay in Josh MacPhee and Erik Reuland's *Realizing the Impossible: Art Against Authority* (Oakland, CA: AK Press, 2007).

16. Not, however, that the audience would probably mind the hypocrisy. I worked for a short time at a newsstand in Seattle, and on one Buy Nothing Day I was surprised to find a man in front of me about to purchase a copy of *Adbusters*. "You know it's Buy Nothing Day?" I asked him. It appeared to be all he was purchasing, and I intended to suggest I hold his purchase for tomorrow.

"Yes," he told me and laughed. "But I think they would forgive me."

17. Author interview, November 2003.

4. Playing Fair

1. Terri Kapsalis, "Making Babies the American Girl® Way," *The Baffler*, no. 15 (2002), 29.

2. Dave Newbart, "Pilsen Teens Tell Mattel to Play Nice," *Chicago Sun-Times*, March 30, 2005, 3 (sidebar).

3. Christina Brinkley, "The Selling of Nicki: Overscheduled Skier with a Cute Dog," *Wall Street Journal*, December 30, 2006, 1.

4. Ibid.; Philip P. Pan, "Worked Till They Drop," *Washington Post*, May 13, 2002, available at www.washingtonpost.com/ac2/wp-dyn/A8254-2002May 12?language-printer (accessed August 26, 2006).

5. International Center for Corporate Accountability, *Audit Report of Mattel's Vendor Plants: Compliance with Mattel's Global Manufacturing Principles*, 2006, available at www.ICCA-corporateaccountability.org (accessed August 26, 2006).

6. Ben Ho, "Death from Overwork New Issue in China," *CSR Asia Weekly*, June 28, 2006, available at www.csr-asia.com/index.php?p=6998 (accessed August 26, 2006).

7. Pan, "Worked Till They Drop."

8. Abigail Goldman, "Mattel Struggles to Balance Profit with Morality," *Los Angeles Times*, November 28, 2004, available at seattletimes.nwsource.com/cgi-bin/PrintStory.pl?document_id=2002102845&zsection_id=268448413&slug=toys28&date=20041128 (accessed August 26, 2006).

9. Goldman, "Mattel Struggles."

10. Mattel Web site, "Global Manufacturing Principles," www.mattel.com/about_us/corp_responsiblity/cr_global.asp (accessed November 10, 2006).

11. International Center for Corporate Accountability, *Audit Report of Mattel's Vendor Plants*. The plant I describe here is referred to in the report as Plant 7, one of seven plants listed in the report.

12. National Labor Committee, *Toys of Misery: A Report on the Toy Industry in China* (New York: December 2001), 9, available at www .nclnet.org/campaigns/china/chinatoys01.pdf (accessed November 10, 2006).

13. Shortly before Christmas 2004 the American Girl Place was packed with girls and their mothers. One girl had apparently become separated from her mother, who, concerned, began yelling her name, "Samantha!" At least three different human girls responded to the call, while several helpful shoppers pointed to the Samantha doll exhibit and said, "She's right here."

14. Susan S. Alder, *Samantha Learns a Lesson* (Madison, WI: Pleasant Co., 1986), 51. As insipid as these tales are when brought into a real-world setting and held up to Mattel's own standards, they make for a moderately entertaining read—significantly better than the literary fare offered by *Nickelodeon* magazine for example, or the relaunch of *Mad*, both of which seem mere veils for wanton product placement. And yet the constant reiteration of upper-middle-class values throughout each story deserves the full weight of criticism, whether the writer or corporate licenser is to blame.

15. Because of my experience with riot grrrl culture, my definition of "girls" is fairly wide: I included those ranging in age from Fiona to women with children Fiona's age.

16. One of the activities that American Girl Place makes available to young girls through shopping is the opportunity to dress exactly like your doll; more recently, this trend has caught on with the older generation as well, and it's not unusual to see a doll, a girl, and a mom all wearing matching outfits as they stroll along Michigan Avenue toward the store.

17. I was unable to find any published statistics about shoplifting at American Girl Place, and the store is famously unwilling to acknowledge protests against its store. (In fact, one security guard asked if I was "friends with that Reverend Billy guy." When I asked if he'd protested there, she at first told me he hadn't—they never had protesters—and then admitted he might have done something once.) Nor was I able to unearth how many video cameras *most*

stores of this size keep trained on their employees to determine whether the figure quoted me was unusual or not, although I do believe the hundred-and-thirty-per-floor average noted in the text to be preposterously high for the size of American Girl Place. I learned about the four hundred video cameras number and plainclothed store detectives from two store detectives during my detention at American Girl Place.

18. The benefits information came to me through a friend who was an employee of the company in the sales division at the time I was researching American Girl. Shortly thereafter she was terminated for unknown reasons after eight faithful years of employment. Perhaps coincidentally, she got her notice the same day the local newspaper, The *Isthmus*, ran a feature on a reading I was giving in Madison on my Mattel research and experiences at American Girl Place. Although my friend was happy with her job at the time, her stories of forced overtime and the competitive nature of her work environment here in the United States were alarming. She relayed one story of a coworker in the sales division under so much pressure she accidentally left her newborn in the car, where the infant suffocated to death.

19. American Girl Company profile, available at www.americangirl .com/corp/html/aboutpc.html (accessed November 12, 2006).

20. Although I've published several versions of this story, each of which highlights a different ridiculous aspect of this experience, I have so far failed to call sufficient attention to the large number of Chicago police officers brought in to protect Mattel's brand, even after it was clear that I had neither stolen anything nor intended any physical damage to people of property. When I have found myself in actually dangerous situations in Chicago—my house keys and wallet stolen or in the presence of someone intending to do harm—I've often waited a few hours for a single disgruntled officer, or been asked to "file a complaint over the phone." Although, I will acknowledge that on one such occasion I received more specialized treatment: the officer on the other end of the line hinted that he could come protect me for the duration of the evening.

21. In 1998, McLeod trademarked the use of the phrase "Freedom of Expression" in printed matter. He wrote in his 2005 book that although he applied to register the trademark as an ironic comment on the commodification of culture, he hoped it "wasn't actually possible" that they would approve it. They did, and in the ridiculous prank McLeod staged to underscore the absurdity of his new trademark—a letter containing fake infringement threat against a friend posing as the editor of a fictitious zine called *Freedom of Expression*—he penned the following preposterous but telling line: "I didn't go to the trouble, the expense, and the time of trademarking freedom of expression® just to have someone else come along and think they can use it whenever they want." Kembrew McLeod, *Freedom of Expression: Overzealous Copyright Bozos and Other Enemies of Creativity* (New York: Doubleday, 2005), 120.

22. A musical genre consisting of the combination of the parts of two or more songs, usually the instrumental track of one with the vocals from another. Generally, to create a successful mash-up, all the source songs will be extremely popular and still recognizable.

23. See www.nolo.com. Often, although not always, commercial interests supersede those of scholarship and education; if you try to sell the work, it will be difficult to argue for its protection under fair use, although not impossible.

24. All McLeod quotations, unless otherwise noted, were taken from author interviews conducted in August 2005.

25. Koons lost an extremely high-profile copyright infringement lawsuit when he admitted to using a black-and-white postcard image as the sole basis for a wooden sculpture called "String of Puppies," which he commissioned craftspeople to execute and paint in bright colors and then sold three copies of (keeping a fourth for himself), for a combined total of $367,000. Whether Art Rogers, the photographer who sued Koons for that amount, ever succeeded in winning it in full is unclear.

26. In 1996, the American Society of Composers, Authors, and Publishers (ASCAP) tried to collect royalties from the Girl Scouts each time they sang "Puff the Magic Dragon" and "This Land Is Your Land."

Public outrage caused ASCAP to back down, but it charges the group a nominal fee of $1 per year to perform the songs.

27. The feeding frenzy on Napster downloaders was initiated in 2000 when the heavy-metal band Metallica decided to sue Yale University, Indiana University, and the University of Southern California for allowing their students to copy Metallica songs using Napster software. Shortly thereafter A&M, Geffen, Sony, and other record companies successfully sued Napster directly, which quickly forced the company to reconfigure itself as a legitimate enterprise: an online MP3 store that couldn't compete with iTunes when it finally reemerged. In a bizarre PR campaign, the RIAA took out ads featuring the innocent-looking children who had been "caught red-handed" and sued as a warning to other potential downloaders (though the practice, and similar campaigns, still thrive)—a strange and mean-spirited display of aggression toward youth whose dollars they nonetheless court.

28. McLeod, *Freedom of Expression*, 8.

29. Author interview with McLaren, August 2005. *Stay Free!* was an infrequent publication focused on American media, consumer culture, and sometimes McLaren's neighborhood of Park Slope, Brooklyn.

30. The exhibition occasionally still travels. Check www.illegal-art.org.

31. Bob Levin, "The Pirate and the Mouse," *Comics Journal* nos. 238 and 239, October and November 2001.

32. Naomi Klein, *No Logo* (New York: Picador, 2002), 181.

33. It should be noted that these cards are now available on my Web site, www.anneelizabethmoore.com, although it should also be noted that I first confirmed with Marjorie Heins that a fair use defense might apply in a copyright infringement case before making them available.

34. McLeod, *Freedom of Expression*, 8.

35. Marjorie Heins and Tricia Beckles, *Will Fair Use Survive?: Free Expression in the Age of Copyright Control* (New York: Brennan Center for Justice, 2005), 36.

36. Unless otherwise noted, all Forsythe comments are taken from a September 2006 author interview.

37. It perhaps says something about my method of play that I recall finding this symbol in a couple of Barbies' private areas pretty early on in
my childhood. It was, in fact, my introduction to the term "copyright," although it would be several years before I had any knowledge of what it meant. Also, it might explain why I link the term in
my mind with lesbianism.

38. Bill Werde, "Judges Says Artist Can Make Fun of Barbie," *New York
Times*, June 28, 2004. available at www.nytimes.com/2004/06/28/
national/28barbie.html?ex=1246161600&en=2ecd3 c8338e2855c&
ei=5090&partner=rssuserland (accessed September 5, 2006)

39. Ibid.

5. The Master's Blueprints

1 Snarky parentheticals in the original. Yaris Web site, www.yaris
works.com/drive_it_yourself.php (accessed September 13, 2006).

2. Laura Blum and Steve McClellan, "Companies Serious about
'Mocketing,'" *BrandWeek*, June 26, 2006, available at www.brand
week.com/bw/news/recent_display.jsp?vnu_content_id=1002727
897 (accessed August 4, 2006).

3. Rob Walker, "Pabst Unsold," www.robwalker.net. A similar version
of the story appeared in the June 22, 2003, issue of the *New York Times
Magazine*, although this version comes from the category "Journal of
Murketing" (accessed August 4, 2006).

4. David Oglivy, *Confessions of an Advertising Man* (London: Southbank
Publishing, 2004), 156.

5. I am indebted to Alex Wreck, creator of this great zine, for first
pointing out how weird it was that her zine appeared in advertisements for both the Bumbershoot InkSpot workshops and Starbucks.

6. Naomi Klein, *No Logo* (New York: Picador, 2002), 45.

7. Blum and McClellan, "Companies Serious," quoting Barbara Zack,
managing director and chief marketing strategic officer at IAG Research in New York, a firm that daily measures the effectiveness of all
ads and product placements on television.

8. Author interview, 2005.

9. Weiden+Kennedy also run a studio art residency program out of their Portland, Oregon, headquarters, which I discovered while interviewing the amazing and otherwise thoroughly independent artist Khaela Maricich from Olympia, Washington, who, in between music performances as the Blow offered advice on a print ad campaign for vodka (she suggested, I believe, "unicorns").

10. Author interview, 2003.

11. Author interview, 2003.

12. Stephen Thompson, *The Onion*, September 2, 1997, available at www .avclub.com/content/node/23291 (accessed September 26, 2006).

13. Negativland, *Dispepsi* (Concord, CA: Seeland Records, 1997).

14. This information came in the form of a press release, as cited in the band's own press materials at www.negativland.com, although Naomi Klein notes that it was an *Entertainment Weekly* reporter who first elicited the quote. Klein, *No Logo*, 288.

15. Kevin Roberts, *Lovemarks: The Future Beyond Brands* (New York: Powerhouse Books, 2004), 18.

16. This conversation took place in October 2006.

17. I'm grateful to Rob Walker for alerting me to this story. It prompted the hilarious notion that somewhere there existed a dedicated sect of edge traditionalists up in arms about the change in edgy. It should probably be noted that both my work and I have both been called edgy on more than one occasion. I hope that when this book is reviewed it is at least called "new edgy," because I don't think my ego could handle being some kind of old, outmoded, unstylish edgy.

18. As to the built-in safety features of edginess, we can look to the ad campaigns for a new kind of Ford car, the Edge. "The Edge is Never Dull," is the car's slogan. It has all-wheel drive and a feature called Roll Stability Control (RSC). Potential purchasers are urged to "stay sharp with the edge" and "put dull in the rearview mirror." Note that even from the edge (Edge) you can always keep an eye on dull. Also, note how stable the Edge truly is. Four-wheel traction and one single feature named both with the word "stability" and the word "control." Rob Walker also reminded me that, in the mid-1990s, it was popular to name radio stations "The Edge," and one still exists in

Dallas, Texas—although its main claim to edginess is a Web site link to pictures of half-naked white women. Also, it's a Clear Channel affiliate, and so plays music much akin to what you could hear if you turned on your radio right now. Another Edge station in Scottsdale, Arizona holds *American Idol*–watching parties, which is an activity I struggle to define as anything other than "mainstream." United Christian Broadcasters also runs a station called The Edge. "As the radio ministry grinds day-in day-out we've met and had thumbs-up time with great people hanging with us on The Edge. These guys play hard . . . and pray hard . . . on The Edge!" they say on their Web site.

19. Roberts, *Lovemarks*, 18.

20. Klein, *No Logo*, 288.

21. Available at www.guerillamedia.net.

22. Ibid.

23. Larissa MacFarquhar, "The Populist," *New Yorker*, February 16–23, 2004.

24. Rob Walker, "Anti-Fan Club," *New York Times Magazine*, November 26, 2006, 26.

25. Craig Baldwin, *Sonic Outlaws*, Other Cinema DVD, 1995–2005.

26. Creative Commons is a not-for-profit organization that offers flexible alternatives to copyright law. Rick Prelinger interview available at creativecommons.org/getcontent/features/rick.

27. It's the same image used on the cover of at least one edition of Guy Debord's *Society of the Spectacle*, the Situationists' most famous text and a central one for culture jammers.

6. The Filmmakers

1. "Underground Spawns Cool Swag and Avatars," Starwars.com, June 15, 2005, available at www.starwars.com/episode-iii/release/publicity/news20050615.html.

2. Author interview, January 2007.

3. Author interview, January 2007.

4. Peter Keogh, review of *Star Wars Episode 1: The Phantom Menace*,

Boston Phoenix, May 24, 1999, www.filmvault.com/filmvault/boston/s/starwarsepisodeitl.html (accessed June 6, 2006).

5. Ibid., 152.

6. John Seabrook, *Nobrow: The Culture of Marketing, the Marketing of Culture* (New York: Vintage Books, 2001), 153.

7. Frank Ahrens, "Star Wars Marketing Targets Young Children," Associated Press, May 16, 2005, available at www.commercialexploitation.org/news/articles/starwarsmarketing.htm (accessed January 22, 2007).

8. We even traded zines in the late nineties, as we both recalled (although I have since donated my collection to various zine libraries across the country).

9. As this book went to press in late spring 2007, the USPS announced a rate hike that would go into effect July 15, overturning the findings of their own Postal Regulatory Commission to approve a 758-page plan submitted by Time-Warner that suggested a rate hike for bulk mail, the mail service often used by periodicals. Now, Time-Warner makes a lot of periodicals—*Time, Entertainment Weekly, People, Mad,* etc.—so this might seem strange; but what they were proposing was a rate hike that would be carried primarily by magazines that didn't send that many issues out at a time. Under their plan, small-circulation magazines (like *The Nation, The Progressive, Mother Jones, The New Republic*) face between 30 and 40 percent higher rates; the largest face less than ten. *The Nation* alone estimated their rates would increase by $500,000, a number that would quickly put them out of business. A rallying cry went up from independent publishers everywhere. A bulk-mail rate hike that favors large-circulation periodicals stands in direct opposition to all that the postal service was originally established to do: provide the widest number of people the widest range of access to the most diverse viewpoints available. Even more strange was that it came at the exact moment the USPS had initiated a marketing campaign for a single piece of mass media. You guessed it: Star Wars. Across the country, in hundreds of cities, for an unknown cost, mailboxes were done over in R2D2 drag. An "unprecedented promotion," the Star Wars

Web site proclaimed of the thirty-year anniversary celebrational coup of an entire arm of the government (Star Wars.com, May 5, 2007).

10. Author interview, August 2006.

11. Steve Mount, "Frequently Asked Questions," January 19, 2000, available at Steve Mount's relocated Web site, www.saltyrain.com/tatooine/mountl.html (accessed January 9, 2007).

12. Steve Mount has helpfully posted the original e-mail from Lucasfilm for all interested parties on his site at www.saltyrain.com/tatooine/lucasfilml.txt (accessed April 10, 2007).

13. Steve Mount, "Steve Mount's Letter to Lucasfilm," January 19, 2000, available at www.saltyrain.com/tatooine/mountl.html (accessed January 9, 2007).

14. Author interview, January 2007.

15. Ibid.

16. Mount, "Steve Mount's Letter to Lucasfilm."

17. Colin Hulme, "Costume Wars: Copyright Storm Over the Troopers," *Journal of the Law Society of Scotland*, November 15, 2006, available at www.journalonline.co.uk/article/1003639.aspx (accessed January 4, 2007).

18. "Lucasfilm Ltd Wins Major Copyright Infringement Lawsuit Against Star Wars Stormtrooper Pirate," press release, October 11, 2006, available at www.lucasfilm.com/press/news/news20061011.html (accessed January 4, 2007).

19. "YouTube and Fan-Made Star Wars Videos," Starwars.com, August 2, 2006, blogs.starwars.com/lucasonline/54 (accessed January 4, 2006).

20. Amy Harmon, "Star Wars Fan Films Come Tumbling Back to Earth," *New York Times*, April 28, 2002, available at select.nytimes.com/search/restricted/article?res=F20717FB345B0C7B8EDDAD08 94DA404482 (accessed January 9, 2007).

21. Ibid.

22. Ibid., 152.

23. The connection between Lucas and Campbell is so oft repeated that the Bill Moyers PBS miniseries *Joseph Campbell: The Power of Myth*

was filmed at Skywalker Ranch, and featured discussions of his influence over the successful film series and interviews with George
Lucas. *Salon*, however, published an excellent essay arguing that the
connection was not as sound as all that. See Steven Hart, "Galactic
Gasbag: Beneath All the Pseudo-Mythic Joseph Campbell Hogwash,
the Roots of George Lucas' Empire Lie Not in 'The Odyssey' but in
Classic and Pulp 20th Century Sci-fi," *Salon.com*, dir.salon.com/
story/ent/movies/feature/2002/04/10/lucas/print.html (accessed
April 10, 2007).

24. Davis D. Cohen, "Is the Force Still With Him?" *Variety*, February 13,
    2005, available at www.variety.com/article/VR1117917816.html?
    categoryid=13&cs=1&query=India na+Jones+ (accessed January
    10, 2007).

25. Although, Jon hastened to add, not in costume.

26. My research on this was not terribly scientific. I e-mailed the sixteen
    people I communicate with most regularly who have devoted their
    lives to independent media creation and were likely to be aware of
    the barrage of advertising that might go into making them *want* to
    see the film. It is probably clear from the remainder of this chapter
    that I was fairly certain most of them would have seen the film by the
    time I spoke to them.

27. Brandon Gray, " 'Sith' Destroys Single Day Record," *Box Office Mojo*,
    May 20, 2005, www.boxofficemojo.com/news/?id=1824&p=.htm
    (accessed September 26, 2006).

28. Lea Goldman and Kiri Blakely, "The Celebrity 100," *Forbes*, June 15,
    2006, available at www.forbes.com/list/2005/53/rank_1.html (ac-
    cessed December 30, 2005).

7. The Athletic Shoe Company

1. Randall Rothenberg, *Where Suckers Moon: The Life and Death of an
   Advertising Campaign* (Vintage: New York, 1995), 183.

2. Ibid.

3. Rothenberg, *Where Suckers Moon*, 203.

4. Elizabeth L. Bland and Elaine Dutka, "Wanna Buy a Revolution?"

Time, May 18, 1987, available at www.time.com/time/magazine/article/0,9171,964404,00.html (accessed August 22, 2006).

5. Rothenberg, *Where Suckers Moon*, 215.

6. "Brash guerilla marketer" comes from Stanley Holmes with Aaron Bernstein, "The New Nike," *BusinessWeek*, September 20, 2004, available at www.businessweek.com/magazine/content/04_38/b3900001_mz001.htm (accessed August 22, 2006); "Ambush of all ambushes" comes from Abram Sauer, "Ambush Marketing: Steals the Show," *Brandchannel*, May 27, 2002, available at www.brandchannel.com/features_effect.asp?pf_id=98 (accessed January 23, 2007).

7. Holmes with Bernstein, "The New Nike."

8. Sauer, "Ambush Marketing."

9. Alicia Rebensdorf, "Capitalizing on the Anti-Capitalist Movement," *Alternet*, August 7, 2001, www.alternet.org/globalization/11295/ (accessed August 22, 2006).

10. Jordan Robertson, "How Nike Got Street Cred," *Business 2.0*, available at money.cnn.com/magazines/business2/business2_archive/2004/05/01/368253/index.htm (accessed August 22, 2006).

11. Daniel Sinker, *We Owe You Nothing: Punk Planet, the Collected Interviews* (New York: Akashic, 2001), 24.

12. Ibid.

13. Tiffany Montgomery, "Nike Tries on Skateboard Shoes," *Orange County Register*, posted to the Skateboard Directory, www.skateboarddirectory.com, September 12, 2002, available at skateboarddirectory.com/articles/480267_nike_tries_on_skateboard.html (accessed January 23, 2007).

14. Maria Hampton, "How Nike Conquered Skateboard Culture," *Adbusters*, May/June 2006, available at 2006, available at adbusters.org/the_magazine/65/How_Nike_Conquered_Skateboard_Culture.html (accessed August 22, 2006).

15. "Kevin Imamura," *The Hundreds*, previously available online at www.thehundreds.com/chronicles/kevinimamura.html (accessed August 25, 2006). (This page appears to have been removed.) *The Hundreds* is a lifestyle print and online zine project focused on Los Angeles skateboard, punk, and hip-hop brand-based fashion.

16. Shannon McMahon, "Skating to the Top: Sport's Footwear Gains Popularity, Even Among Those Who Have Never Owned a Board," *San Diego Union-Tribune*, September 25, 2005, available at www.signonsandiego.com/news/business/20050925-9999-mzlb25skate.html (accessed March 21, 2007).

17. Ibid.

18. Ibid.

19. Ibid.

20. Saba Haider, "Popularity Extraordinaire," *Transworld Business*, January 26, 2004, www.twsbiz.com/twbiz/industrynews/article/0,21214,708254,00.html.

21. Montgomery, "Nike Tries on Skateboard Shoes."

22. Robertson, "How Nike Got Street Cred."

23. Letter from Nike Skateboarding to Minor Threat, Dischord Records, and fans of both, June 27, 2005, www.nike.com/nikeskateboarding/v2/letter/index.html (accessed August 22, 2006).

24. Sinker, 16.

25. Rothenberg, *Where Suckers Moon*, 416

26. "Minor Threat vs. Major Threat," June 28, 2005, Movable Walls, www.tinypineapple.com/chris/archives/minor_threat_vs_major_threat.html (accessed August 22, 2006).

27. All of MacKaye's quotes are taken from a 2005 author interview unless otherwise noted.

28. Alec Bourgeoise author interview 2005.

29. Bland and Dutka, "Wanna Buy a Revolution?"

30. Naomi Klein, *No Logo* (New York: Picador, 2002), 74.

31. "Minor Threat vs. Major Threat," Movable Walls.

32. Author e-mail interviews, March and August 2006.

8. The Male Perfumers

1. In a predictably absurd turnabout, similar pressure washers have recently been used to spray ads into dirty sidewalks, leaving behind a stenciled image made out of extremely clean sidewalk. See

"Clean Advertising," September 27, 2006, brentter.com/?p=44 for more.

2. Author interview, August 2006.

3. See Critical Massive Web site, www.criticalmassive.com/start_about.html (accessed August 7, 2006).

4. Rob Walker, "Nissan's Game of Tag," *Slate*, August 11, 2003, www.slate.com/toolbar.aspx?action=print&id=2086789 (accessed August 6, 2006).

5. "PlayStation Ads, Disguised as Graffiti, Spark Controversy," *USA Today*, December 29, 2005, www.usatoday.com/money/advertising/2005-12-29-graffiti-ads_x.htm (accessed August 1, 2006).

6. Arshad Mohammed, "Verizon Fined by District for Chalk-on-Sidewalk Advertising," *Washington Post*, April 1, 2006, www.washingtonpost.com/wp-dyn/content/article/2006/03/31/AR2006033101792_pf.html (accessed June 1, 2006).

7. "Guerilla Marketing: Street Graffiti," *Event Marketer*, October 21, 2003, www.eventmarketer.com/viewmedia.asp?prmMID=415 (accessed August 25, 2003).

8. "PlayStation Ads," *USA Today*.

9. Ryan Singel, "Sony Draws Ire with PSP Graffiti," *Wired News*, December 5, 2005, www.wired.com/news/culture/0,1284,69741,00.html (accessed February 19, 2007).

10. "Guerilla Marketing," *Event Marketer*.

11. Scott Johnson author interview, August 2006.

12. Johnson—who kindly tolerated my questions for some months after our original interview—continues: "As for the question of ethics, even though I'm in the advertising business, I do think it's unethical for companies to besmirch our urban landscapes with marketing graffiti. Graffiti simply becomes another form of signage for companies. I tend to believe that the quality of a civilization is inversely proportional to the number of signs it feels compelled to display."

13. Author interview, July 2006.

14. Author interview, November 2005. Parts of this interview were

originally published in my story "Black Market," *Punk Planet* 70, November/December 2005.

15. Natalie Hope McDonald, "Naked City: When the Street Is for Sale," *Philadelphia City Paper*, January 12–18, 2006, available at www.city paper.net/articles/2006-01-12/naked.shtml (accessed June 1, 2006).

16. Zachary, posting on the open forum at Joystiq, a news site for videogame discussion, www.joystiq.com/2005/11/17/sony-psp-advertising-hits-the-streets/(accessed August 21, 2006).

17. Deeko is a blog and news site devoted to videogame culture. Although the discussion of the PSP campaign is no longer online, they were previously posted to www.deeko.com/forums/archive/index.php?t-514.html (accessed August 21, 2006).

18. McDonald, "Naked City."

19. See www.popgadget.net/2005/11/sony_psp_corpor.php#015213. Interestingly, she also claims that when she first called to complain about the campaign, Sony told her they had nothing to do with it.

20. Tracy Clark-Flory, "Teen Boys Buy Lady-Luring Spray," *Salon.com*, April 6, 2006 www.salon.com/mwt/broadsheet/2006/04/06/axe/print.html (accessed August 21, 2006).

21. Ann Friedman, "The Violence Effect," Feministing.com, June 21, 2005, feministing.com/archives/003440.html (accessed December 24, 2006).

22. Clark-Flory, "Teen Boys."

23. Lori Aratani, "Teen Boys Picking Up on a Scent: Body Spray," *Washington Post*, April 3, 2006, B01, www.washingtonpost.com/wp-dyn/content/article/2006/04/02/AR2006040201235_pf.html (accessed August 21, 2006).

24. Irene Tejaratchi, Ryan Singel, and eee were all generous enough to supply images of the regraffitied graffiti for an article I wrote on the PSP campaign. Anne Elizabeth Moore, "Game Over," *Punk Planet* 72, March/April 2006.

25. "Time Inc. Graffiti Board Completed," Adrants.com, June 30, 2005, www.adrants.com/2005/06/time-inc-graffiti-board-completed.php (accessed April 3, 2006).

26. Author interview, August 2006.

27. Ibid.
28. Jake Dobkin, "Opinionist: Corporate Graffiti Sucks Balls," Gothamist
.com, November 20, 2005, www.gothamist.com/archives/2005/
11/20/opinionist_corp.php (accessed April 7, 2006).
29. Even one graffiti Web site claimed to have been fooled. The Wooster
Collective, a Web site devoted to documenting innovative street art
projects throughout the world, originally posted images from the
campaign as legitimate graffiti. That the site has direct links to the
corporate advertising world, however—one of its two publishers also
runs the marketing service company ElectricArtists in New York—
has raised some doubts about whether their mistake was intentional
obfuscation.
30. "Guerilla Marketing," *Event Marketer.*

9. The Pharmaceutical Manufacturers

1. Most of this story appeared in an Ouch! pamphlet called *The Cave of*
Pain, written by L. Vanderbilt, illustrated by F. Eces, published by
Tylenol. (One participant recalled it was probably distributed in
Tokion, Giant Robot, and *Transworld Skateboarding* but couldn't be certain.) Intended to be read as a zine, the half-size format (the term for
several folded 8½-inch × 11-inch pieces of paper saddle-stitched together) was a full-color, professionally printed, thoroughly branded
enterprise that featured the Ouch! name and Tylenol on the cover.
Of course, the content was also thoroughly branded; Team Ouch! are
the stars of the story. Constructus's quote, however, as well as the
ending to this story, were taken from an earlier, unpublished version
of the same Ouch! project called *Attack of the Suits.* Embellishments
have been devised here in the retelling, but the story—particularly
the funny bits—remains the property of Vanderbilt. Or, maybe,
Tylenol.
2. Faith Popcorn bio, the Harry Walker Agency, 2002, available at
www.harrywalker.com/speakers_template_printer.cfm?Spea_ID=
178 (accessed March 21, 2007).
3. Faith Popcorn, *Eveolution: The Eight Truths of Marketing to Women*

(New York: Hyperion, 2000), as quoted in "Trendsetters," *Craftrends*, March, 2001, available at www.craftrends.com/trendsetters.htm (accessed July 15, 2005).

4. Maureen Tkacik, "New York World," *New York Observer*, February 28, 2005.

5. "What is Ouch," www.ouchthewebsite.com/whatisouch/what .jhtml (accessed August 16, 2006).

6. "Advertising drugs is a special art . . . [P]hysical discomfort is no joking matter to the sufferer." David Oglivy, *Confessions of an Advertising Man* (London: Southbank Publishing, 2004), 170.

7. Faith Popcorn, quoted in Julia Boorstin, "The Pill Whose Name Goes Unspoken," CNNMoney.com, September 20, 2004, money .cnn.com/magazines/fortune/fortune_archive/2004/09/20/3811 67.index.htm (accessed July 6, 2006).

8. Boorstin, "Pill Whose Name."

9. Dan Nadel, "Bad Medicine," *Print*, July/August 2005, 112.

10. Author interview, 2005.

11. Nadel, "Bad Medicine," 112.

12. Bob Meher, "The Pain of Youth: Tylenol Goes Underground to Woo the 18–29 Set," *Chicago Reader*, February 11, 2005, www .chicagoreader.com/TheMeter/050211.html (accessed February 20, 2007).

13. Author interview, 2005.

14. Tokion 2006 Media Kit. Request one for yourself by sending an e-mail to usmail@tokion.com.

15. "What is Ouch."

16. Naomi Klein, *No Logo* (New York: Picador, 2000), 43.

17. Nadel, "Bad Medicine," 114.

18. Anonymous author interview, February 2007.

19. L. Vanderbilt, *Attack of the Suits* (New York: McNeil, 2004), 12.

20. E-mail forwarded anonymously following the publication of the *Punk Planet* article.

21. Sorry, the interview's still anonymous. For the record, though, I spoke to nearly all of the artists who worked on the Ouch! campaign, both on and off the record. For some reason they were

much more willing to come forward than the project organizers themselves.

22. Boorstin, "Pill Whose Name." Although it is the only one I could locate, $2.5 million for the entire Ouch! campaign is possibly an early and incomplete figure.

23. And yes, one of my editors suggested this example.

24. Meher, "Pain of Youth."

25. Although the *Print* article stated that the "Tylenol Bowl" nickname first appeared in a press release, Mimms recalls it as a paid advertisement.

10. I Love Monkey

1. Jim Welte, "Sony BMG Posts Profit," MP3.com, January 26, 2006, www.mp3.com/news/stories/3031.html&ref_id=48929&ref_type _id=1 (accessed October 8, 2006).

2. "Consolidated Financial Results for the Third Quarter Ended December 31, 2006," Sony Web site, www.sony.net/SonyInfo/IR/ financial/fr/06q3_sony.pdf (accessed February 6, 2007).

3. All quotes originally appeared on Radiofreeohio.org, the Web site listeners were urged to check during the pirate-style break-ins. The text was removed shortly after the Web site was found to be registered to Clear Channel and then posted to *Stay Free!* magazine's blog, blog.stayfreemagazine.org, where some of it can still be read today .blog.stayfreemagazine.org/2005/05/radio_free_clea.html (accessed February 26, 2007).

4. BzzAgent Welcome Kit (Boston, 2006), n.p. This document is mailed to new agents along with the BzzAgent Code of Conduct and a handy guide called "Example of a Good BzzReport." Among the elements of a good BzzReport: location, BzzTarget, product description, and the BzzTarget's response.

5. Again, I hesitate to speculate too seriously as to why, although the Neopets virtual world's spate of available characters is replete with cute baby animals, and there is no end to the fashion accessories you can buy for them. To my mind this indicates clear desire for the girls'

market (a conjecture bolstered also by the existence of word-of-mouth agencies that exist solely for girls: Girls Intelligence Agency and even the new Tremor-for-moms group, VocalPoint). Again, I can only posit that a long history of economic disparity in wages between men and women is behind women's greater willingness to provide free labor in exchange for the gifts or social standing these organizations supply.

6. Frequently Asked Questions, Neopets Web site, info.neopets.com/presskit/faqs.html#1 (accessed February 23, 2007).

7. "Executive Summary Pre-Post Neopets Ad Campaign Market Research Study," a PDF download from the Neopets Web site, available at: info.neopets.com/presskit/articles/research/immersive_gen_research.pdf (accessed February 26, 2007).

8. Terms and Conditions, BzzAgent Web site, www.bzzagent.com/pages/Page.do?page=Terms_Conditions (accessed March 3, 2007).

9. The American Marketing Association's "Dictionary of Marketing Terms" is an online dictionary available at www.marketingpower.com (accessed February 25, 2007).

10. Terms and Conditions, BzzAgent Web site.

11. Brian Del Vecchio, "*Love Monkey*: Not Hardcore," Institute of Hybernautics blog, hybernaut.com/love-monkey (accessed August 21, 2006).

12. "CBS Breaks Up with 'Love Monkey,' " Zap2it. com, Friday, February 10, 2006, tv.zap2it.com/tveditorial/tve_main/1,1002,271%7C99968%7C1%7C,00.html (accessed March 21, 2007).

13. I am indebted here to Roman Mars's *Punk Planet* story "Radio Free of Ethics" (*Punk Planet* 70, November/December 2005, 71) both for my understanding of this Clear Channel campaign and my use of the term "radio wonks."

14. Robert Levine, "That Rebellious Voice Is No Pirate After All," *New York Times*, May 30, 2005, sec. C, 4.

15. Greg Levine, "Scott's Wal-Mart: Opportunity Knocks in Poor Zones," *Forbes*, April 4, 2006, available at www.forbes.com/2006/04/04/wmt-opportunity-zones-cx_gl_0404autofacescan12_print.html (accessed February 13, 2007).

16. Wal-Mart Watch, "Divide and Conquer: Dirty Tricks Gain Wal-Mart Entry into America's Third Largest City," walmartwatch .com/reports/shameless/shameless_chicago (accessed February 6, 2007).

17. "Coldplay Lead Rock TV Takeover," *Rolling Stone*, December 15, 2005, available at www.rollingstone.com/artists/teddygeiger/ articles/story/8957456/coldplay_lead_rock_tv_takeover (accessed February 5, 2005).

18. "Wal-Mart Launches First Jobs and Opportunity Zone in Chicago's Austin Community," *Windy City Word*, January 23, 2007, available at www.windycityword.com/news/Article/Article.asp?NewsID=755 86&sID=33 (accessed February 6, 2007).

19. Ibid.

20. On February 10, I went to the Wal-Mart on North Avenue and scoured the store for the "Small Business Spotlight" for close to an hour but found nothing. I asked several employees, who could not help me, and finally began an argument with the second assistant manager, Veronica, the customer service representative quoted here, had called for me. I cited the news stories, but the Small Business Spotlight rang no bells for Veronica. While she smartly asked if I'd brought the stories with me, I hadn't. "I was pretty sure I wouldn't need to provide documentation of something that was supposedly happening in this store to people who worked here," I explained. Veronica was very nice about the apparent confusion but could really only offer me the number of the district office—(708) 488-8510—if I wanted to find out more.

11. Taking Dissent Off the Market

1. Stanley Holmes with Aaron Bernstein, "The New Nike," *Business-Week*, September 20, 2004, available at www.businessweek.com/ magazine/content/04_38/b3900001_mz001.htm (accessed August 22, 2006).

2. This came to light in a conversation with Ryan over a year after the original *Punk Planet* article appeared. He'd apparently taken same

guff about the article and wanted to clarify this seemingly small but entirely relevant point.

3. Author interview with Christen Carter, September 2006.

4. Jean Halliday, "Yaris," Advertising Age's *Marketing 50 Awards*, special insert, November 13, 2006, 2.

5. Kathleen M. Joyce, "Marketer's Salary Survey," July 1, 2005, *Promo*, online at promomagazine.com/research/salary/marketing_hanging _tough (accessed March 11, 2007).

6. Libby Copeland, "The Mark of Borf: With Graffitist's Arrest, Police Put a Name to the Familiar Face," *Washington Post*, July 14, 2005, available at www.washingtonpost.com/wp-dyn/content/article/ 2005/07/13/AR2005071302448.html (accessed January 19, 2007).

7. Arshad Mohammad, "Verizon Fined by District for Chalk-on-Sidewalk Advertising," *Washington Post*, April 1, 2006, D01, available at www.washingtonpost.com/wp-dyn/content/article/2006/03/ 31/AR2006033101792.html (accessed April 10, 2007).

8. William Gibson, *Pattern Recognition* (New York: Putnam, 2003).

9. Rob Walker, "The Hidden (in Plain Sight) Persuaders," *New York Times Magazine*, December 5, 2004, available at www.nytimes .com/2004/12/05/magazine/05BUZZ.html?ex=1259989200&en =db8 7e6e46659a643&ei=5088&partner=rssnyt (accessed January 19, 2007).

10. *Punk Planet* 71, January/February 2007, 22.

11. Parts of this interview were previously published in my article "Our Profit Margin Could Be Your Life," *In These Times,* May 2007.

INDEX